FISH

A Memoir of a Boy in a Man's Prison

T. J. PARSELL

CARROLL & GRAF PUBLISHERS
NEW YORK

For Tom Wasik,
the greatest psychotherapist in the world,
who holds me tight and keeps me safe at night.

FISH
A Memoir of a Boy in a Man's Prison

Carroll & Graf Publishers
An Imprint of Avalon Publishing Group, Inc.
245 West 17th Street, 11th Floor
New York, NY 10011

AVALON
publishing group incorporated

Fish \\fish\ n, a: *Prison slang for a new inmate,* b: *A memoir.*

Contents

Fish is an accurate memoir of events in my life that took place over twenty-five years ago. I have changed the names and identifying details of others who were involved in those events. The names and identifying characteristics here are not accurate as to any living individuals known to me. I have used the real names of members of my family and some prison officials.

Prologue

State Prison of Southern Michigan
Jackson, Michigan
April 15, 1978

The office was in a converted prison cell. The bars had been removed and replaced with gray painted cinderblocks. The door had a large window that was covered from the inside with old rusty blinds that hadn't been cleaned in some time. At eye level, the word PSYCHOLOGIST was stenciled on the glass.

When I entered the office, he pointed to a wood chair in the corner and told me to take a seat. He looked like the guidance counselor at my high school. He was in his thirties with dark brown hair. A corduroy jacket hung from the back of his chair. He pulled a file from the stack on his shelf. "1-5-3-0-5-2, Parsell. Is that you?"

"Yes sir," I said, my voice slightly cracking.

He didn't look up as he flipped through the file, scanning the pages of what was to become my prison record. The size of the folder was impressive, considering I had been there only a few days. He read the Pre-sentence Report. "You have a control hold," he announced, still not lifting his head.

"What's that?"

"It says here that you still have an armed robbery pending."

"Yeah, I don't go back for sentencing on that until June."

"Well, its only April," he said, closing the file. He read something on the cover and opened it again. "It means you're going inside."

"Inside?" It didn't make sense. Inside meant *inside the walls* of maximum security. "My lawyer said I would go to a camp," I said.

He didn't respond; he just continued reading the file.

"Ever been fucked?" he asked abruptly.

"Excuse me?"

"Fucked," he repeated. It was the first time he looked up from his desk.

I blinked, not sure I was hearing what he said. I looked over at the closed door and then back again, too stunned to respond.

He swiveled his chair around so that he faced me and tossed the file onto his desk. "You have a control hold," he said, "because you have a capital offense case pending." He placed his hands behind his head and studied me as I sat there staring back at him.

"What do you mean, capital offense case?" I asked, grateful he changed the subject.

"Any crime that carries up to life is considered a capital offense case. Because you have an armed robbery pending, and because armed robbery carries up to a maximum of life, we have to send you inside until you're sentenced."

He eyed my tall but skinny, hundred and forty-eight pound frame.

"Armed robbery," he said slowly. "You're a pretty dangerous guy."

"Not really," I said, ignoring his sarcasm.

"What did you rob?"

"A Photo Mat," I answered, almost sheepishly.

He was silent.

It started out as a joke. I hadn't actually intended to rob the place.

"It was with a toy gun," I added.

He still didn't say anything.

He just sat there looking at me.

My lawyer said it didn't matter that the gun wasn't real. As long as the girl inside the photo booth thought it was real, it was considered armed robbery. I was hoping it'd make a difference here, so that I wouldn't be sent inside.

"So," he said, leaning back in his chair. "Ever suck a dick?"

"Fuck, no," I said.

"Well, you will."

"No, I won't."

He was silent again, for a long moment. The hum of the electric clock seemed to overpower the noise from the crowded cellblock just beyond the door. Seven Block was quarantined, where they assigned the *fish*—new inmates. We were kept locked down until we were classified and shipped to whatever prison we were to serve our time. The psychologist was the last step before we met with the Classification Committee.

"You're going to M-R until your case is adjudicated," he announced.

I had heard about M-R, The Michigan Reformatory, while I was in the county jail. It's where they sent young inmates who were serving a lot of time. Someone once told me, "Whatever you do, don't let them send you to M-R." Inmates called it Gladiator School. "Where motherfuckers fight each other off with broomstick handles and garbage can lids."

"A pretty boy like you," the psychologist added, "you'll need to get a man."

"Fuck *that*!" I said, my eyes darted to the floor. I could feel my face burning.

"If you don't get a man, you'll be open game."

"They'll have to kill me first," I said, sitting up in my chair.

"That can be arranged," he said, calmly.

He was enjoying the volley.

I didn't know what to say next, or how he'd respond to it. I studied the books that were sloppily arranged on the shelf above his desk. I was afraid to let my eyes look at him, fearing what they might reveal.

"Your life means nothing to one of these cons who's serving a life sentence. You'll suck dick, or you'll get your throat slit. And then they'll fuck you."

Now I was getting scared, and angry. This prick was having too much fun with me, and I didn't know what to do, but mostly I was scared. I couldn't believe they'd send me to M-R. I was definitely *not* a dangerous guy. Up until a few weeks ago, I was still living with my parents and reading comic books.

"Fuck you," I screamed. "They'll just have to kill me, You Mother-fucker!"

"OK," he said calmly. He got up and walked to the door. "You can have a seat in the bullpen." He tossed my file into a metal basket and opened the door.

"Williams," he called out, reading from the clipboard on the wall. "1-5-3-2-9-7."

A black inmate got up from the floor of the crowded bullpen and crossed the hall. The psychologist shut the door to begin his next evaluation, and I sat in the space that Williams had just cleared, struggling not to let anything show in my face. I'd learn later, he wrote in my file that I was violent and dangerous and recommended I be sent to M-R.

"Yo! White boy," a black inmate with cornrows said. "What'd he say?"

"He said I'm going to M-R," I shrugged, pretending it didn't bother me.

"Damn, Homey! You're too motherfuckin' pretty to be going to no M-R."

"Broomstick handles and garbage can lids," another blurted. "You're goin' to Gladiator School."

"Nah," Cornrows said. "How old are you, Blood?"

"Seventeen," I replied.

"Nah." He said, shaking his head confidently. "They'll send you to Riverside. There's no way they'll send some pretty white boy like you to M-R. No way."

1

Camp Dearborn

Color of Eyes: Blue   Color of Hair: Red now, is Blond (8 weeks)
Complexion: Peaches and Cream

Remarks: A darling baby boy who smiles and talks to his mommy like
crazy. A sweet little bundle of joy. Timmy, at 8 weeks, you are
Mommy's precious doll. I hope you will always make me as
happy and lovable as you due [sic] right now.

First said 'Daddy': 10 Mos. Da Da   First said 'Momma': 11 Mos.

Other First Words: See, Hurt   First put together words: I don't want to

SOURCE: Mom's entries in my Baby Book.

As a boy, I spent my summers at Camp Dearborn. It was located in Milford, Michigan, about thirty-five miles northwest of Detroit. The camp was owned by the City of Dearborn and reserved for the use by its residents.

Dearborn was the birthplace of Henry Ford and home to The Ford Motor Company, where my Dad worked as a painter. During the week Dad stayed at home, while my Mom, older brother and sister and I were out at camp.

On 625 acres of rolling hills, trees and man-made beaches, the campsites offered electric hook-up for tents, pop-up campers and trailers like my Dad's recently painted Air Stream. There were six manmade lakes, paddle and row-boats, a large swimming pool, and playground equipment in the shape of giant rocket ships. I remember climbing up through the four levels of the spacecraft where I could navigate to far off galaxies with a large metal steering wheel. I wanted to be the astronaut who landed the first mission on the moon. Two chambers below was the emergency evacuation slide for when Mom called me to dinner or when Dad had arrived for the weekend. From the top of the ship, I could see our trailer at the foot of the hill. It looked like a giant blue marshmallow, ready for roasting on one of the many campfires that were held at night.

After dinner, I went up the hill with Mom to the shower house where she washed dishes in one of the deep outdoor sinks. It was where the real toilets were, like the kind we had at home. I hated the brown stinky outhouses that were located throughout the park. I was scared of bugs, especially spiders, and I was afraid of falling into the hole. The real toilets flushed and they didn't have all the creepy crawlers.

In the kitchen of our trailer, next to the fridge, Mom had taped all my ribbons to the Friday night talent shows. Mom loved showing them off. I had a ukulele with four strings, and I sang like Elvis Presley and the Beatles and everyone in the camp knew me.

"Hey! There's our little Beatle," someone said, as I walked with Dad down by the paddleboats. I wasn't even in school yet and I was already famous. Dad patted me on the head and rustled my blond hair. My sister had Dad's black hair, but I got his blue eyes.

My favorite song was "She Loves You" and to my young ears, I sang it as good as the Beatles. Mom cut my bangs so I looked just like them. And even before I got up on stage, the audience would start to clap and giggle. They loved my song so much that I'd been singing it all summer.

I won the talent show every week, except the last one, when Connie and her girlfriend won. I didn't think it was fair, because they couldn't even finish their song.

Connie and Laurie were two years older than me and had been practicing all week. I wanted to help, but they kept shooing me away. They rehearsed their routine, so they shook their fingers and then rocked their arms like they were cradling a baby. But at show time, they forgot their moves and stopped doing it the way they had practiced. They looked like Connie's Chatty Cathy doll the way Mom made them costumes on her sewing machine, using blue pastel crepe paper and flowers to hide the pins. They wore their bathing suits underneath, because the talent show was right after swim class.

"Miss Polly had a Dolly . . . That was Sick Sick Sick," They pointed their fingers and shook them in unison. Connie started to giggle while Laura kept on singing. *"Who called up the Doctor to Come Quick, Quick, Quick!"* Then Laura began to giggle and they had to start over. They kept starting over and then cracking up and pretty soon they had everyone laughing. The audience loved them. But I still don't think they should give ribbons for giggling. It didn't take any talent to do that.

The next morning, Connie's Chatty Cathy was found floating in the creek.

When my older brother Ricky wasn't away at big kid's camp, Mom made him look after me. Other times, I'd follow him around, even when he didn't know I was doing it. I loved to spy on him. One time, I caught him and cousin Donnie smoking a cigarette. I watched from the base of the Rocket, as they hid on the side of the ugly-brown outhouse.

A moment or two later, when a grown-up lady went inside the outhouse, they got down on the ground and yelled up through the floor boards, "Hey Lady! We're working down here!" The woman inside screamed and the boys ran off laughing.

When Rick discovered that I was following him, he yelled at me to go back to the trailer, but I threatened to tell on them for smoking and he let me come along. We pulled that trick at the outhouse many times that summer. It was always good for a scream.

The canteen was where we ate when Mom didn't feel like cooking. They served hot dogs and hamburgers and the greatest french fries God ever put on earth. They were crinkle cut—the kind with ridges, and were best when you got them while hot. But not too hot or they'd burn the roof of your mouth. The ketchup was in a large plastic jug, but I needed someone to get it because it was up on the counter and too high for me to reach. The ketchup was always warm so I couldn't use it to cool my fries. I would sit and wait, testing with my tongue every few minutes. But that could be dangerous, because the longer it took for them to cool, the greater the risk that one of my cousins would come along and want some. "It's always polite to share," Mom would say. I hated being polite.

Mom didn't like it when the Parsells were out at the camp. I heard her say once that she thought they were a bad influence on Dad. Dad had five brothers and sisters, a couple of cousins plus all their kids. He always seemed happier when they were around.

Dad and Uncle Billy were the only ones who lived in Dearborn; so they had to sneak the rest of them in. They didn't have a trailer either, so they slept in tents. With twenty-six cousins, it wasn't easy getting everyone in. Dad and Uncle Billy would remove the Camp Dearborn sticker from the inside windshield of their cars and share it. Or they'd take turns driving in and out—smuggling the rest of our clan into the park.

At night, they stayed up late drinking and sometimes got so loud it was hard to sleep, but then everyone slept in the next morning and that made it easier to stay up again the next night.

Inside our trailer, I slept on the upper bunk, where I'd watch the bugs fly around the light just outside the door. In the mornings, there were always a few trapped inside the globe. I wondered how they got in there, and how stupid they were for not going back out the same way they came in.

Mom didn't like all the drinking, especially around us kids. She had grown up with a mother who drank a lot and she didn't want us growing up the same way. Mom was only fifteen when she ran off to marry my Dad. She told my Grandpa that she was perfectly capable of raising a family of her own, because she already had. Mom was the oldest of four kids, and when her Mom passed out on the sofa by three in the afternoon—Mom had to look after the others.

My grandparents were married on October 29, 1929. Mom said the stock market's crash that day did little to dampen the spirits of her parents' wedding. The O'Rourkes and The Costellos. My grandma, being the Costello, had fourteen brothers and sisters. All of them eventually died of one form of alcoholism or another.

Mom said the O'Rourkes were very different from the Costellos. They didn't mix well at all, mostly because of the drinking. "The Costello reunions were always the same," Mom would say. "They'd start out falling down laughing and they'd end up falling down drunk." Mom, being the oldest, felt responsible and now that she had her own family—the Parsells were continuing the same tradition.

Mom and Dad argued a lot about the Parsells. I heard them screaming once about *choosing* and they were both very angry. That was when Mom would start breaking things. She'd grab a plate from the counter or a flowerpot from the window and smash it on the floor. It would scare me and I'd start to cry. She promised me she wouldn't do it anymore, but I knew she couldn't help herself when she got mad at Dad.

Mom said I had a strong mind and that all I had to do was force myself to think about something else. I thought about ice cream and candy and birthdays and Christmas. I thought about G.I. Joe and Tigger and 31 Flavors ice cream. And how hard it was to choose with so many flavors.

Dad said that Mom usually got her way, especially when she wouldn't speak to him for days at a time. My aunts and uncles went camping in Irish Hills. It was about a hundred miles away. And for as long as they stayed away, peace would reign, but they eventually returned and the parties continued. Mom said she didn't know how much more she could take. She wanted a different life, but Dad seemed content with the one he had. It was the harbinger of a divorce.

2

Last Chance for Romance

*In front of our trailer was an old fashion farm-hand water pump with a
long cast-iron handle. I liked helping my older brother pump until the
water gushed from the spout. It took both of us to carry the five-gallon jug
back inside. I couldn't believe that water could be so heavy. Ricky could
have carried it himself, but he let me help because he knew I was sad he was
going away.*

*Boys Camp was just up the hill and in the woods, but I wouldn't see
him again for two whole weeks. He said he was going to get away from
me, but I knew he went for the merit badges. Last time he got one for
fishing, rifling, horsemanship, and cowboy crafts. I wished I could've
gone too, but you had to be ten and I was almost five.*

*I hated the taste of well water. Mom said I'd get used to it, but even
with wild-berry Kool-Aid mixed inside it tasted like the time I got my
tongue stuck to the swing set in the middle of winter.*

On my last night before going to prison, my brother Rick took me into
Detroit to buy me a hooker. As we made the forty-five minute trip downtown, Donna Summer's "Last Dance" played on the radio of my brother's
van. We sang along, modifying the lyrics to suit our adventure, laughing and
enjoying our last few hours together.

It was my last chance for romance, and Rick knew where to take me. I
was nervous about going downtown. I didn't know anything about Detroit,
except for the Hudson's Thanksgiving Day Parade and vague recollections
of the Boblo Boat down on the riverfront. But that was before things started
to crumble at home and our parents got a divorce. The boat would take us

up the Detroit River to Boblo Island, an amusement park somewhere between Michigan and Canada. That was also before the race riots of the late 1960s, from which, Detroit never seemed to recover. The city was now mostly black.

As we exited the expressway, we drove past a row of burned-out buildings. I had always thought *Race Riots* was an odd expression, since there was only one race involved, but Detroit was a city that had been looted—gutted of jobs and money. What was left behind continued to decay, but the city's problems started long before those separations.

The whites had moved to the suburbs, where it was thought of as safe, and the mayor of our town was determined to keep it that way. *Keep Dearborn Clean* was the slogan displayed on the sides of police cars, which really meant Keep Dearborn White.

Mayor Oriville Hubbard was the longest serving mayor in the history of Dearborn, a small working-class suburb that bordered Detroit. He was an outspoken separatist, who once told the *New York Times*, "I don't hate niggers. Hell, I don't even dislike them. I just don't think whites should have to live with them—that's all."

Dad said that if blacks got caught driving through Dearborn after dark, they were arrested and held in the jail for seventy-two hours—the maximum allowable by law until the police had to charge them with a crime or let them go. It was supposed to send the message that even if just driving through, they weren't welcome in Dearborn.

Fortunately for my brother and me, the police in Detroit were still mostly white, so we didn't run the same risk as the blacks did for just driving around at night.

Rick was five years older than me. He was bigger and stronger, and had always looked out for me. And this last night was no exception. He intended for this to be the best night, given the circumstances, wanting to send me off in style.

He had Mom's Irish freckles and Dad's sense of humor. As he tapped on the steering wheel to the beat of the tune, the tattoos on his knuckles danced under the strobe of the passing streetlamps.

I had always worshipped him. When I first started school, they let the kindergarten class out five minutes earlier than the older grades, so I ran as fast as I could to the other side of the building and into his fifth grade classroom.

"Is Rrrrricky heeeeerrrrrrrrre," I'd sing, hanging onto each syllable as if each one gave comfort until the time passed and we could walk home together. The first time I did this, the kids in his class stared at me in a stunned silence, before erupting in laughter, which I mistook for encouragement. Rick complained to Mom and Dad, but otherwise he was a pretty good sport about it, and I learned how to wait for him, silently, just outside the door. It was the same way we used to hide, underneath our beds, when Mom was mad at Dad and smashing things all over the house.

Sometimes, Rick and cousin Gordon would ditch me by running into the woods next to our school. I wasn't allowed to go into the woods, so I'd sit down on the grass and wait for them to come back to get me. I loved being with him, even when I was old enough to walk home alone. If anyone ever tried bullying me, they left me alone once they found out Ricky was my big brother. He was a tough kid, and everyone knew it.

He was upset I was going to prison. For weeks he kept telling me, over and over, "If anyone tries to fuck with you, just pick up a chair or a pipe or anything you can get your hands on, and blast them over the head with it. Don't take no shit from nobody," he'd say. "You let them know, right up front, that you're not to be fucked with! It's very important. You gotta let them know right way." He had a look in his eye that scared me, but it was his fear, not mine, that frightened me most.

He was always good at figuring me out, so if he sensed he was making me scared, he'd change the subject or tell one of his funny stories from when he served time. It usually worked. He had a way of making it sound more like an adventure, than a punishment or something to be feared.

Rick hated Sharon, our stepmom, as much as I did. He ran away from home when he was thirteen and was placed in a reform school. When Dad wasn't working, or off on another bender, he'd take us up to visit him on weekends. We'd stop on the way, at a supermarket, and pick up candy and fruit, but we weren't allowed to have any ourselves, because it was for Ricky. It was a good thing I loved him, because it never seemed fair that the treats should go to the one who had gotten into trouble. Inside the visiting room, we'd sit and watch him eat, as he told us stories about what went on in there.

He could always spin a tale that would make us laugh. Reform school didn't sound like such a bad place. He confided in me once that it was better than being at home.

Dad reminisced about what it was like when he had been sent there. He and Uncle Ronnie served a couple of years for breaking into a store when they were kids.

When the state wouldn't let Rick come home for the Christmas holiday, Dad helped him escape by holding the front door open as he was leaving the visiting room. Ricky ran out the door, and Dad yelled after him. "Rick! Don't do it," in a bogus attempt to look like he was surprised. A few minutes later, Dad picked him up down the road, at a spot where they had agreed to meet.

After the holidays were over, Dad took him downtown to sign up for the military. Dad had to do the same thing, when he was eighteen, except that a judge gave him the army as an ultimatum. Otherwise, he would have gone to jail.

Rick said the Air Force was also better than being at home, but then he got a dishonorable discharge for giving a "blanket party" to a snitch. That's when you throw a blanket over someone and beat the shit out of him. Later, when Rick went to prison, he never did say if prison was better than being at home.

But on my last night, Rick laid off the advice. We had set aside the time for fun and laughter and enjoying each other's company for the last time. We started drinking at his apartment around three, and then he took me for a steak dinner at The Ponderosa. Afterward, he smoked a joint, and I drank more beers.

Rick liked country music, but since it was my night, he let me listen to whatever I wanted on the radio. I loved the new sounds of disco. It had a beat and a rhythm that felt sinful and bad, and something else I couldn't explain. It had a feeling of forbidden access, maybe because it was black, and whites didn't listen to black music.

My friends all listened to rock and roll. They liked the Detroit bands like Alice Cooper, Ted Nugent, Bob Seger and The Silver Bullet Band. I liked rock and roll as well, but I was fascinated with disco. Though I wished I had the courage to listen to what I wanted to without caring what others thought of me. "Turn off that nigger shit," one of my friends sneered. After that, I only listened to disco when I was alone.

I had seen *Saturday Night Fever* a few months earlier and fantasized about dancing like John Travolta on a lighted dance floor. The Bee Gees were all the rage, but I'd grown tired of them. They were missing something that black girls like Thelma Houston or Donna Summer had. The way the music made me feel free and afraid all at the same time felt almost sexual.

I couldn't understand why Ricky liked country music. He'd taken his wife Belinda to see Conway Twitty for her birthday. It all seemed so cornball and hillbilly to me, yet ever since he served time in a Florida prison, he liked Hank Williams and Loretta Lynn and complained how Willie Nelson and Waylon Jennings were renegades who were out to ruin country music. I didn't know what he was talking about, and I didn't care. As long as he liked it and didn't try forcing it on me, I was OK with it.

We picked up a black woman, named Candy, on Woodward Avenue. It was in an area known for prostitutes between Six- and Eight-Mile Roads. She had on a leopard-skin miniskirt and rust-colored lipstick that was outlined in a darker brown.

"Don't give her the money until you come," Rick yelled, after having gone first. He zipped up his fly as he walked into the diner to have coffee with her pimp.

As soon as I stepped inside the van, she asked me for the money.

I was nervous, so I gave her the fifteen dollars Rick had negotiated. I pulled down my jeans, past the knees, and leaned back against the side of the wheel well. The carpet was soiled and felt coarse and gritty on the cheeks of my ass. I tried as hard as I could, as did she, but we couldn't seem to get it up. No matter how hard I tried to concentrate, Donna Summer's lyrics kept beating in my head. *"Will you be my Mr. Right? Can you fill my appetite? I can't be sure that you're the one for me."*

I was too ashamed to admit it at the time, but the fact that she was a black woman, or that she had on way too much make-up—had nothing to do with it. It was because she was a woman. I couldn't tell this to my brother; I could barely admit it to myself. It was usually only when drunk that I could face this truth about myself, and even then, it was difficult. I could always blame it on the booze, since it was only when I drank that this desire would surface. Well, sometimes it came up in my fantasies, but then I'd tell myself it was just a phase I was going through. There weren't any queers in my part of town, and I didn't know of any other part that had them either. It was the Midwest in the 1970s and people didn't talk about these things, especially not in my neighborhood, unless it was the butt of a joke.

Queers were what you called a sissy, or a friend that pissed you off. Or it was something you heard about that happened in prison. Maybe that's what my brother was so concerned about. Perhaps that's why he seemed so afraid. Or maybe that was why I felt so drawn there. I don't know. You just didn't talk about these things. That's why, the next morning, I couldn't tell Rick what happened that night, or rather, *what didn't happen*.

My head was hurting from the hangover of my last dance.

3

The Absence of Drama

As I was leaving for court in the morning, Rick came out of the house and called to me.

Sharon started to say something, but stopped herself. Instead, she got into the car and started it. Rick handed me a carton of cigarettes, and Sharon looked away.

My brother and I stared at each other for a long moment, neither of us knowing what to say. It had all been said before. He looked down at his feet and back up again. As usual, he was trying to hold it together. None of us were any good at emotional stuff.

"Remember what I told you," he said. It was his last piece of advice. "No matter what happens in there, Little Brother. It'll be your memories that hold you together."

I looked at him and nodded.

"Up here," he said, thumping the side of my head. "And in here," he gently pressed my chest.

"Not more than four years," the judge ordered, "and no less than two and a half." He scribbled in the folder and passed the file to the clerk seated on his left.

"You are hereby remanded to the Michigan Department of Corrections."

I was disappointed that I didn't get a *May God have mercy on your soul*, or even a *May you rot in hell* final admonishment. It all seemed so horribly lacking in drama. I was just another number. The bailiff was calling the next case before the Sheriff deputy could get his handcuffs on my wrist. The judge didn't look up at me. There was a huge stack of manila folders and dark brown files in front of him. It was sentencing day, and the court had a full docket. They were using an abandoned wing of the Wayne County Hospital as overflow to the congested courts in downtown Detroit.

I looked over at Sharon, she was blowing her nose into a hankie as she turned and walked out. Our eyes didn't meet, so I wasn't sure if there were tears. Dad couldn't get off work that day, or perhaps he couldn't bear to— we knew I was going to prison.

The deputy took me into the back, through a large set of double doors, to a holding cell. A long metal bench was attached to the wall. He unlocked my handcuffs and ordered me to take everything from my pockets and place it onto a table. I removed my wallet and a pack of gum from my right front pocket. I had three quarters and two dimes in the other. I took a pack of cigarettes and a green lighter from my shirt and placed it onto the table next to the carton my brother had given me that morning. He said they would hold me at the county jail a few days until I was transferred to the state prison.

The deputy told me to remove my belt and shoe laces, so I couldn't hang myself, and to place my hands on the wall while he patted me down. He unlocked the cell, ordered me in, and closed the barred door with a clunk. The vibrations echoed off the walls. I tried to ignore the metallic sound of the turning tumblers and the thud of the locking bolt.

I fumbled for a cigarette and asked the deputy for a light, not knowing how long it would be before he'd be back again. He kept my lighter, which was considered contraband, and gave me a book of matches from his shirt pocket and told me to keep them.

"Thanks," I said. My hand slightly shook as I took the matches.

Behind him, a deputy entered with another prisoner. As each new inmate was placed inside the cell, I tried harder not to think about the sound of the turning bolt that slammed into the steel jam I'd gotten myself into. It had been almost a year since I was arrested for sneaking into a hotel room at my after school job at The Airport Inn.

Using a stolen passkey, a buddy and I had gone to the hotel to find an empty room to sleep in. We had been out late drinking and didn't want to go home and risk waking our parents. Sharon was such a light sleeper that when I was younger, she could hear cereal being poured into a bowl and she'd wake up screaming. She made me stand in the corner or kneel at the foot of her bed until she was ready to get up. So if I just didn't go home at night, no one would have cared that I wasn't there.

I was supposed to get probation, but since I was out on bail at the time I was caught for another crime, the judge wouldn't honor my plea bargain. Part of the deal with probation is that you can't get into any more trouble. So I blew it, before I was even sentenced.

My lawyer said, "Don't worry about it. When you come back for the Photo Mat, the judge will probably give you the same amount of time as he did on this sentence."

I guess the biggest problem I had with what he had to say, was the word *probably*. I was worried about it, because everything was happening so quickly. He was a court-appointed attorney, and so far, things hadn't worked out exactly as he said they would. But that wasn't his fault, he was quick to point out, since I was the one who had gotten arrested again.

"Trust me," he said. "You'll go to a minimum-security camp, and with good time, you'll be back on the streets in no time."

My brother was helpful, in terms of coaching me on how to carry myself once I got to prison, but he wouldn't come to court for any of my hearings because he had warrants out for his arrest involving unpaid child support and traffic tickets. So I had been mostly alone. At least Sharon came for my sentencing. She had to drive past the courthouse on her way to work.

The more crowded it got inside the holding pen, the more I realized how must worse my situation was than I'd ever imagined. There was no way out of it now.

Trust me, the lawyer said. He was *probably* right.

4

Who's Angrier than Who?

When we heard Dad's horn outside, I said to my sister Connie, "I looked the last time. It's your turn to look."

We were living at Grandpa's house, on Cook Street, and I was still in the first grade.

Connie walked over to the window and slowly lifted the blinds.

"Is she there?" I asked.

Connie dropped her head and sighed.

We were hoping that Dad's new girlfriend, Sharon, wasn't there or that her two boys, at least, would be off with their own Dad.

"Time to go," Mom yelled from the bathroom, where she was putting on makeup. "Tell your Dad if he doesn't pay me the child-support he owes—he's not getting you kids next weekend."

"Don't tell him," Connie whispered.

After my parents were divorced, we went out to Camp Dearborn with my Dad, Sharon, and her two boys, Bobby and Billy. Bobby was my age, now almost eight, and Billy was a year younger. We no longer had money for things like crepe paper costumes, ice cream, and french fries at the canteen. I stopped competing in the Talent Show. It wasn't the same going there by myself. We ate our meals at the trailer that Dad had rented (the Bank repossessed the big Marshmallow), and Sharon even washed out our straws to save extra money. Bobby said I couldn't sing anyway, and when I tried to argue with him, he asked if I wanted to fight about it. Ricky was away at Boys Camp for what would be his last time.

Connie said Bobby was mean because his dad used to beat him. I didn't care. I wished I could've beaten him too, but he was tough and mean like his mother.

Sharon and I didn't get along well at all. Particularly since I told her what my mom had told me to say. "My momma says she don't want some old broad hitting me! She said she's my momma and if there's any spanking to be done—she'll do it —NOT YOU!"

I stood there with my fists balled at the sides, matching her stare glare for glare.

I didn't know it was possible to see anyone get as angry as Sharon got. Part of what made her mad was that my mom was actually older than her.

Sharon's eyes turned as red as her face as she let out a low rumble that seemed to shake the entire trailer. "Dale," she yelled, back to where my Dad was sleeping. "You better come get him, before I kill him."

Bobby came running in, and Sharon yelled at him to go back outside.

I was terrified to say anything else, so I just stood there trembling, waiting for Dad.

Ricky had been living with them for a couple of months, but Connie and I hadn't been told we were moving in with them for good until just then. Mom said later, she didn't have the heart to tell me, and Dad just thought we had known about it.

Mom couldn't handle us alone anymore. She was studying for her GED so she could get a job with the phone company. In the meanwhile, she worked as a cocktail waitress at the Dearborn Lounge and always came home late. When Dad offered to take us—Mom said OK.

Sharon was the exact opposite of my mom. She screamed and yelled and always seemed mad about something, especially when Dad disappeared for days at a time. Connie said Dad was still heartbroken over Mom's affair. And that Sharon's ex-husband used to beat Sharon up as well. "That's why she's mad all the time," Connie said.

I guess in fairness to Sharon, I was like any other young kid in my situation—she was replacing my mother, so I hated her and I never cut her a break. It probably skewed my perceptions of her.

Dad still only came to camp on weekends, and most of that time was spent sleeping. At night, he sat around the campfires with my aunts and uncles laughing and drinking. "You kids go off and play," they'd say. They didn't like us hanging around when there was so much for us to do there. The camp was ideal for them, because they didn't need a babysitter. There were now twenty-eight of us kids, counting Bobby and Billy and my various cousins.

At the paddleboat lake, there were all types of boats you could rent for a quarter, and each family got two free for every week they stayed in the park. I loved the ones that were shaped like a bicycle. It straddled two pontoons and was faster than all of the others. I used to get on it and pedal as hard as I could, pretending that my hat would catch wind, like in the *Flying Nun,* and carry me away from there.

I just wanted to be back home with my mom.

5

Chain Reactions

On Saturday nights, the camp held teenage dances on the tennis courts next to the canteen. Only a few of my cousins were old enough to go, but that didn't stop the rest of us. We hid on the hill and watched from the shadows.

They looked pretty silly there, especially when they slow-danced, the way they hugged each other and pivoted like they were wind-up toy soldiers. When the beat of the records picked up, they looked even sillier, thrashing their arms about with their thumbs extended, like they didn't know which side of the road they wanted to hitchhike down.

Diana Ross and the Supremes, Petula Clark, and Simon & Garfunkle filled the hot summer air with music that was cool and groovy and spoiled only by the sounds of the electric bug zappers that surrounded the canteen.

We threw small pebbles at the electrified metal grid and giggled as it buzzed. No one could see us hiding unless it was a full moon, and even then it took the glow from the bug zapper's ultraviolent lights to be seen.

Ricky said they were called "ultraviolent" because of the way they vaporized flying insects.

When I arrived at the County Jail, it was just after 6:30. There were twenty-three of us who were transferred downtown. We entered the receiving area joined together by a chain. Our wrists were affixed, every few feet, by handcuffs that were welded to the shackles. We were placed in the first of four holding cells along the right wall. There was a control booth in the center area and a matching set of bullpens on the opposite side of the room. The deputies sorted prisoners based on whether we were sentenced to prison or to county jail time. Sentences of a year or more went to the state prison, and sentences of less than a year either stayed in the county jail or were sent to The Detroit House of Corrections.

The holding cell was dark and crowded. There were over thirty of us, in a space that was large enough for maybe fifteen or twenty men. It reeked of urine. There was a sink and toilet attached to the back wall and an open partition that provided little privacy. There was no toilet paper in sight. Some of the inmates where yelling to the holding cells across the room and others where just yelling. I prayed it wouldn't take long to get us through intake and into our own cells. I was hungry and regretted not eating the stale bologna sandwich they gave us earlier at the Hospital/Courthouse.

As soon as the bars slid shut on our cell, the metal gates to the loading dock opened, and another group was led in on chains. There must have been thirty of us in the pen, but only four of us were white. I sat on the floor, with my back against the wall, avoiding eye contact with anyone. I absently chewed my nails as I tried to pretend it was all routine, like I'd been through before and wasn't fazed, but I was too afraid to look up and see if anyone noticed. It was hard to think with all the noise. The large metal gate opening, inmates yelling, electric cell doors opening and closing, and the sounds of heavy chains crashing to the floor. An inmate kicked the metal tab on the wall, and the toilet made a whoosh as it flushed the rust-colored water down the filthy suck-hole at the bottom of the stainless steel bowl. It continued sucking air long after the water receded and then spit back, noisily, water that was just as filthy.

A deputy came to the front of the cell, "OK, Listen up. When I call out your name, step to the front of the cell."

"Hey Dep! Can I ask you somethin'?" a stocky black inmate pleaded.

"Williams, Johnson, Taylor," the deputy read from a clipboard, holding a pen in his right hand as he went down his list. "Miller, Hughes, Jackson."

"Yo, Dep!" the black man persisted, "Please! I have a quick question."

"Walters, Parsell, Pierce." He looked to his right and yelled, "Open Five!" Two deputies came over and joined him. All three of them were white.

I followed as each man stepped from the cell. The deputy with the clipboard checked off our names. The other two deputies motioned us to the right and ordered us to line up, turn in and face the holding cell with our backs to them.

"Officer! Please, just one quick question."

"Close five!" the deputy yelled, not looking up. The gate jolted forward and closed on Holding Cell Five. "OK Maggots, let's go."

They led us past the other cells and into an open area. There was a counter to the right with stacks of blue plastic bins and to the left a long cinderblock bench. The deputy told us to take a seat and to remove our shoes. My shoelaces were still with my other belongings that were taken at the courthouse, including my carton of cigarettes.

One at a time, we were called into the next room where there was a black curtain tacked to the wall, opposite a large Bell & Howell camera. The deputy handed me a letter board that read, Wayne County Jail. My name was spelled out in tiny letters. March 3, 1978, was indicated below.

"Hold it just under your chin," the deputy ordered.

I'd seen this a hundred times before, in the movies, but it felt chilling to see my name written along the felt grove. I was startled by a loud thump and dropped the board. The plastic letters scattered to the floor, but I couldn't see them because the large flash had temporarily blinded me.

"Oh Jesus," the deputy said under his breath. "Why the fuck don't they put these on a chain?" He came out from behind the camera and kicked the letters off to the side. I flinched, half expecting him to hit me. I guessed he could tell it was my first time.

After he reconstructed the board and took a profile, he led me to the next room where he placed a thin white piece of cardboard on an easel at the edge of the counter. He clamped a metal frame down to hold it into place, squeezed a dab of ink from a tube and used a small roller to spread it evenly across the smooth surface of the template.

"Relax," he said, ordering me to stand behind him, "and let me guide your hand."

He took my index finger and rolled it, left-to-right, onto the inked surface and then repeated the same motion onto the marked section of the cardboard. He captured each impression with a swiftness and precision of someone who'd been doing this a long time. When he was done, he handed me a piece of tissue, which was barely large enough to clean one hand. He didn't seem to care. "Have a seat out front," he said.

Next, I was handed a blue storage bin and told to take off my clothes and place them inside. The deputy pointed to the bench where two black inmates were sitting naked. A third nude inmate was standing up, his back to me, with his arms stretched to the side.

"OK, good," a deputy in front of him said, as the prisoner complied with each command. "Now open your mouth and lift your tongue . . . OK . . . Good. Run your fingers through your hair . . . Shake it . . . Good . . . Lift up your balls . . . OK . . . Turn around and bend over . . . Spread your cheeks . . . Wider . . . OK. Let me see the bottom of your feet. Good . . . Have a seat on the bench."

The deputy ran through his routine like the one who had taken my fingerprints. As if he was working at The Fisher Body Plant—just putting in an eight-hour shift as the endless stream of chassis came down the line. The first inmate sat down, and the deputy pointed to the next. "Open your mouth," he said. "Lift up your tongue . . . Run your hands through your hair . . . Good . . . Lift up your balls . . ."

I could feel the blood draining from my face. I was afraid to take off my clothes, especially in front of everyone, but I didn't have a choice. I couldn't pass on the shower and take an F for the day, like I used to do in gym class on days when I wasn't sure I'd get through a shower without a boner embarrassing me. One time, when a kid looked over and noticed, he called me a fag. I wanted to die. So on school days, I'd jerk off right before I caught the bus, hoping it would relieve enough pressure to get me through the mornings, but gym wasn't until second period, which was usually enough time for my balls to regenerate and spring my shaft to an unmanageable attention.

When I was at risk of failing the entire semester, I tried to relieve myself in the bathroom right before gym, but there wasn't enough time in between classes, and people kept coming in. I was afraid they'd look between the cracks of the stall or from the shadows on the floor and see what I was doing. A couple of times, I slipped out of first period early, but there were always one or two guys in the bathroom, sneaking a smoke. So I kept failing gym and had to retake it. It was a stupid requirement for graduation.

So at the county jail, taking an F wasn't an option, and even worse, I was too hungover that morning to do anything before I left for court. I was hoping my hangover would get me through it, but it was awfully late in the day. I was really frightened, because there was now a lot more at stake than just being called a fag.

I set the bin down and slowly took off my clothes, hoping the deputy would finish with the others and take them away before it was my turn for the humiliating butt check. I was down to my underwear when he ordered the other three into the showers.

As they walked off, three more naked inmates carrying bedrolls and clothes brushed past heading out toward the bullpens. I tossed my underwear into the bin and sat back on the bench, cupping my shriveled source of embarrassment with both hands.

The other deputy stepped away, so I was left there, sitting alone. Goose bumps rolled over me as if a cold chill had swept the room. I shivered slightly, but my face felt warm.

Three more inmates were led in, handed blue bins and told to take a seat on the bench. I scooted over, hanging on for dear life. I clenched my chattering teeth, but my heart was pounding, "Please God, GET ME THE FUCK OUT OF HERE!"

6

Safety in Numbers

On an Easter morning, when my dad was a kid, he got up early before his brothers and sisters were awake. He ate the ears off everyone's chocolate Easter bunny. Everyone's that is except for my Aunt Diane's.

Aunt Diane got blamed, but my Dad got caught, because he was the only one who wasn't crying.

There were several televisions located throughout Camp Dearborn. They were locked up, during the day, in large wooden cabinets. Our whole clan gathered around the TVs at night to watch our favorite shows: *Wagon Train*, *Tarzan*, and *Batman & Robin*.

Around the big Totem Pole, during the day, we fought over who got to play *Wagon Train*'s Chris Hale or Barnaby West and who had to be the scouts that went out looking for Indians. The older cousins liked being the Indians, but we had to stop playing because they started taking the game too seriously. On TV, the Indians would capture the scouts and torture them, leaving them tied up in the desert to dehydrate and wither away.

"Where's Billy?" Sharon asked, as she rustled us up for dinner. She had made Sloppy Joes, which were Billy's favorite.

Someone had tied him to a tree and forgot about him. When we found him, he was blindfolded and gagged with two red Indian bandanas. Sharon got mad, and we weren't allowed to play anymore, even though the real reason it happened was because Billy squealed on Ricky and Donny for stealing watermelons out of the creek.

After a few summers, we got bored with these games and sought out more exciting adventures. Given the size of our clan, we developed quite a reputation as we grew older. Cousins Donnie, Marty, and my brother Rick were all teenagers now, but they thought the dances were too square. As we hid on the hill, they used their slingshots and took turns nailing kids in the butt. Bobby and I brought along our peashooters, but they didn't work as well. When Rick took out one of the bug zappers, the camp counselors were on to us.

Occasionally, someone would chase us, but we rarely got caught. One night, when cousin Jamie got nabbed by some kid who tried to take him back to the canteen, the kid ran away quickly when he saw how many of us there were.

Meanwhile, our parents spent nights around the campfire bragging about their own youthful adventures. Like the time Dad and Uncle Ronnie went down the street in the middle of the night pushing cars into the road. People didn't lock their cars back then, so they slipped the gears into neutral and shoved each one down the driveway. When they were done, they banged on a door at the end of the block and then ran into the woods, where they watched in laughter as each house alerted the next and a string of porch lights lit up the neighborhood.

My favorite story involved my Dad putting a bag over his head and robbing the neighborhood paperboy, who happened to be his half-cousin. "I know that's you, Dale!" the kid bellyached, as he handed over his money. "I'm telling your Mom."

They laughed hysterically every time that story was told, as if they hadn't heard it a hundred times before. I guess everything sounded funny when you were happy and drinking. In spite of their own craziness, my family always had a good time when they were together.

Of course, we kids tried to copy our parent's pranks. One of my favorites was to go around at night unplugging trailers. It was especially fun to peep through the window to see what the people were doing. Like when they were playing poker—we'd watch as they raised one another back and forth and then, *Boom*, just as they were about to show their hand—we'd pull the old plug and run.

For a longest time, I wanted to be a lawyer when I grew up. *Perry Mason* was my favorite show on TV. I wanted to be just like him. My Dad said you had to be smart to be a lawyer, but since he never finished the sixth grade—and most of my family had no schooling beyond high school—we didn't know how long it would take in school to become one. Some folks had TVs inside their trailers, and I remember watching from the window while Perry Mason, played by Raymond Burr, cross-examined a witness to elicit a last-minute confession. All of the show's hour-long leads would come down to these last few critical moments, when Perry would have the witness quivering on the stand. His secretary, Della Street, or Paul Drake, his private eye, would hand Perry an envelope then, just as the witness was about to confess— BAM . . . we'd pull the plug. "Oh Shit! You dirty little bastards!" Off into the darkness we'd run.

A lot of our pranks weren't as much fun if we weren't chased afterward. In fact, being chased was one of the most enjoyable things we did together. I liked the rush that came with it—my heart pounding and the shortness of breath. It made my whole body tingle. Like ridding a roller coaster or watching a scary movie—it made you jump, but then it made you laugh, and you wanted to go again.

There were several pavilions, where groups held family picnics that included a variety of games and prizes. We'd sneak in on the fun and share in the ice cream, watermelon, and potato sack races. Since the camp supervised most of the activities, over time, we got to know the games pretty well. Once, after cousin Rusty won several prizes in a row, including the dance contest, someone wanted to know whose little boy he was, and his cover was blown. We didn't get into too much trouble, though, since it was Uncle Ronnie's idea in the first place. That night, we heard our parents laughing about it.

When Dad's grandma ran out of money, she was forced to move in with Grandpa. Grandpa had rented her house to a hillbilly who stopped taking care of the place, and when Grandpa went to talk him—the man threatened Grandpa with a shotgun. When Dad and Uncle Ronnie found out about it, they went there at night and moved the outhouse back a few feet. They covered the hole with a piece of cardboard and kicked dirt on top of it to make it look like the ground. Then they started a fire behind it and tossed a couple stones at the house to get the man's attention. When the man saw the fire, he ran out and fell into the hole. Dad and Ronnie and a couple of cousins then pissed on the man, telling him that if he didn't move out, they'd kill him next time. I didn't know if they were serious, but Uncle Ronnie said the tenant moved out that very week.

We laughed as much our parents did when Uncle Ronnie repeated that story, but soon they chased us away. We were forced to sit around our own fires and think up our own capers. Sometimes, we laughed so hard at the idea that pulling off the prank wasn't as much fun. We loved it when we could make each other laugh, because in that moment, it meant someone was paying attention. For that fleeting instant, we knew we were loved.

7

Early Induction to an Inverted World

I was given a clean set of underwear, a pair of gray socks, dark green pants with a worn-out waistband, and a pullover shirt that had Wayne County Jail stenciled on back. I got through showering without incident—I didn't know how I thought I'd get an erection when I was so frightened—but then the size of my pants was about three sizes too big, which I wouldn't know until after I was told to walk into the next bullpen *buck naked* to put them on. When I entered the cell, the other inmates were already dressed and sitting on benches that ran along the sidewalls. I took an empty space on the left and got dressed quickly.

A parade of naked men followed me, each entering the bullpen with bedroll and clothing in hand—their private parts pivoting from side to side. By the time the cell was full, there were two or three dozen of us. Most of them were black, well muscled, in their twenties to early thirties. I felt smaller and skinnier, and paler than ever.

I tried not to be too obvious, but I couldn't help sneaking a look. To my young eyes, everyone's dick seemed enormous. These were grown men, and I couldn't imagine what they'd look like when sporting a boner. I had run out of nails to chew, and my right leg bounced nervously as I tried to distract my attention.

I thought about music and measure and the melody of a metronome. How calming its cadence could be. I thought about the black and white of a piano keyboard, and how I'd always wanted to play. For the first time, I got a glimpse of what it must have been like for a black man, who suddenly found himself in an all-white neighborhood. I thought about old Mayor Hubbard and how it was best not to mention where I was from.

There were three whites in the holding cell, not counting me, and over twenty or thirty blacks. The other whites were older than me, in their early twenties, and one of them looked like a biker. He was big and burly, with curly brown hair and a scraggly beard. He asked for a cigarette, and when I gave him one, he didn't even bother to say thanks. His manner was cold, and his eyes were mean, but when he stepped back from the bars and almost tripped over a black guy, he suddenly looked a lot less threatening.

"Hey! Watch where you're goin', you big ass redneck."

"Hey, fuck you," the biker shot back.

The black guy and two others jumped to their feet.

"Yeah? What are you gonna do about it?"

Two more blacks stood up.

"Yeah, honky. What are you gonna do?"

A flash of fear registered in the biker's eyes.

"Nothing" he said quickly, brandishing a pathetic smile.

The biker was missing teeth, which gave the impression he wasn't so meek, but he didn't stand a chance.

"All right then," the black guy said, slowly backing down. He looked over at one of the others. "Someone's got to teach these woods."

The biker took a seat on the floor, looking more like a defeated fat guy.

The other two whites looked away, disavowing any connection.

Wood was short for peckerwood. It was used like "nigger" or "coon," "porch monkeys" and "spooks"—except peckerwood was a word blacks called whites, along with honky and rednecks, crackers and ghosts. But on that side of the bars, only blacks spoke those words aloud. The jail was located in downtown Detroit, where the whites were highly outnumbered.

It felt like I'd walked inside a photographic negative, where all the values were reversed.

The bullpen was quiet.

An inmate at the back of the cell broke the silence.

"There was this fag in here once," he said. "Called herself Angela Davis."

"I knew her," another said, referring to *her* as naturally as if she were a woman.

"*She* sucked off the whole bullpen," he said.

"The whole bullpen," the con next to him said. "No shit?"

"Square business!" He nodded. "Went right around this cell. Must've blown a dozen guys."

"I remember that," another said. "She sucked a mean dick."

"She sure did. And then, when she was done . . ." he paused, holding everyone's attention. "The bitch dropped her drawers and wanted to get fucked!"

The others laughed, and shook their heads, saying things like, "Damn!" or "Shit! Can you believe that? You'd think one dick would be enough."

"Uh, uh." The guy shook his head. "That bitch loved to suck dick!"

"She sure did," the other said, rubbing his crotch. "And I sure could use her now."

To my right, the convicts who were standing at the front of the bullpen looked out at reception with their hands resting on the cross section of bars. It was dark inside our cell, and the deputies didn't seem interested in what went on in there.

I was glad I was dressed. My right leg continued to bounce.

When the heavy metal door of the cellblock slammed shut, a shudder went through my body. A sudden jolt of panic made me want to scream out to the guards, *"I was just kidding! I wasn't really going to rob that Photomat. Could I please go home now?"*

But it was too late. The guards were already gone.

It was ten o'clock by the time they moved me upstairs. I was placed in a cellblock with mostly white, nonviolent offenders. They no longer segregated by race, the deputy had told me, but they did try to separate first-time offenders. I was six foot two, but at a hundred and forty-eight pounds, I wasn't much more than skin and bones.

On some level, I was still half expecting my parents to show up and take me home—hoping I'd learned my lesson. That maybe this was all just part of a Scared Straight program that I had heard about, where they took teenagers inside a prison to frighten them away from crime. But the reality of my situation was as cold as the metal slab that would cradle me to sleep that night.

I started to cry, but quickly muffled it. I was certain that if the other inmates heard me, they'd see me for what I was—a sniffling coward who was pretending to be something he's not. Or worse, they would see for me for what I was.

"Never!" My brother Rick smacked me on the chin the night before. "Never, let them know what you're thinking."

I could still almost smell the tobacco on his finger, from when he shook it in my face. He was imitating Marlon Brando in *The Godfather*. We shared a love of gangster films, but in that moment, I was alone in my cell, and the wall of my emotional front was about as thin as the cheap mattress that was folded over my bunk.

Inside the cell, a steel toilet and sink were attached to the back wall. Smoke rings burned on the ceiling spelled out the words Fuck and You and Hell and Here. Simon, '77 was scratched on the sidewall. It reeked of bleach and ammonia, piss and damp cigarettes. And, like the bullpens downstairs, there wasn't any toilet paper in sight.

By the time we got upstairs, we had missed dinner, so it would be morning before I'd eat again. I was hungry, but the pang of anxiety quickly took over. For the first time in over twelve hours, I was alone. I could finally drop the tough guy, this-doesn't-faze-me, I've-been-through-it-all-before act. It probably wasn't working anyway, but I had to keep it up. Ricky had been coaching me for weeks. *My God! What's going to happen to me?*

I unfolded the mattress across the steel frame and wrapped the sheet around it. They didn't have pillows in the county jail, so I folded the end of the pad under itself to prop my head. I'd rather my feet dangle on cold metal than sleep with my head lying flat.

I stared up at the ceiling and tried to imagine how someone had scorched the letters that formed each word. It would have taken too many matches. Perhaps they burned their sheets?

I lit a cigarette with my last match and thought about my brother. I wondered what he was doing and whether he missed me.

The lights went out with a buzz and a thump. The light from the catwalk cast shadows in my cell. The silhouette of bars, pitched on angles, criss-crossed the walls.

The next morning, the lights came back on with the same buzz and thump that accompanied darkness. I hadn't slept well, tossing and turning on the slab, my head full of visions of street fights and gladiators, drag queens and bikers. It felt like I'd just fallen asleep.

I lay awake for several minutes, wondering if I'd be transferred to Jackson today. An old timer, down in the bullpen, had mentioned the economy and prisons and a shortage of beds. I drifted back to sleep, but the sound of the door to my cell sliding open and scuffling feet woke me up. I looked out and saw several inmates running past my cell.

I jumped up to look out.

Inmates at the end of the cellblock were grabbing milk, juice, and small wax paper bags from the cross-section of the bars. Breakfast consisted of three white-powdered donuts, a half pint of milk and a four-ounce container of orange juice. I walked down to get it, but when I got there, there was only a carton of milk left.

"You snooze—You lose," a white inmate said. He was holding an orange juice and milk, but someone had taken his bag as well. "You gotta get here quick or some motherfucker steals your donuts, man."

I took the milk from the bars and looked to see if I could spot a deputy through the small opening in the outer door.

"Don't even bother to call the deps, Little Bro." He walked back toward his cell, "They really don't give a fuck."

I was hungry. I hadn't eaten since the steak dinner my brother bought me two days earlier. The next morning, when the light came on, I was up and ready for the mad breakfast derby. When the deputies pulled the brake, like a horse bolting from the starting gate, I was off and running to get my three powdered rings from the cross-section of the finishing line. Win, Place, or Show, I was sure to get mine. But this time, when I arrived at the front of the line, the same white guy from the day before, was there to greet me. As I took my share, I watched him snatch two bags of donuts and stuff them into his underwear, grab a third in his hand and quickly pull his shirt down to hide it.

He shot me a look that said, *don't you dare say a fucking word.*

As I walked back toward my cell, I overheard him telling the new fish behind me, "You snooze—you lose, Little Brother. But don't even bother to tell the deputies. They really don't give a fuck."

31

8

The Big Blue Wagon Ride

The Detroit Free Press was delivered in the morning, *The Detroit News* in the afternoon. I once won a sales contest by delivering the paper as early as anyone wanted it. I converted several *News* customers to *Free Press* accounts by delivering before 6:00 A.M. The papers were ready as early as 3:00, but I preferred getting them at 4:00. That way, I could be back in bed by 5:30 to catch an extra hour of sleep before school. Even in the summer, I was up and out before dawn. I loved how peaceful it was, being alone on the street, with the solitary sound of my rusty red wagon's rickety wheels.

"Does anyone have a cigarette?" I yelled through the screen of the hippies' home. They were early on my route and often still up when I got there by 4:15.

"Who's that?" one of them asked.

"It's the paperboy!" a guy yelled from the couch.

From the porch, I watched as he passed a joint to the gal sitting on his lap. She was in cut-off jeans, with filthy feet, and her long brown hair looked as scattered as her speech.

"How cute," she stammered, handing the joint toward me. "Do ya wanna hit, toke smoke off of this?"

Her name was Crystal, but she sometimes answered to Joy.

"Na," I said. "But I'll take a cigarette."

Her eyes looked red and watery.

Zingy, the guy who let me in, must have used the same barber.

I was about to turn fourteen, and like most kids in my neighborhood, I had started smoking that year. I didn't like it at first, but we all thought it was cool to smoke Kools. The hippies were always good for a cigarette, or a beer, and if I wanted it, pot, but it made me feel stupid and fearful, so I stuck to the smokes and an occasional brew.

Pretty soon, the hippies' home became a regular hangout for me.

An aging poster of Jimi Hendrix hung on the wall above a large stack of albums. A beat-up sofa, a beanbag chair, a few overstuffed pillows, and three dead houseplants completed the living room. An uneven beaded curtain hung from the doorway that led to the kitchen. The quadraphonic stereo was their only decent possession. They said things like *shedding the shackles of social conformity* and *ridding the mind of material illusions.* The house reeked of patchouli incense that camouflaged the smell of marijuana.

I loved having older friends, and even better, it made some of the younger ones jealous. My brother was away in the military, and they somehow made missing him easier—even when they ragged on me about the Vietnam War. It didn't seem to matter that my brother was in Texas, or that the war had ended earlier that year.

The hippies were good tippers too—that is, when they paid their bill. Each week when it came time to collect, they'd pass a hat and fill it with coins, cigarettes, and joints. I gave the pot to my friends, keeping the cigarettes for myself. Most of the time, there wasn't enough change to cover the cost of the paper, but since I never saw anyone reading it, I figured it was a fair trade. I enjoyed their company and with the cost of cigarettes and beer I came out ahead, especially when my other friends and I needed someone to "buy." The drinking age in Michigan was eighteen.

Every third or fourth morning, I'd find the hippies had crashed, and the house lay quiet. Bodies were strewn on the sofa, sprawled on the floor, and sometimes even in the hall. One time, when I went to use the bathroom, there was someone sleeping in the tub. On these occasions, I'd just step over the bodies, grab a beer from the fridge, a cigarette from the table, and toss the paper onto a chair.

It was on one such morning that I discovered my first addiction—*stealing cars.* There, next to the cigarettes, an overflowing ashtray, and a baggy of green and white pills, lay a set of car keys. Out the kitchen window, their rusty blue station wagon sat tempting me in the drive. It was a 1968 powder blue, Ford LTD station wagon.

Well, if I'm old enough to smoke and old enough to drink, then why shouldn't I be able to drive? I stared at the keys and the bag of drugs on the table. "One pill makes you larger," Ziggy would say, quoting Jefferson Airplane. I'd have it back before they'd wake up and they'd never know it was gone. And besides, I'd probably have my papers delivered in half the time.

I grabbed the canvas sack from my little red wagon and tossed it onto the passenger seat of the Blue. I didn't want to risk waking them with the sound of the starting engine or the muffler that needed replacing, so like my Dad and Uncle's prank of years before, where they pushed all those cars down their driveways, I slipped the transmission into neutral and gave it a shove. I was wrong about the time it took to deliver my papers. I was done in a third of the time. I could have finished sooner, except that I pulled into each driveway along my route, tossing the paper onto the porch or lawn. It was riskier doing it that way, but since everyone was asleep—no one was the wiser.

Instead of returning the car back when I had finished, I drove around awhile enjoying my newfound freedom. Driving came easily to me. I'd been driving a mini-bike since I was eleven, and now driving a car was way too much fun to have to wait two or three more years till I was old enough for Driver's Ed. *Down with the established order!*

My sister was in summer school, so I decided to go home and pick her up. "Do you want a ride to school?" I asked, beaming. She hated taking the bus, especially on hot humid mornings, but she struggled to comprehend what I was saying.

"It belongs to the hippies," I said. "They're letting me *borrow* it."

It was sort of true, I thought. I was *just borrowing it*, and considering the way they were all passed out, they were in a sense *letting me*.

It was 7:30 in the morning, and they often slept till noon, but since I wasn't sure when they had crashed, I figured I had until about nine o'clock. Connie didn't have to be at school until 8:30, so we picked up her girlfriends along the way. They were fifteen, and I wished it wasn't so early, so that my friends could see me driving around with three older girls.

We were on the other side of town when I realized how much gas we'd used. I wanted to make sure there was enough in the tank so they wouldn't know I had taken it. But when I pulled into the gas station, I misjudged the right front corner of the car and the bumper caught the edge of the pump. It collapsed rather easily. Too easily, and when I put the car in reverse to back up, I stepped on the gas too hard, squealing the tires, and hit a pick-up truck behind me. Inside the wagon, the girls were screaming so loud, I couldn't hear the screeching and grinding of the ignition as I tried to re-start the engine, even though it was already running. Everyone at the station had stopped, as if frozen in place, and stared at us. I slammed the transmission into park and leapt from the car.

"I'll go call the police," I shouted and quickly ran from the scene.

Two attendants were right on my tail and caught me before I got far. When they brought me back, I noticed Connie and her girlfriends walking off through an adjacent lot.

"Connie!" I screamed. "Please don't leave me!"

"Oh yeah?" She and her friends screamed, flipping me a finger. "You left us!"

I was arrested and brought to the police station, where they took me into the back. They sat me at an empty desk and called my dad. About twenty minutes later, I heard my name mentioned in conversation out at the front desk. I strained to listen to what they were saying. The voices were low and familiar, though not my dad. I couldn't make it out at first, until I heard one of the hippies say, "No. That's OK. We don't want to press charges. He's our paperboy."

9

Prison Transfer

The black and white vans had gold emblems on the two front doors, with round stirrups on each tip of the six-pointed star. It was the official seal of the Wayne County Sheriff. PRISONER TRANSFER, KEEP BACK 500 FEET emblazoned the rear. Inside, two black padded benches ran vertically along each side, with metal hoops on the floor, for the stringing of chains. Six transports were to be filled from the secure loading dock that morning, all of them headed for the State Prison of Southern Michigan.

It felt like we were cattle being herded into separate corrals, the way they kept moving us from one bullpen to another. We were shifted three times, as they sorted out the prisoners who were going to court from those who were going to prison. I didn't notice anyone being sorted out to go home.

They returned our street clothes, and I was finally given the carton of cigarettes they took from me after sentencing. I couldn't wait to open them. It had been hours since I last took a drag off a short, and a day and half since I last smoked a whole cigarette. A short was the end of a cigarette where a puff or two remained before the fire hit the filter.

"Save me shorts?" you'd ask a fellow inmate as he lit up, but you had to ask quickly, or someone else would beat you to it.

Cigarettes were in short supply, and the deputies liked keeping it that way. It was one of the few outside luxuries we were allowed. There was no reason they couldn't have given them back to me the night I arrived from court. They hardly mattered to me now, since we couldn't smoke inside the vans. The other inmates warned that my cigarettes would be tossed out when we got to Jackson. I didn't know if I could believe them, but everyone kept hitting me up. "C'mon man, the motherfuckers are just gonna throw 'em out."

After seeing one or two others do the same, I started handing them out. We chain-smoked while we waited to be called to the transport chains.

Someone said we'd get a bag of Bull Durham and some rolling papers inside our toiletry kits at Jackson. I'd read about Bull Durham, in a Louis L'Amour western, and was surprised it still existed. It was a roll-your-own tobacco that came in a drawstring pouch. "That shit is nasty," an inmate said. "It's like smokin' shit rolled in toilet paper."

After the Bull Durham, we had to wait for commissary, which could take awhile, until whatever personal money we might have had, was transferred from the county jail. I had twenty-eight dollars in my wallet the day I came in.

I was amazed at how much these guys knew about jailing. Almost more than my brother. I had only been there three days, but I felt like I knew what to expect once we got to Jackson. It was as if these guys had been doing time their whole lives. They said we were going to Quarantine, and that's where the state would figure out which prison they would send us to. There were dozens of prisons in the state, and since I had only been sentenced to two and half years, they said I'd probably go to camp. I wondered what the camps were like.

Rooster, a tall talkative black guy, said the camps sucked and he preferred doing time inside, where there were more programs and things to do. But I figured he was just jealous, because he couldn't go. Rooster was twenty-five and had been in prison once before. He was serving ten years for armed robbery and liked to brag about how he and his rap-partner knocked off jewelry stores on the east side of Detroit, using a sawed-off shotgun and a 9mm pistol. But only nonviolent inmates with a couple of years to serve could go to camp.

According to the guys in the bullpen, there weren't any walls or fences at the camps, so other than a new prison term, there wasn't anything that kept you from walking away. Inmates referred to running off, as breaking camp, but it carried up to five years, which was stacked on top of whatever time you were already serving. Meaning, you'd have to finish the full term of your original sentence, before you would begin serving the added time. It was enough to keep most from running away.

I doubted I'd ever escape, but somehow knowing that I could if I wanted to was comforting. The temptation was even a little scary, but I wouldn't want to get more time.

There was a lot of energy in the bullpens that morning. It seemed as if the inmates were excited to be going to prison, but it had more to do with getting out of the county jail. Doing time in the county was the hardest kind of time to serve. "It's the worst," an inmate said, "because all you have to do here is wait. You're either waiting to go to court, or you're waiting to go to prison, but there's nothing else to do, but wait."

"It's so tight up in this motherfucker," a black inmate said, "that the only thing you have to do—is to get on each other's nerves. You can't even get a job assignment. You got no yard. You got no nothin'. It's enough to drive a motherfucker insane." He'd been there for almost year, held without bail for murder, and then his trial kept getting postponed. "I finally copped a plea," he said, "accepting more time than I wanted, but I just couldn't take it no more." He was sentenced to ten to fifteen years for manslaughter.

The bullpen was loud and energetic. Everyone, it seemed, was in high spirits, because at least once we got to prison, we'd be allowed out of our cellblocks during the day. Even if it was just to walk the yard, or perform a work detail, it was better than sitting around all day counting the time. Yet we'd had to get through Quarantine and Inmate Classification first. "But even then," an inmate said, "they let you out of your cell for an hour of yard each day."

I don't think there was much that could've been said to raise my own spirits. I was quiet and apprehensive.

They brought us down at about 5:30 that morning, before the breakfast wagon had come around with our donuts and milk. I didn't like orange juice, so I was able to trade it for a cigarette the day before. I was hoping they wouldn't forget about us, and the deputies would bring it to us in the bullpen. But they didn't. "They never do," Randy, the donut thief said. "They really don't give a fuck." He was also going to Jackson that day.

As we sat waiting in the last holding pen, out of the corner of my eye, I'd noticed something crawling on the wall. I turned my head to look, but it stopped moving. It was small bug, about an inch and half long, that had the same copper coloring as the rust stained walls. At first glance, it looked to have eight legs, but its body was flat and the two front legs turned out to be feelers. Its front tentacles were swinging back and forth, in a stiff, almost mechanical fashion. When it moved quickly, I jumped, and a large black man sitting across from me raised his voice. "It's a fucking cockroach," he said impatiently.

Embarrassed at my skittishness, I looked over and smiled.

"Stupid ass white boy. Ain't you seen a cockroach before?"

When I didn't answer, he looked left to make eye contact with someone and then shook his head. His look echoing his thought, "Stupid ass white boy."

Having grown up in the suburbs, I had never seen a cockroach before, but now that I had, this guy in the bullpen seemed to overshadow its creepiness. His name, I would learn, was Moseley. And going forward—I hoped to avoid them both, but as luck would have it—we were linked together by handcuff and chain.

Moseley didn't care much for white boys. He was enormous in size, well over six feet six, and his skin was so dark it almost looked purple. The chain that connected us would be looped through hooks on the floorboard of the transport. Our other hand was bound at the belly by a chain that was wrapped tightly at the waist and joined by another, which connected to the shackles at our feet—*Belly chains and leg irons*. It was a good thing they had us enter the vans from the loading dock, because I couldn't have stepped up from ground level. And I hoped they had the same set-up at Jackson, because my hands and feet were bound so tightly, I wouldn't be able to break a fall, and the last thing I'd want to do was take Moseley with me.

I was the only white guy inside my van. I noticed three or four others in the bullpens that morning. With six transports holding up to ten prisoners in each, I wondered why they didn't get a bus.

Jackson Prison was about ninety minutes from Detroit, but it seemed like we arrived in minutes. When the van pulled off I-96 and onto Cooper Street, the prison was to the right. I turned around to look out, but it was hard to twist with all those chains.

I looked down and noticed my wrist was loose in the handcuff that was attached to the chain, so I brought it up to my other hand to see if I could wiggle free. Bunching my fingers together and pressing my thumb into my palm, I tried to make my hand the same size as my wrist. I squeezed the little finger around, and with my right hand that was attached at the waist I was able to push the cuff down to the bump at the base of my thumb. It felt like it was cutting into my skin, but it didn't break the surface, and the van got quiet as they watched me work. I leaned forward to spit, but missed, and it landed on my jeans. I spit again, and that time it smacked, perfectly, on the back of my hand. I rubbed the spit around the thumb and joint and was able to slip the metal cuff free.

I was fairly pleased with myself, as one or two other smiled on, but then Moseley spoke up. "You're a regular fuckin' Houdini. So now what are you going to do?"

I shrugged. If only I could do the same with my other hand, my ankles and the chain that was looped and locked at the waist. Then all I'd have to do is figure a way out of the van, all without alerting the two armed deputies in the front and the others that were trailing behind. At least I didn't have to worry about falling from the van. It also meant I could now twist around to get a good view of the prison.

Through a dark brown cluster of cedar trees, I could see part of the main complex. Covering nearly sixty acres, Jackson was the world's largest walled prison. But my anticipation turned sour, as the van made its way onto a circular drive and past a large arrowed sign that read: INMATE RECEIVING.

I felt a sudden urge to scream, but I kept my head silently turned out the window, afraid my face would betray me. I could not let the inmates see how the sight of the prison's massive walls hit me like I was entering a slaughterhouse. The chain at my waist was squeezing all the air from my stomach, up and out from the lungs. Suddenly, for the first time, I wanted to escape. And as Moseley had said, I was beginning to feel like a regular Houdini. But it was Houdini at the very end, in the movie version, where he was trapped inside a water tank and as everyone looked on, no one could see he was drowning.

10

Convict Orientation

One day on my paper route, a headline story jumped out at me. A terrorist group had kidnapped Patty Hearst, a young newspaper heiress. The story caught my attention because a year earlier, while on vacation in California, we had taken a tour of San Simeon—her grandfather's mansion. It sat on top of a hill, from which William Randolph Hearst once owned the land as far as anyone could see.

It was hard to fathom that he made all that money from selling newspapers. And then, later on that year, Patty Hearst was arrested for robbing a bank with the very people who had kidnapped her. She had become one of them.

We entered the prison through a side door. The sound of the electric gate hummed like a swarm of angry bees. Through large double doors and a barred gate, we entered the bubble of the State Prison of Southern Michigan. It was called the bubble, because it was the only portion of the prison that extended out from the structure's five towering walls. It was the reception center for all new inmates serving state time. Over the next six weeks, we would be quarantined until the Classification Committee determined where we would be sent to serve our time.

The bubble was also the entry point for visitors, although they entered through a different door, and once inside, were ushered past metal detectors and taken to the visiting room beneath a large rotunda. I noticed the rotunda as we came up the drive. It was set back beyond the bubble. On top, a large cupola doubled as a gun tower.

It had been easy to step from the van, as I loosely held on to the handcuff that was fastened to the chain. The deputies hadn't notice I'd slipped free, or if they had, they didn't care. Their twelve-gauge shotguns served as a good deterrent.

Before clearing the first chamber, I felt consumed by the noise, the echoes, the sound of distant screams and a dank, cold metallic odor that billowed out from deep within. My heart bounced as the first gate pounded shut. Each new set of bars waited for the ones behind to close. Inside, the air felt oddly still. It was hard to breathe. The last gate opened with a hiss and a wheeze, as the hydraulic pressure released the sliding rack.

I had suffered from asthma when I was younger, but it was triggered by allergies. My doctor said it was my lungs' way of rejecting something my body couldn't handle.

Several vans from other counties had already arrived, so the holding cells were full. There were close to a hundred fish waiting to be issued new prison numbers. If you had been though before, they'd place a B in front of your old number, indicating it was your second time, a C meant your third, and so on. Assuming I got out alive, I was already determined that there'd be no prefix added to mine.

The intake process was similar to the county jail. We were strip searched, fingerprinted, photographed, and showered. The only difference being, we were peppered with a delousing powder, which got into my eyes. It burned, and the redness must have shown in the numerous photographs they'd taken. One set for Lansing, the state capital; two more for the FBI, one was attached to my file, and the last one in the form of an prisoner ID "You look like my kid," one of the guards said, as he handed it to me. "He's a sophomore at Jackson High." I was surprised by his friendliness and how casual he seemed. *Never get friendly with the guards,* my brother warned, *the inmates will think you're a snitch.* Looking down at the photograph, the irritation in my eyes appeared as fear, which I knew I needed to hide. I never did take a good class picture.

I was a senior at the time, and I didn't like being compared to a sophomore, but I was skinny and my face was hairless. I looked younger than seventeen. With the exception of a few zits, which the food in the county jail didn't help, my skin was smooth.

"Move over there," the guard ordered, pointing to the next counter. His friendliness had disappeared. "Give them your file, so they can run a check for warrants and control holds."

Next, we saw the Quartermaster, who gave us our bedroll and clothes. State Blues, the inmates called them. They were a pair of dark blue pants and matching shirt. They wore like pajamas and looked like the uniform of a garbage man, but at least they weren't stripes and our numbers weren't printed above the shirt pockets. State Blues were the mark of fish, because as soon as most inmates were shipped to wherever they did their time, they'd immediately send for their street clothes.

"Only scrubs and fish wore State Blues," an inmate with a B-number said. *Scrubs* were guys who were poor, didn't have family on the outside, or lacked the game necessary to hustle some clothes. *Hustle some* meant stealing them from an open cell, snatching them off a weaker convict, or "getting some fat chick on the outside to buy them."

Later on, when my brother Rick came to visit, I couldn't believe the number of overweight girls in the visiting room, kissing and holding hands with young muscular inmates. Occasionally, the chaplain would be called to perform a wedding, and the inmate would be granted a one-time-only conjugal visit. Rick said as soon as these guys got out, they'd dump them for skinnier girls, but in the meantime, their hefty welfare checks helped beef up the inmates' lean, 50-cent-a-day job pressing license plates in the prison factory. And the girls didn't seem to mind all the foreplay they were getting in the visiting room.

The state shoes were like the kind my brother wore before being tossed out of the Air Force. I remembered, sadly, how he'd pay me to polish them and how proud I was that I could spit-shine them so well his staff sergeant could see his own reflection. But the state shoes had a dull shine. They looked downtrodden and miserable. Perhaps it was because inmates were forced to make them in one of the prison industries.

The classification process would take six weeks and would include a physical, educational and vocational testing, a psychological exam, and a hearing with the classification committee. But Inmate Classification should have been called Convict Orientation, considering how we were all being educated. Inmates who had been there before, explained to the rest of us how things were done. The men with older numbers, a B or C prefix, were treated with respect. While we were in the bullpen, however, we were all in the same position, so those who knew something were quick to brag about it.

There were dozens of prisons and camps in the state and four different levels of security: Minimum, Medium, Close-Custody, and Maximum.

A memo, posted on the inside wall of the bullpen, explained classification:

> **Security Assignments are made in accordance with severity of crime, perceived dangerousness of inmate, length of incarceration, and past history of escape or violence.**
>
> **Major concerns for the Committee include: limiting security risks, assessment of rehabilitation needs and maintaining the good order & security of all institutions within the Michigan Department of Corrections (MDOC).**

As I read this, an inmate standing next to me translated: "However much time a motherfucker's got?—That's where they're sending his ass." Meaning, the longer the prison term—the higher the security.

I wondered why they didn't just say that, so everyone would understand, but then Rooster stood up and started imitating a southern lawyer.

"Irregardless of what this particular memorandum stipulates," he said, "Convict Classifications—are primarily determined—by the length of your adjudications."

"In other words," he grabbed his crotch, "The longer the dick—the longer the ride." He gave his pelvis a slight thrust, and everyone laughed.

"Man, sit your Perry Mason ass down, fool," the first guy said, smiling. "And mother-fuck all that mumbo jumbo M-D-O-C bullshit." He pointed at the memo. "It's very simple: If you're doing less than two years, you're going to camp. Up to five—medium-security. Anything higher, and you're going inside."

When inmates talked about going inside, they meant inside the walls of a close-custody prison. Inmates with long sentences, up to and including life, were sent there. They were surrounded by walls, motion sensors, razor wire, and gun towers. The older cons went to Jackson, while those of us under twenty-five went to the Michigan Reformatory (a.k.a. Gladiator School). At this point, I didn't know if the name the inmates had given the place was real or not, but I didn't want to find out.

Inmates with terms of up to five years were sent to medium-security. These prisons were surrounded by fences and gun towers, or armed jeeps patrolled the perimeter. Inmates who had been serving longer sentences inside the walls were transferred down to medium as soon as they got within five years of parole. Once they reached within two years, they were eligible for the camp program.

When I was called from the bullpen the second time, I was handed a document entitled, *Inmate Outdates*. Outdates were the earliest release dates we could be granted a parole. Good Time, time off for good behavior, had already been calculated.

"It don't mean you're getting out then," a guard said, "It just means them are the dates you could get out, assuming you don't lose no good time."

"They do it that way," an inmate with a B-number said, "because when they take the good time back from your ass, they figure you'll miss it more."

But for the moment, I was preoccupied with trying to figure out if, *don't lose no good time* was a triple negative, and if so, did that mean I didn't want to *don't lose no*, or if I wanted to not *don't lose some?*

There were two types of good time, regular and special, and release dates were noted for each. No one could tell me why there were two kinds of good time, but as the same inmate suspected, "It's so the motherfuckers can have two different things to take away from your ass."

The way it was calculated, I only had to serve nine months for every year of my sentence. So my two-and-a-half to four years worked out to roughly twenty-two months. A little more than the *"year and a half, tops!"* my court appointed attorney assured me I'd *only* have to serve. My early release date was January 9, 1980. As I read this, my heart felt like it had fallen from a gun tower. The numbers looked alien—nineteen and then an eight-zero. Up until that moment, I'd never thought about the *eighties* before. It was barely 1978, and it was too hard to comprehend. I put it away. My release was a long way off, and anything could happen by then.

When I returned to the bullpen, I scooted over to where the white inmates had flocked. There were one or two others scattered about, but less than ten total, counting the three or four who'd already gone in. No one seemed to notice I'd moved, except for Moseley, who'd been keeping a steady eye on me.

Other than Tree Jumpers, Chesters, drug dealers, and smugglers, inmates with prison terms of less than two years were sent to camp. Inmates with a history of escape were also barred. A Tree Jumper was a rapist, and a Chester, a child molester, named after the *Hustler* magazine cartoon, *Chester The Molester.* I asked an inmate why rapists were called Tree Jumpers and he said, "Imagine a motherfucker hiding up in a tree, just waiting for some fine young female to come walking along . . ."

Inmates didn't like rapists. They figured if the only way a man could get some was to take it, then he wasn't a real man in the first place. And a Chester was worse. On the inmate hierarchy, a child molester was just a fraction of an inch above a snitch. State law didn't allow child molesters in the camp program, and anywhere else for that matter—they were sent to lock-up for their own protection. Otherwise they would be killed. Lock-up involved going into protective custody, where an inmate would spend his entire prison term in solitary confinement.

Listening to the guys talk in the bullpen that morning, I got the impression that they would put up with quite a lot, but raping kids was not one of them. It was a sad irony, as I'd learn soon enough, that while rape outside the walls was so looked down upon, inside it was almost a validation of one's own manhood.

When Rooster was called out and left, the other black inmates started talking about him. "Cock-a-fuckin'-doodle-do. Can that nigger talk or what?"

A few others laughed.

"That's how he got his nickname," someone else said. "'Cause every morning, that motherfucker is up at the crack of dawn, his mouth a cacklin'."

When the next con was called from the bullpen, a white inmate who was sitting off to himself, got up and walked out.

"That boy is fuckin'," I overhead a con whisper.

"No shit?" the guy next to him said. "Why didn't you say something?"

"Yeah, " another black inmate said, reaching into his pants and groping himself. "I could've used some face."

"He's with Little Chet," the first one said, "over on the North Side. He's just coming back from court." The other two nodded and dropped the conversation.

I didn't know who Little Chet was, but judging by the way the others had backed off, Little Chet must have been well respected.

Fucking meant someone was taking it up the ass, or sucking dick. And Little Chet must have been that boy's man. It was my first introduction to the efficiency of the inmate grapevine. Inmates had little else to do but talk, so information flowed quickly. If someone was fucking or snitching, was a Tree Jumper or a Chester, inmates made certain that other inmates knew about it.

"It's one of the greatest communication devices ever known," Rooster bragged, later that morning. "It you ever want to know what time it is about someone, or something, all you have to do is Telephone, Telegraph, or Tell an Inmate."

After a while, I thought the inmates would run out of things to talk about, but that morning, there was plenty. They went on, non-stop, about the differences in classification, prisons, and how the system worked. I kept to myself and listened intently. Over my first months inside, I'd become as familiar with these workings as some of the old timers. That first day, however, I gathered as many details as I could. But no matter how much I learned, nothing would prepare me for what I was to face in the days that followed.

The longer a prison sentence, the higher the security, and the higher the security, the greater the violence. Close-custody prisons were the most dangerous, because the state had the least control over inmate behavior. In a minimum-security, where most inmates were within a few months of parole, the state held good time and early release dates as leverage, so violence was minimal. But in the higher custodies, where no one was going home for years—maybe never—convicts could give a fuck about the rules.

Inmates who weren't seeing the Parole Board for a decade or more, believed they'd have plenty of time to clean up their records, once they were transferred to a lower security prison that didn't demand as much violence. Many believed it was not a good thing to go to the Parole Board without any misconduct reports in your file. "They'll call you conwise," an inmate said, "and they'll give you a flop." (A denial of parole in six- or twelve-month increments.) "It's always better to have a few tickets," he said, "Cause otherwise, they'll think you'd been laying low and you're trying to manipulate."

As for inmates who were never seeing a parole—those inmates serving life—they had nothing to lose. What could the state do, give them another life sentence? There was no death penalty in Michigan, so there was no death row. Inmates who caused too much trouble in close-custody were sent to Marquette, the state's only maximum-security prison.

Marquette was located off the shores of Lake Superior in the upper tip of the Upper Peninsula of Michigan, where legend had it security was so tight that inmates were welded into their cells. Only the most violent prisoners were shipped there, after having killed someone while at another prison. I doubt they were actually spot-welded in, but as Rooster put it, "They might as well be, 'cause unless a motherfucker's got him some snow shoes—he ain't goin' nowhere."

Convicts liked the word motherfucker a lot. They used it mostly when referring to other inmates, but *These* Motherfuckers or *The* Motherfucker usually meant The Man, Authority, The Courts, or The System. It was the function words like the or these, or the singular or plural form that indicated which motherfucker they were referring to. *Some motherfucker* could be either, like "Some motherfucker stole my shit" or "Some motherfucker jammed me up, sending me down for a dime" (meaning they were set up and sent to prison for a ten-year stretch).

They talked about time in terms of nickels and dimes, and serving a quarter-deuce (twenty-five years to life). Now that's a motherfucker, because with a quarter-deuce you won't see the parole board until after you've finished serving the full twenty-five. By then, it's very possible, because you've spent so much time here—you may not want to leave this motherfucker.

11

Quarantine

The largest part of Jackson Prison, called Central Complex, was home to over 6,000 inmates. Each was housed inside massive cellblocks that contained up to 600 prisoners each. Seven Block, one of the largest, was reserved for Quarantine. The very site of which, made me forget my hunger, which had been haunting me since sentencing. It was hollow inside, with five tiers of cells that went on for almost a mile. On each floor a set of catwalks overlooked the base while another separated the back of the cells from the exterior wall. Several windows were either open or broken, letting in the damp winter cold. Nevertheless, it was hot where we had entered at base, and the air felt static and old. I was struck by the sight of birds flying around in the vast open space, in between the tiers.

At base level, there was a large cluster of tables where the inmates had their meals. Cantilevered from the second tier above, was a control desk where a lone guard sat, observing the area from his station. A black telephone and stacks of paper were on his desk. There were two horizontal openings some 80 feet above where armed guards could maintain control by shooting at the inmates below.

Noise echoed from everywhere making it hard to hear anyone. Screaming, yelling, the rumble of rollers, the pulling of release breaks, and the sounds of a hundred sliding cell doors. The high-pitched squeal of squeaky wheels and the scrape of mop buckets being pushed by porters. Occasionally, a metal food tray crashed to the floor, or another was slammed into the dishwasher that was just beyond the chow line.

As we entered the chow area from the intake bubble, inmates from one of the floors above were already sitting down, while others waited in line. Everyone stopped to look. The heavy metal door closed behind me, heading off any impulse to run. Whistles and catcalls came from everywhere, and a round of applause broke out from the tables.

The guard motioned us to the serving line, even though we hadn't been taken to our cells yet. "You guys go ahead to chow," he yelled, "but stay together. I don't want to have to come looking for you later."

Fat chance of that, I thought.

I couldn't show it, but I was shaking inside of my state shoes.

Never, let them know what you're thinking.

Suddenly, I wasn't hungry.

As we walked between the tables, someone grabbed my ass. I spun around, but the inmates sitting nearby all looked away. The cons on the other side of the table looked up, but said nothing. They seemed to be measuring my reaction.

"That's a pretty motherfucker there," I heard one of them say.

"I'm gotta get some of that," another yelled.

They all laughed.

"We're gonna need to put this one on Two-Special," one of the guards said, looking at me. Two-Special was the group of cells just to the right of the guard's station. It was where they placed inmates that needed extra supervision.

"They put pretty young prisoners and sissies in those cells," Randy, the donut thief said. "So that nothing happens to them."

With over a hundred cells in each row, it was hard for the guards to see what went on after the first ten or fifteen, especially with the chain-link fence on the outside of each catwalk. The caging was installed to keep prisoners from either jumping, or being thrown from the upper tiers. The base floor was solid concrete.

I didn't know what to think about being placed on Two-Special. I was told it was where they put the fags, and I didn't want people to think I was one of them. At least up until that point, at best, I would have considered my sexual orientation undecided. And if anyone were to find out, I would be the one to decide what exactly I was. But it was beginning to feel like some of my choices were quickly being taken away.

"You've got to watch yourself, little bro," Randy whispered. "Your pretty blue eyes and long curly hair might be too much for these motherfuckers. They're going to want some of that fine white booty."

"Fuck that," I said. I grabbed my crotch like I had seen done back at the county jail. "They can have some of this fine white dick."

"Oh, now, now," he quipped. "That's just a little white handle to turn you over with." He and the guy next to him laughed.

They were both in their twenties and bigger than me, so they didn't have the same worries.

"Yeah, well, they can pull on this all day long then 'cause I ain't giving up shit."

Randy tousled my hair and smiled. "Just stick close to me kid, I got your back." He leaned over and checked out my ass.

"Fuck you too," I said.

He and the other laughed.

I smiled too, but I didn't think it was funny. One of those guys at the table had grabbed my ass, and I knew they were testing me, as Rick said they would. I didn't know which one had done it and I couldn't have taken them all on, so I just pretended it hadn't happened. I knew that was probably a mistake, but I didn't know what else to do.

Lunch was a watered-down stew, with potatoes and carrots, a few celery bits and a shredded piece of meat that looked pretty creepy. The roll was stale, and the coleslaw had started to turn sour. But the Kool-Aid, unsweetened in a metal cup, tasted like well water. But that and a skinny piece of yellow cake, topped in a dark brown chocolate, was the only thing I could swallow. Randy said they mixed something called saltpeter into the Kool-Aid to keep us from wanting to fuck each other. I looked over at the other tables, where someone had grabbed my ass and hoped that this was true. But later on, when the library cart came around, I read in the dictionary that it was used for curing a different kind of meat.

As we waited for the guard to come back, I tore off a piece of my bread and tossed it to the floor. I watched as one of the birds sat at an empty table, patiently perched, waiting for a moment when no one was looking. I turned my head for only a second, and when I looked back, both bird and bread were gone.

In the first three cells of Two-Special, there were three black drag queens. Charlene, Tiffany, and Lisa Marie. Lisa Marie was a pre-op transsexual, who already had breasts. She looked just like a woman, except for her genitals, so Charlene and Tiffany started calling her Miss Thing.

I was never clear which of the other two was who, and all three made me too uncomfortable to ask. All three were in their twenties, with exaggerated feminine features: arched eyebrows, long hair and nails, and tin-sounding voices intended to imitate women. I felt embarrassed to walk past their cells. I didn't want to look in, but at the same time I couldn't help myself. All three stared back in uncharacteristic silence. They usually had something to say about everyone, but with me, they just stared quietly.

I was placed in a cell a few down from theirs. In between, were several white guys who looked young and mostly frightened. I hoped I did a better job hiding my fear.

The drag queens' cells were filled with all the trappings of a wealthy prisoner: cigarettes and coffee, commissary items, potato chips, pastries, and bags of candy. The inmates called the goods Zoos Zoos and Wham Whams. I don't know if those were the names of specific treats, or just the slang, but it was the currency of prison, along with drugs and homemade liquor. As far as material goods were concerned, the queens were well treated. The more time an inmate had to serve, the sooner his fantasies were replaced. Drag queens were the closest thing to women some of these guys would see for a long time, and there weren't that many of them to go around, so they were in high demand. I often smelled pot coming from the direction of their cells, and I noticed they were called to the infirmary on a daily basis. Inmate clerks inside the walls prepared the call-out lists, so the "girls" left each morning and returned late in the afternoons, often with fresh boxes filled from the commissary.

Once lights went out that night, I saw something crawl up my wall. It was a cockroach, the size of the one I'd seen that morning at the county jail. I killed it quickly with my heavy state shoe, but no sooner had I smashed that one, then a few more appeared. There were two walls in my cell, one on each side, and a rack of bars at the front and back. The guards walked both catwalks, sometimes sneaking up on inmates, to catch them violating rules.

I smashed a couple more cockroaches and then jumped when I saw another, on the wall just above my bed. After killing a dozen or so, and sitting there poised to get the next, a mouse with a long tail ran through my cell. It could have been a rat, but I'd never seen one of those before either. I let out a yelp, and the guard at the front desk flashed his light.

"No noise over there, 208, or you'll be spending the night in The Rock."

The Rock was the holding cell next to the guard's station. Talking and noise was forbidden at night, so with the exception of an occasional animal noise that the inmates loved to let out, like a cow's moo or a hyena's laugh, the first few minutes after lights out, the convicts pretty much respected the rule. But during those first few minutes, the guards snuck around, tracking the sounds. Some nights it would be barking dogs and cats' meows, while other nights it was lions, monkeys, and bears.

It was a nightly game that ended with a handful of inmates sitting upright, on the rock-hard floor, until the 6:00 A.M. shift change. It usually took only one night in The Rock for an inmate to give in and respect the rule. But still, each night, there were several minutes of animal cries that echoed up the long stacked rows of cages.

After seeing the mouse, or rat, I climbed under my covers and tucked the sides of the gray blanket between my mattress and slab. I pulled the covers over my head, grabbing the slack around my neck and cried silently. It was going to be a long six weeks until I would be sent to camp. In the morning, I'd ask the guy in the cell next to me if cockroaches bite, or if rats could climb walls. But at that moment, I hated myself for being such a sissy.

If the days were long, the nights were even longer. I'd been there for over five weeks, and nothing had progressed with my classification. With the exception of a once-weekly shower, inmates on Two-Special were not allowed out of their cells. The sliding bars were top locked by a dead bolt at the top of the door, which prevented it from opening when the guards pulled the release brake at the end of the tier. At chow times, the others went down to base while our meals were delivered, usually cold, on Styrofoam plates.

The other inmates were also allowed out of their cells for yard, which made the guy in the cell next to mine pretty angry. He kept saying we were supposed to get an hour of yard every day. "It's in the fuckin' constitution, man. This is crude and unusual punishment!" But the only thing crude was his daily ranting about the injustice of it all.

"Stay out of prison," a guard told him, "and you can play in the yard all you want.

At least we didn't have to worry about someone grabbing our asses.

Inmates would occasionally stop at my cell and stare, or ask me my name or what I was in for, but the guards would appear and order them along. I welcomed the company, at first, but they were never allowed to stay long enough for a conversation. Sometimes, in passing, one of them would say something rude like "That punk is gonna need a man" or "There's no bigger joy than a pretty white boy."

I tried to escape into reading, but the library cart only came twice and by the time it reached us on Two-Special, there were only a few books left. They were usually titles that no one there would ever read, like *Scruples* by Judith Krantz.

I read *Black Gangster* by Donald Goines, which I was able to trade later for a Louis L'Amour western—I read the latter twice out of boredom. I traded the western for *The Drifters* by James Michener, and was taken away to Europe, by way of Canada, and to the running of the bulls in Spain. It was the highlight of my six weeks stay in Quarantine, and I read the book twice, gladly.

I tried to sleep away my days, but the noise was maddening. There was a constant drone of inmates yelling, sliding cell doors banging closed, and the shuffling back and forth of convicts between program testing, the yard, and chow. I eventually learned to ignore it, but the only time I felt solitude was lying awake late at night.

For the once-weekly shower, we were paraded in our towels upstairs where we waited in line for one of the six open stalls at the end of tier three. They were in plain sight, between the two long rows of cells, so that anyone in the cellblock could look up and watch. Privacy was something you forfeited in prison, but I guess it was preferable to showering in a dark room somewhere and being afraid to pick up the soap, like so many back home had joked.

The guards gave us three minutes to shower, at which point, they'd shut off the water. If you still had soap on you, you'd have to use your towel to wipe it off. The green state soap didn't lather much, and even when thoroughly rinsed, your skin still felt greasy.

At first, I was nervous about showering in the open, but my erections were no longer a problem. Since jerking off was about the only thing we had for entertainment, it was probably the real reason I preferred staying up at night. Occasionally, a guard came along taking count with a flashlight and would catch me. But since most other cons were doing the same thing, I'm sure he was used to seeing it. I felt pretty embarrassed, the first time he saw me, but he didn't seem fazed at all.

Late one morning, I was startled by the guard's routine check of the prison bars. Guards ran their wooden batons along the face of each cell, above and below each cross-section, to ensure that no one was slowing hacking away at them. I say slowly, because the guards did this check every Saturday morning, so that if an inmate did have a saw, he needed to cut through the bars pretty quickly. The guy in the cell next to me said the bars had rollers on the inside, which would spin, preventing a saw from gripping and cutting through to the other side. The guard's baton would make a clunk if it hit a broken bar.

The spot check seemed silly, because even if an inmate were able to get out of his cell, he still had nowhere to go; he'd need to get out of the block and then over the wall and past the razor wire and motion sensors and gun towers and dogs. I wondered what would happen if someone came in with a helicopter, but it would have to be bulletproof, since the guards would shoot at it from the towers. And tunneling wasn't an option, since we didn't get any yard time on Two-Special.

The guy next to me was also seventeen. He was shorter than me, about five foot eleven, and couldn't have weighed more than 130 pounds. He had short, dark brown hair and large hazel eyes, which seemed out of proportion with his face. An inmate porter commented on how he looked like a grasshopper, and from then on, the name stuck.

Grasshopper was serving time for arson. He grew up in Genesee County, in the upper part of the state. "The problem with getting jammed in the sticks," he said, "is that you end up getting sentenced by hicks."

Even though it was his first offense—and the only thing he had burned down was an abandoned building—the judge decided to make an example of him by sentencing him to eight years in prison.

"It's not like nobody got hurt or nothin'," Grasshopper said. He was worried about his classification, because even with good time, he'd have to serve seventy-two months, which meant he might have to go inside for a year until he could transfer to a medium security. "I know what happens to guys like me. If they send me inside, I'll never make it."

Grasshopper was pretty, by anyone's standards, and I was hoping the Classification Committee would take that into account. But arson was considered a violent crime so his chances didn't look good. He'd already had his physical and was now waiting to see the psychologist, before his final hearing.

With all the noise, it was hard to hear each other, so we stood at the back of our cells and yelled from around the wall. I purchased a small mirror from the commissary when my money from the county jail finally landed in my account, which only took four weeks. We used our mirrors to see one another as we spoke—sticking them out of the bars and tilting it at the other. Somehow, it was easier to hear, when I could see his lips moving.

The guy on the other side of me, who never talked much anyway, said even less after he returned from the psychologist. I wondered if he, too, was being sent inside.

A guard with a clipboard came by my cell and said I was scheduled for my physical the next morning. He told me not to eat breakfast, because they'd be taking blood. I hated needles and giving blood, but was happy to see the process finally moving along.

I fell asleep early that evening, but was awakened by whistling and cheering, catcalls and the sound of the laugher. I sprang to the front of my cell to see, and there on the tier above, in between the two long rows of cells, were the three black drag queens.

In an effort to avoid problems, the guards showered the queens separately. So there they were in all their glory with their hands held high in the air. They were facing the wall and shaking their butts, while the cellblock went nuts with laughter. They turned in unison to face the open block. Their dicks were stuffed between their legs so that all you saw were their pubic hairs. It looked like they had real pussies, and from where I was standing, they looked liked women, especially Lisa Marie. They shimmied forward with their legs together and danced, their movements in sync with one another. The energy felt almost electric the way it sliced through the boredom and enlivened the giant birdcage. Even the guards, who were standing on the opposite catwalk, looked up and laughed, shaking their heads.

"I could use one of them bitches right about now," an inmate said, walking past my cell. "Shit, I'm tired of jerkin' off."

I was embarrassed by the drag queens. I didn't understand it, but they frightened me, and I felt ashamed for them. I wasn't like them in any way. I had no desire to be anything that flamboyant. No matter what thoughts I may have had about my identity, I was not going to be turned into one of those.

Turned-out was the expression for someone who was "turned" gay. To be turned-out, a guy was either raped or pressed into having sex. Men were expected to defend their manhood, and if it were lost, they would need another man to protect them. For a weaker con, the choice of having to do it with one was a better than having to do it with many. Or sometimes, inmates were even tricked into it by another punk or queen.

"There's this queen in here named Geraldine," Grasshopper told me. "She was huge! I saw her when I went inside for my physical. She was about six foot six, and weighed close to three hundred pounds."

I had first heard about Geraldine back at the county jail. Her reputation was almost legendary, and though I had never seen her myself, most inmates claimed that they had.

The story went that Geraldine had a thing for white boys. She loved to suck their dicks. According to legend, she'd trick them into her house (which is what inmates called their cells) and she'd hide them under her bed where she'd give them the best head they'd ever had.

"She's quite experienced," Grasshopper bragged, as if he'd sampled her trade. "She's probably sucked hundreds of dicks in her day, especially in here, where there's an endless and eager supply."

I was surprised he was talking about it so freely, given all his fears, but maybe if he joked about it, he wouldn't seem so afraid.

"Anyway, she'd suck their dick, and then when she was done, her voice would get all full of bass, and she'd say," Grasshopper dropped his voice real low, "OK, motherfucker. It's my turn."

"The only problem was," he said, "these white boys were straight, so as soon as they'd start to object and say something like, 'But Miss Geraldine, I'm not that way . . .' BAM! Miss Geraldine would knock 'em out."

Grasshopper paused to laugh. "And then, when they woke up, the white boys would say something like, 'God damn! That bitch hit me so hard my asshole hurts.'"

The next morning, we were escorted to the infirmary. Two of the drag queens from Two-Special were in our group. I wondered why the guards weren't suspicious of all the appointments they had to see the doctor. The inmate clerks kept putting them on the call-out list.

"I'm a diabetic," I heard one of them say.

"Sugar needs her sugar," the other explained.

I didn't know if she was referring to insulin shots or the Zoos Zoos and Wham Whams they returned with later.

To the right of the infirmary, I noticed a building that had a major pharmaceutical company's name posted over the doorway.

"That's where they're testing the Swine Flu vaccine," one of the old timers told us. "They pay inmates to test new drugs and run experiments on their asses."

"Cheaper than chimpanzees," another said.

Rooster laughed. "Ain't no fuckin' way. I ain't gonna be a guinea pig for nobody."

"Medical records have a funny way of disappearin'," the old timer said.

Inside the infirmary, an inmate clerk explained the program. It was a clinic that paid inmates to participate in Phase I and Phase II drug trials. The clinic measured side affects and inmates were paid up to two dollars a day. It was good pay, he said, considering most jobs paid about fifty cents a day. The money came in handy for those who had no other income.

"Oh yeah?" an inmate said. "When your dick falls off, then what do you do?"

"You better hold onto that," Rooster said. "These motherfuckers done took everything else."

The old timer said they measured side affects, but they didn't say they'd treat 'em. "They just *record and measure*," he said, "as your nuts roll off the side of the catwalk."

"Yeah," Rooster added, "They'll wanna see how high they'll bounce from base."

Everyone laughed, until the old timer told us about a study down south, where a bunch of blacks were infected with syphilis as scientists sat back and watched, even after a cure, as some of the men in the study went blind and died. Or another one, down in Ohio, where inmates had cancer cells injected into their arms and a few weeks later, so they could study cancer growth, researchers cut parts of their arms off.

None of those things had anything to do with this particular pharmaceutical company, but the inmates didn't care. To them, it was all the same thing. "Just put me back in my hamster cage," Rooster said, "and leave me the fuck alone."

Some inmates looked a little skeptical. "It's been in all the papers," the old timer said, "don't any of y'all dumb asses know how to read?" He was old and black, so he could get away with talking like that. "You silly ass jitterbugs are too busy boostin' records and bustin' caps, that none of you all don't know nothin'. These motherfuckers will have you ass strung out so bad, your own momma won't recognize ya."

"Now that's some fucked up shit there," one of the younger blacks said.

"It sure is, son. Your own momma won't know you."

"Oh, don't bring my momma into this, Pops, or we'll be boostin' that silly old ass of yours. And the only thing we'll be bustin'—is that head."

Boostin' was the term for stealing, and bustin' caps meant firing a gun.

"The Man just wants to see the black man eradicated," Moseley said, "it's as simple as that. If we can't shoot 'em off the streets, we'll send 'em to prison, and if that's not enough, we'll poison their asses. But either way, we're gettin' rid of the niggers."

I once heard that if you weren't a racist when you went into prison—you would be by the time you got out. Again, I was suddenly aware of how many blacks there were in the room, and how few whites.

I was surprised that private companies like Upjohn and Park/Davis had a laboratory in Jackson prison. The pay they were offering inmates wasn't much, but the old timer said they wouldn't pay more because they considered it unethical.

"Unethical?" It was the first time I spoke up, but I was surprised by what he said. "If they paid any more," he looked over at me. "They'd be afraid it would fuck their results. If inmates are making too much—they might not report their problems out of fear of being dropped from the study."

Two dollars a day wasn't more than enough to buy smokes and a couple of extras at the inmate store. It hardly seemed worth it, considering you had no idea what you were getting yourself into. And what really seemed unethical was that inmates would be reduced to selling their bodies for commissary. But just then, the drag queens got up and went into a room marked X-ray. They weren't seen again until later in the day, when the returned to Quarantine, each carrying a box of goodies.

I glanced back and noticed Moseley was staring at me.

A few minutes later, an inmate with a clipboard came out and called my name. He brought me inside a room where I was given a physical. They took my temperature and a vial of blood. That was it. I waited nearly six weeks to have an inmate nurse stick a needle in my arm and a thermometer under my tongue. It was all the recording and measuring necessary.

Later that evening, I would meet with the prison psychologist, the one who had informed me that I was not going to a camp. He said I was being sent *inside* until my case was adjudicated.

"Ever been fucked?" he asked abruptly.

"Excuse me?"

"Fucked," he repeated. It was the first time he looked up from his desk.

12

Riverside Correctional Facility

As the state van made its exit from I-96 and headed north on a small two-lane highway, a gas station and a McDonald's blemished the landscape of open fields and farmland. The men inside the van, who were mostly from Detroit, tried to swallow up and devour everything they could see, hear, and smell, and squirrel it away for the oncoming famine. A sign warned motorists—Prison Area: Do Not Pick Up Hitchhikers. I wondered how long it would be before I had another Big Mac.

We passed a State Police Post and a small airstrip for private planes. Nestled among the hills and rolling farms, the city of Ionia was home to the world's largest free county fair, where the best in livestock, poultry, and agricultural displays could be viewed. Ionia was also home to four state penitentiaries. The Department of Corrections was the region's largest employer.

"If you're from Ionia," one of the cons in the van said, "you either worked the pigs or you were a pig." The guard smacked his baton against the caged partition and startled the offending inmate. Everyone laughed, including both guards.

We traveled another mile and then turned left. The Michigan Reformatory could be seen in the distance and the van got quiet as we took in the sight. Built in 1876, M-R was the oldest prison in the State of Michigan and boasted one of the largest cellblocks in the world. Its forty-five-foot high concrete walls and soaring gun towers loomed on a hill like an evil fortress. It looked as menacing as its reputation claimed.

Fortunately for me, the van turned left again and headed up a winding landscaped drive. In spite of what that psychologist had said to me, the

Classification Committee determined I was too young and vulnerable for Gladiator School. Instead, they sent me to Riverside Correctional Facility until I was sentenced for robbing the Photo Mat.

Riverside was a close-custody prison for inmates serving long sentences, usually ten or more years, who were either very young or old, mentally ill, or in need of protection for some other reason. Protection cases included ex-cops, informants, child molesters, and homosexuals. Riverside was notorious for having lots of sissies.

Formerly known as The Ionia State Hospital, and later The State Asylum for the Criminally Insane, the Department of Corrections had acquired the property a year earlier, and it looked like a mental hospital. It was an aging complex of several large buildings, surrounded by newly installed gun towers and twenty-five-foot-high barbed-wire fences. There were four housing units designated for each class of inmates: one building for those over the age of fifty, another for those under twenty-one, one for the mentally ill—referred to as bugs by the other inmates—and the last unit which was shared by segregation, the infirmary and the hole.

The housing unit for inmates under twenty-one was a bit of a misnomer, since there were only a few inmates who were actually that young. In fact, with the exception of the geriatric and bug wards, most inmates at Riverside were in their thirties.

I was housed in 10 Building, the unit for younger inmates. It was an aged yellow two-story brick building with small block-shaped windows that opened on pivot hinges guided by steel brackets. The openings were large enough to allow for a breeze, but not nearly wide enough for someone to squeeze free. I wondered what would happen in a fire, but the buildings' all-brick and steel construction left little chance for that to occur.

Each floor contained several dormitories and a small number of individual rooms. Though highly coveted, individual cells were issued in order of seniority. Inmates placed their name on a list with the unit counselor and waited for one of the small 8 x 10 foot digs to become available. If you received a ticket, a misconduct report for a violation of the rules, you were placed at the bottom of the list. It normally took years to earn the privilege of a room. This meant that fish were automatically assigned to the dorms.

The dormitories housed eighteen men. There were nine double bunks, eighteen lockers, and a toilet and sink in each. But the toilets were used for the purposes of taking a piss, as the inmates insisted you go down the hall, to the main can, if you needed to take a dump. As one inmate put it, "'Cause don't nobody want to smell a motherfucker's shit when they're trying to cop some Zs."

Some inmates had televisions and radios, but the use of headphones was required at all times, except when walking the yard. The yard was a noisy place where the sounds of competing radios bellowed from all directions. Most of the music was rhythm and blues or the new sound of disco. Even the white guys listened to what back home was called black music.

The day I arrived at Riverside, we sat in the control center for what seemed like hours, repeating many of the same processes we went through in Quarantine at Jackson. We were strip-searched, fingerprinted, photographed, and issued bedrolls. The Deputy Warden gave us an inmate handbook and told us to "familiarize ourselves with the rules." The opening chapter, echoing the Department of Corrections emphasis on rehabilitation, stated that we were to be considered residents, not inmates.

The Deputy Warden, who had a body shaped like a coke bottle, spoke to us in a slow, deliberate, well-rehearsed speech.

"You were sent to prison as punishment, not *for punishment*. So while you are here, you'll be required to participate in programming. Including school. We want you focusing on the betterment of yourselves, so that when you get out, you stay out." But since Riverside had just opened, they hadn't yet worked out all of the job assignments and construction on the new school space was behind schedule. This, along with inadequate staffing, would explain the lack of structure that I would experience later.

"You'll meet with your unit counselors as soon as we get these things sorted out," he said. "In the meantime, none of you are going nowhere anytime soon."

To get to 10 Building, we had to cross the main yard. As three guards led our group, I noticed that activity in the yard had come to a subtle, yet definite stop. Conversations ceased as inmates took us in. They pointed and nodded, leaning toward one another to make comments. Some of them yelled things, like pretty boy or sweetie, but I kept my focus on the ground in front of me.

One of the cons in our group pointed to a building on the northeast corner of the yard. "That's where the old-timers are housed." We turned right and headed toward 10 Building. The guards led us up the steps and through the door. None of the inmates in our group were taken on to 11 Building, the mental ward, so I took that to mean there weren't any bugs among us.

Another guard met us, and the group was cut in half and told to step to the side. The rest of us were ordered to follow up the stairs. On the second floor, we were taken down a long glazed-bricked hallway where dormitories appeared, every twenty to thirty feet, on the left-hand side. Through the narrow windows of the painted steel doors, I could see the first set of bunk beds, which blocked the view of most of the room.

At the end of the corridor was the guard's station. One guard handed paperwork to another while a third guard led us into the dayroom.

Inside the dayroom, there were several orange fiberglass-molded rocking chairs arranged in slapdash rows in front of a television that had been mounted from the ceiling. Two inmates were watching a soap opera while one of them sipped from a plastic tumbler. To the left, a doorway opened onto the poolroom. The partition wall that separated the rooms was lined halfway up with glass. The inmates shooting pool stopped their game and came to the windows to gawk. We couldn't hear what they said, but several more inmates got up and joined in. While I couldn't hear clearly, the one word that came through was *fish*.

The guard walked us through the dayroom and into the smaller card room where he ordered us to take a seat at one of the tables. He went back to the office.

"Hey Slim," a black inmate said, tapping on the window from the TV side of the partition. I wasn't sure, but it appeared he was looking at me. One of the inmates sitting behind him whispered something, and they both laughed. They were staring in my direction. I turned and looked behind me, thinking they couldn't mean me, but there was no one there. I looked down at my fingernails and pretended not to notice them.

A few minutes later, the guard returned with a clipboard and a handful of keys dangling on long nylon strings. You were only allowed inside your own dormitory, to which we were each issued a key.

The guard read through several pages of orientation notes.

"There are four counts a day," he said, "One at 6 A.M., one at 4 P.M., one at 9:30, and the last one at midnight. At count times, you are to be in your dorms and on your bunk or you will be considered AWOL, and you will be shot." He paused to look at us. "And," he added, as if being shot wasn't enough, "you'll be issued a misconduct report."

Several of us looked at each other.

"The mess hall is in the basement," he said, "meal times and menus are posted on the bulletin board just outside the officer's station." Meal times alternated depending on floor. We were to be in our dorms at eleven and lights-out was 11:30. We would meet with the unit counselor, and those appointments would be posted on the board. He said the rest of the rules were listed in the inmate handbook.

"I thought we were residents," one of the inmates said.

"You're a bunch of convicts," he said. "I don't care what that book says. Just make sure you familiarize yourselves with the rules." He then read off our names and numbers from his clipboard. "1-5-3-0-5-2, Parsell."

"Here," I said, raising my hand.

"Dorm 1013, South." He handed me a key

"Thank you," I said, realizing how out of place my politeness sounded.

"This is the north side. The south side is through that door." He pointed to the southwest corner of the dayroom, behind the two inmates in front of the TV. Having lost interest in the fish, they were now engrossed in *The Young and The Restless*.

The guard finished handing out keys, ordered us to grab our bedroll, and then he and another guard split us into groups. We walked through the door that led to the south side. It was an exact duplicate of the north. There were two inmates shooting pool on the other side of the partition while *The Price Is Right* played to an empty day room.

We crossed the dull floors and continued down a hallway to the right. The guard stopped and directed one of the inmates into the first dorm and then took two others and me to the second. My key chain had a brass ring on it that indicated the building, floor, dorm, and bunk: 10 Building, 2nd floor, Dorm 13, Bunk D. I was on the upper. Young Blood had the lower. Young Blood was an eighteen-year-old black kid from Detroit, whose cell was across from mine in Jackson.

A short, pudgy, white guy in his early twenties jumped down from his bunk.

"Hi," he said, smiling. "I'm Bottoms." He had shoulder-length, dirty blond hair, and his skin was greasy. His eyes had a bright gleam.

"Hi," I said, extending my hand. "I'm Tim."

We shook awkwardly as he tried to grasp my hand by the thumb.

Young Blood gave him a disinterested nod.

"You guys just come through the Bubble?" He asked.

"Yeah," Young Blood said, studying him as he undid his bedroll.

"What's your number?" He asked, still smiling.

Prison numbers were unique to each inmate, issued sequentially as you entered the system, so inmates could tell how long you'd been down by how high your number was.

"1-5-2-9-7-4," Young Blood said, not looking up as he made his bed.

"What's yours?" Bottoms looked at me.

"1-5-3-0-5-2." I came in a few days later than Young Blood, so mine was higher.

"God Damn!" Bottoms blurted. "The numbers are up to one-fifty-three!"

"Fish-ass motherfuckers," said a dark-skinned black man, as he came out from the bunk next to Bottoms. "I'm Frank," he said. He was friendly, but not smiling.

Frank was about 6 feet 5 inches tall and looked as though he weighed twice as much as me. "You motherfuckers are gonna get the floor wet," he said.

I must have looked puzzled.

"He means your drippin' wet," Bottoms said, "fresh out of the tank."

I smiled and nodded.

Bottoms smiled back.

Curious about what I'd heard about gays earlier, I asked, "Hey? Are there a lot of fags in here?"

Bottom's sparkle turned to a dull gaze as he focused his eyes to the floor. "Nah," he said softly, as if to shrug. He backed away and turned to his bunk.

I was embarrassed I asked the question. I hoped I didn't seem eager to meet any sissies. Seeing that Young Blood was finished, I unfolded my bedroll and began making my bed.

• • •

"Hungarian goulash, string beans, cornbread and grape drink," read the menu for that night's dinner. The full week's menu was attached to the bulletin board just outside the north side dayroom. Carrot cake was the dessert. It sounded pretty good after the bologna sandwiches we were given when we arrived. Corn fritters were on the menu for tomorrow's breakfast. I had never had corn fritters before. I wondered what they were. Corn for breakfast didn't sound very good.

Without a sound, an older man appeared to my left. I had finished lunch and was onto tomorrow's dinner menu before I had noticed him standing there smiling. His eyes were sparkling with the same flicker of light in his eyes that Bottoms had back in the dorm.

"Hello," I said, returning my gaze to the bulletin board. I moved onto Wednesday morning's menu. He didn't say anything, just stood there as quietly as he had appeared.

Thursday, Dinner: liver and onions, peas, scallop potatoes and grape drink. I made a grimace: even the dessert, lemon meringue pie, were foods that I hated. It looked like the grape drink was the only thing on the menu that I could have. Maybe they serve bread. I was just doing what I always did when I was frightened—I focused my mind on something else.

The guy was still staring at me.

"Liver," I said with a scowl, looking back at him.

"I'm Chet," he volunteered, "What's your name?"

"Tim," I was embarrassed by his intense stare. I wondered if he was stoned.

"Tim," he slowly repeated. "Where are you from, Tim?"

"Westland," it was a suburb just west of Detroit.

"Oh, I lived in Inkster for a few years when I was younger." His voice was gentle and reassuring. "How old are you?"

"Seventeen."

He let out a long whistle, "Sev—en—teen!" he said, stretching out each syllable of the word. He was considerably older. "You're a baby!" His voice held a hint of affection.

I smiled.

"I've got kids your age," his eyes drifted off my shoulder and into the distance, "somewhere."

I smiled back at him. I was pretty young compared to everybody I had seen so far.

"Why, how old are you?"

"What are you in for kid?" he interrupted. I wasn't sure he had heard my question.

"How much time do you have?" he asked.

"Two and half to four," I answered. I still hadn't grasped the reality of it.

"How come they sent you here?"

"I have to go back to court for an armed robbery," I said. "I haven't been sentenced yet."

"A control hold," he nodded, his face relaxing. "When's your court date?"

"I don't know," I shrugged.

His tone was encouraging. "What did you rob?"

"A Photo Mat," I said, matching his smile with a slightly embarrassed grin. It looked as though someone had turned up a dimmer switch in Chet's eyes. An inmate walked by us and yelled to Chet.

"Scandalous," the black inmate blurted. He smiled at Chet, but ignored me.

"You are just plain scandalous, Dawg!" He said, shaking his head. He opened the dayroom door and once more bellowed, "Scandalous!"

Chet looked at me reassuringly. "Pay no mind to him. That boy is half a bug, and his Thorazine must be running low."

"What's Thorazine?"

"Bug juice. It's what they give the bugs to keep 'em calm. Do you want some?"

"No!" I said quickly. I wasn't sure he was joking.

Chet just looked at me silently nodding his head, as though he was studying me.

"I don't do drugs."

"You don't do drugs?" There was a trace of doubt and surprise in his voice leading me to believe that he was serious about his offer of Thorazine.

"No."

"Never?" he probed with a puzzled look. "What about reefer?"

"Nah, it makes me paranoid."

"Do you drink?" He sounded like he was running down a checklist in his head.

"Oh yeah," I responded, smiling, "like a fish."

Chet smiled, and the flicker returned.

"Well, then," he said with delight, "have I got a party for you! I've got a batch coming off tomorrow. We'll have a welcoming party."

"Really!" I whispered excitedly. "You've got booze in here?" I had heard that inmates made their own liquor. I remembered a scene in the movie, *The Longest Yard*, where Burt Reynolds and another inmate had booze hidden in a plastic bag inside their cell toilet. But that was the movies.

"Spud juice, my boy. The best brew this side of Jackson."

"Wow! How do you make it?"

Squinting his eyes, Chet bent forward and imitated an Asian accent. "Ancient Chinese secret," he said. We both laughed because he was imitating an old laundry detergent commercial.

"Don't listen to that lying motherfucker," blurted a voice so close behind me that I felt a breath on the back of my neck. Startled, I turned around. "This boy wouldn't know how to brew spud juice if his momma's life depended on it." He was a black man with sideburns and a thick mustache that came down past the sides of his mouth. He looked like the actor in the television show, *The Mod Squad*, except that his hair was wavy and cut closer to his scalp.

Chet shot back at him from over my shoulder, "Oh, now don't you bring my mother into this, Boy!" He said it with an extra emphasis on the word *boy*. The man broke a smile that displayed a perfect set of teeth that were nicely framed by his mustache and dark brown skin.

"Oh, I'll bring your mother into this all right," he said as he brought his full attention to me. He was standing fairly close. I looked down at his feet; he was wearing worn-down brown leather slippers. Perhaps that was why I hadn't heard him when he walked up behind me.

He smiled broadly at Chet. It was clear they were friends. "And I've got your boy," he said, as he grabbed his crotch and squeezed it, "hanging right here."

I laughed, nervously, and was glad they were friends just teasing each other.

Chet put his hand on my shoulder, "Meet my newly adopted son," he said with a paternal pride, "This here, is Tim."

"Well, well, well." He was studying me intently. "Mr. Blue Eyes."

Embarrassed, I smiled, and we shook hands. This time I locked thumbs as we shook. As I tried to take my hand back, he grasped my hand like a regular handshake and held it for a second and then cupped his fingers and glided the tips across the surface of my palm and then curled his fingers and interlocked them with the last joints of my fingers. His hand awkwardly slid off of mine as I unsure what I was supposed to do. He looked down for a second but then smiled as he looked back up at me.

I felt foolish I didn't know the secret handshake.

"He blushes," the man said.

Chet leaned over to my ear and whispered, "This man here is one scandalous Motown motherfucker." He said it loud enough for his friend to hear. "His own momma wouldn't trust him."

"Hey, I'll tell you what," he calmly retorted, "My momma is a big ol' bull dagger, and your momma is her big ass bitch."

Chet and I both laughed.

"I see The Man's sending babies up in here now," he exclaimed, as if the entire north side of the building should be outraged. "How old are you?"

"Seventeen."

"Seventeen!" he exalted. "God Damn! What's your number, Son?"

"1-5-3-0-5-2."

"God Damn!" He raised his voice as if the world should be outraged.

"I got drawers older than this boy," Chet declared from over my shoulder.

I smiled and wondered why they had called them drawers and not underwear.

"The numbers are up to one-fifty-three!" He kept his eyes locked on mine.

"Why? How old are you?" He looked to be as old as Chet.

"Old enough to be your daddy." He looked over at Chet, and they both chuckled.

"How old is that?" I asked, curiously, still smiling.

"I'm almost thirty."

"OOOOOooooooollllldddd," Chet mocked.

He didn't acknowledge Chet's comment.

I did the math in my head and questioned whether it was possible for him to have fathered me at twelve years old.

"Let's go sit into the card room, Tim. I'll introduce you to Taylor here, nice and proper like."

Chet put his hand on my shoulder and led me to the card room, where two black guys were sitting.

"Don't worry about the liver, Kid," Chet boasted. "We don't eat that shit in here."

"That's right!" Taylor said.

"Cook up!" an inmate named Red piped in, loud enough for the guys in the TV room to hear.

"Hey! Let's have roast beef tonight." Taylor said.

"We do our own cook-up," Chet ignored the others.

"Yeah," Red said, leaning over to me. "Do you like meat?"

"Hold up Red," Slide Step said from across the room. "Give that boy some room."

Red was a black man with really dark skin. He was named Red because his eyes always looked bloodshot. They were slanted and gave the appearance that he was almost Asian.

Red threw his hands up at him, as if to say, "What? Did I say anything?"

Slide Step ignored him and looked out into the day room. His feet were propped up on another chair, and he was leaning back with his arms casually crossed in front of him. Slide Step wore a scraggly beard and a knit wool hat stretched over what looked a big ball of hair.

"How old are you," I asked Slide Step, sensing that he was pretty old.

"Thirty." He seemed amused that I was interested in his age.

"Wow, that's pretty old."

He smiled and looked back out into the day room.

Red and Slide Step, like Taylor, were part of Chet's family. Chet explained that you had to have a family if you wanted to survive inside the penitentiary. He said it was very difficult to make it on your own, especially if it was your first time.

When you hook up with a family, he explained, you look out for each other. He said it could be a very cold and lonely place inside these walls. I guess he could tell that I was a little lonely. I was so happy to be out of

Quarantine and to have people to talk to. I was enjoying their company. It was impossible to hold a conversation when you have to yell over to a buddy in the cell next to you. Especially in Seven Block where it was so noisy. So far, I really liked Chet and his family. They were nice to me, and I felt very lucky that he was taking such a liking to me.

Chet wouldn't tell me how old he was, but he hinted that he had served as much time as I had been alive. So he sure knew a lot about jailing. If he came in at my age, he would have to be at least thirty-four. Holy cow!

I was curious about the spud juice that they were cooking up. I wondered how they cooked it and how it tasted. I tried to picture a homemade distillery and wondered if spud juice was like moonshine.

Chet offered me another cigarette, which I accepted.

"Count time," a guard yelled from the open door of the officer's station.

It was the first time that I'd seen a guard since they showed me to my dorm. It was the four o'clock count. We got up from the card room and headed back toward our dorms. Chet handed me the pack of cigarettes he was holding and told me to keep them.

"Thanks." I put them in the pocket of my state blues.

"Are you going to dinner," he asked. "Meet me in the day room and we'll go down together. They're having Hungarian goulash tonight. It's pretty good."

After dinner, I was standing in front of Chet's door. His cell was the first of the three private rooms on the hallway near my dorm. He wanted to show me a picture of a friend of his from The World. That's what inmates called the outside, The World. He handed me a picture of a pretty woman, who was wearing a lot of makeup.

"What do you think?" he asked, studying me as if he were expecting a reaction. I wasn't sure what he was looking for, but I wanted to give it to him.

Red bumped into me from behind and reached for the picture. He looked at me with his face just inches from mine and then down at the picture. "Is that Bobbi?" he asked Chet.

Chet nodded, but kept looking at me.

"It's a man," he said. His eyes showing the delight in knowing he had fooled me.

"Really," I said. I took a closer look. I couldn't tell that Bobbi was a man from the photograph. His tits looked real under the flimsy halter-top he had on. Embarrassed, I didn't know what to say. I thought about my last night with my brother and Candy, the prostitute on Woodward Avenue. Chet and Red studied me as if they expected a particular reaction. I went to hand the picture back; but it slipped from my hand and fell to the floor, sliding under Chet's bed. Red muttered something to Chet as he bent down to pick up the picture. Red's manner made me nervous.

"She worked the streets for me," Chet boasted. He wiped the picture on his sleeve.

I remembered a book I read by Donald Goines, a writer who had done time in Jackson Prison. He described how queers lived like beauty queens in prison. That all it took to have a relationship with one was a couple cartons of cigarettes. Cigarettes were the currency of prison. The older queens cost five packs and up, depending on the merchandise. As long as they gave good head, convicts would be willing to pay.

I couldn't imagine that someone would pay for a drag queen on the outside, unless they didn't know it was man. Bobbi had fooled me. I wondered if he looked as convincing in person.

I stuttered something, self-consciously struggling for the words to excuse myself. "I'll catch you later," I mustered, and quickly headed toward my dorm. Except, I didn't want to go there, so I turned and walked back toward the day room. Chet and Red seemed amused by my sudden nervousness.

The day room was crowded and bustling with the inmates who were free until the nine o'clock count. Inmates playing poker hovered over piles of loose cigarettes, and the convicts in front of the TV were lost in *Gilligan's Island*.

The poolroom was nearly empty, so I decided to shoot some pool. I had played a lot when I was in The World. My brothers and I played while Dad drank with his friends at the bar, and at home we had a pool table in the basement.

Nearby, two guys played a game while two others sat on a bench smoking. They looked up at me when I walked in. I crossed the room and leaned on the windowsill to watch the game.

"How do you sign up to play?" I asked.

No one answered.

The guys on the bench just smoked their cigarettes and watched the game. Out of the corner of my eye, I saw one of the guys lean over and say something to the man next to him.

"Six in the corner," declared the overweight Mexican leaning over the table. He was wearing a pair of state-issued white pants and shirt. He must have worked in the kitchen, as all the guys on the serving line were wearing the same clothes. The Mexican was the only one who wasn't smoking. I opened the window to let in some air.

He hit the cue ball with enough English that it curved backwards after hitting the six in the corner and stopping in front of the two-ball, which was a sitting duck for a shot in the side.

"Sweet," declared one of the cons on the bench.

I wondered if they had heard my question but chose to ignore me. I was too self-conscious to ask again.

Two black guys walked into the room. "Who's next?" one shouted.

"I am," said one of the smokers on the bench.

The two guys looked at me, nodded, and took a seat on the green bench opposite the table. One of them kept staring at me.

Chet appeared outside the room, knocking on the window. He motioned me to come into the day room. I pointed toward the table, indicating I wanted to play, but Chet was insistent.

"It's probably a good idea if you stuck close to me these first couple of days," he said, "until people get to know you're OK."

Chet led me to a set of chairs outside the phone room. It was off the corridor next to south side guard's station.

"I have to call my Moms," Chet said. He pronounced *Moms* as if he had more than one.

"How many do you have?" I asked.

"How many what?"

"Moms," I said with a smirk.

"It's just an expression. Moms." He pronounced it as if it had a Z on the end.

"Momzz," I repeated.

He just smiled.

"Hey White Boy!" one of the black inmates asked, "Where are you from?" He sat opposite me and wore a burgundy skullcap. It had tie-strings hanging on each side, like an old aviators cap. He was thin, but the fierce look in his eyes suggested he was tough.

"Westland."

"Isn't that over near Inkster?"

"Yeah," I said, "I lived right on the border. If you crossed my street, you'd be in Inkster."

"Where's Scatter at?" a guy to his right asked.

"Hey Scatter!" Skullcap yelled down toward the single cells.

"Yo!" echoed back from the end of the long sterile hall.

The building seemed more like a rest home. I was easy to visualize the place as the Psychiatric Hospital it once was. The glazed brick walls and dull floors diffused the fluorescent lighting and created a glow that was fitting for a sanitarium. I half expected to see Jack Nicholson appear at any moment, flanked by a big Indian and a nurse holding a plastic tray with a dispenser filled with bug juice.

Instead, a young black man sprang from one of the rooms. He sauntered up the hallway with a rhythmic swagger. He was holding his crotch in left hand while his right arm swung wildly back and forth in tempo with his body. He was muscular and handsome with light chocolate-colored skin.

His walk was what inmates called *catin'*. It was short for *catwalk*. The way inmates sauntered up and down the tiers of a prison cellblock.

"What's happening? What's happening?" he called out. He increased his beat and tempo as he entered the corridor. Scatter flopped down on the arm-rest of Skullcap's chair.

"Scatter!" Skullcap said, without looking up, "This boy says he's from Inkster."

"No shit!" Scatter looked at me, "You're my homeboy?"

"I lived on the border," I said.

"What school did you go to?" He had a youthful energy.

"Wayne Memorial," I said, smiling.

He was the closest person I'd seen to my age, with the exception of Young Blood, who I rode in with. "How old are you?" I asked.

"Seventeen."

"You ain't no motherfuckin' seventeen," Skullcap said. He looked over and smiled at the guy next to him.

"Almost," Scatter said. He crooked his chin and bunching his lips together. "I will be in September."

"In September," the guy next to them blurted. He got up laughing and went into the phone booth. Scatter scooted over and took his chair.

"Well this is only April, you silly ass jitterbug." Skullcap sipped a hot drink from a plastic tumbler, and set it down on the armrest that Scatter had just warmed. "That ain't no 'Almost.'" His laugh had a heavy S-sound that included a slight whistle.

"Close enough," Scatter played along. He turned to me with the childish look of someone who was caught telling a fib.

He had been in prison since he was fifteen. He was convicted of felony murder.

"My rap partner *accidentally* shot the store manager," Scatter explained.

Felony murder was when someone dies during the commission of a felony. It doesn't matter who dies, or how they die. Everyone involved in the crime goes down. Even if a cop or a shop owner shoots one of the criminals, the other guys involved are charged with murder. The rationale being that if you weren't committing the felony, no one would have died.

"I know this guy who stole a car," Scatter said, explaining the law, "and he was runnin' from the police when he hit some ol' lady crossin' the street."

"BAM!" he said with burst of enthusiasm. "He got sent up for murder."

"That's right," Skullcap said, "even if a motherfucker has a heart attack and shit—your ass is sittin' up in here doin' life."

"Not for a heart attack," Chet said.

"Oh, yes sir," Skullcap said with authority. "If that old bitch crossing the street had a heart attack instead of being hit by the car, they would have still jammed the brother up."

"Now how they gonna know she had a heart attack just 'cause he came flyin' by?" Chet challenged.

I was getting the impression that everyone became a jailhouse lawyer, since they all seemed to know about crimes and court and how the sentencing and procedures went. Or at least everyone had an opinion on it.

"Because," Skullcap said, searching for an answer. "Because . . . The Man is just lookin' for a reason to send a nigger to prison, Dawg. You know what I'm saying?"

The answer seemed to satisfy Chet, or maybe he decided it wasn't worth arguing. He did seem to agree that The Man was always looking for a reason to send someone to prison. The fact remained that Scatter and his rap partner had robbed a supermarket and that his rap partner, according to Scatter, killed the store manager. They were both convicted of felony murder and sentenced to life in prison.

"But regular life," Scatter said. "Not natural life. With natural life, you're down till your ass dies or the governor gives you a pardon."

"Which ain't going to happen," Skullcap said.

"With regular life," Scatter continued, "You see the parole board after ten years." He leaned over playfully to Skullcap, "When I'll be *almost* twenty-six."

Scatter was given his nickname because the inmates said he was so scatterbrained. I wondered why he was sent to prison and not to juvenile hall since he was only fifteen when he and his twenty-four-year-old cousin committed their crime.

The psychiatrist that testified at his trial said a teenager's wiring isn't done yet. They can't rationalize things the same way adults can because their brains and emotional reasoning aren't done yet. The judge didn't buy it so tried him as an adult.

The courts were cracking down on teenagers to solve the gang problems in Detroit. A couple of years earlier, some innocent bystanders were shot and killed at a Kool and The Gang concert at Cobo Hall. They started waving a lot of teenagers over to the adult courts ever since. The mayor eliminated gangs by aggressive sentencing. A large percentage was now over at the Michigan Reformatory.

"Most of them are in Gladiator School," Scatter said. "Doing five, six, and seven natural lives each. They ain't never getting out."

"I've got two cousins over there," Skullcap said, "they were part of the B.K.s," referring to the gang, Black Killers. "One got forty-to-sixty, and the other got six consecutive natural life sentences."

"Now how's a motherfucker going to do six natural life sentences?" Scatter asked.

"They'll bury 'em, " Skullcap answered. "And then they'll dig their black asses up again."

"Shit," he added, again with the half whistle. "Both of them fools ain't but nineteen and twenty years old."

We all sat quietly for a moment.

"The motherfucker wouldn't open the safe, so we shot him," Scatter said, contradicting his earlier claim that the murder had been an accident.

"What are you in for?" Scatter asked.

"Armed robbery," I said. I decided to stop mentioning the larceny, since the robbery sounded better.

Chet handed me a green sheet of paper. It had the official Department of Corrections letterhead and seal on top of it. I took it and looked at Chet.

"What's this," I asked Chet.

"Read it," he said.

I tried, but was distracted by Scatter. It had something to do with a security reclassification.

"What did you rob?" Scatter asked.

"A Photo Mat."

Everyone laughed. Skullcap whistled.

"A Photo Mat," Scatter said. "Homeboy!" He looked down and shook his head.

"With a toy gun," Chet volunteered. They laughed even more.

"You silly ass jitterbugs," Skullcap said. "You should at least go after something that has money in it."

"How much did you get?" Scatter asked.

"About hundred and fifty," I lied, tripling the amount.

"You should have robbed a bunch of 'em!"

"I did!" I announced proudly.

Everyone laughed.

These guys made me comfortable, and I felt like I was being brought into the family. "Hey," I asked. "Do they have a lot of fags in here?"

The room got quiet.

"Well you're here!" Skullcap said. His face hardened as he looked at me.

A guy came out of the phone booth, and the stale unpleasant air filled the corridor. They watched me to see how I would react. Stunned and uneasy, I didn't know what to say. I blinked. My brother warned me that I would be tested, and I knew this was part of it, but I didn't know what to do. In that moment, I had decided that I would never ask that question again.

13

Lasting Impressions

Sharon loved to take us to scary movies.

My mom, on the other hand (though we hardly saw her now), would only take us to see G-rated movies, like The Love bug, Chitty Chitty Bang Bang, *or* The Sound of Music. *Mom didn't agree with Sharon's choice of films, fearing that they would leave a lasting impression. But now I was almost thirteen, Mom gave in and finally agreed to take me to an R-rated movie. I was eager to show I could handle it.*

We saw Papillon, *which was French for* butterfly, *starring Steve McQueen and Dustin Hoffman. It was based on the true story of an innocent man, framed for murder, who was sentenced to life on the penal colony known as Devil's Island. After several attempts at escaping, he was hospitalized in the prison infirmary, where a trustee came onto the ward and placed a red carnation in the mouth of a young prisoner laying on a cot. I shifted in my seat as he ran his hand over the man's bare chest, across his stomach and into his underwear. I was terrified, as I watched this scene unfold, that my Mom could hear my heart pounding. It was the first time I felt a sexual stir; and it was something I would never forget.*

When I was kid and visited my older brother in reform school, he told us stories of how older boys cut holes in the pocket of their jeans and then asked a newbie to help them get something out of it. They would explain they had sprained their finger and couldn't reach for it themselves. The unsuspecting fish would slip their hand inside the pocket only to find a swollen prick poking out from the hole. Ricky said that the longer it took a guy to realize what it was they were holding, the greater the likelihood they would have to service it later.

The thought of it was maddening as my mind vacillated between fear and curiosity. I heard stories about watching your ass when bending over to pick up soap, and about candy bars being left on pillows. Long before Ricky got sent away, Dad tried to scare us from a life of crime by telling us about the booty bandits inside.

Dad and Uncle Ronnie had served time in reform school, when they were kids, for stealing cars and breaking into a business. He said that when he was there, candy bars were left on the pillows of new prisoners, and if a guy ate it, someone who wanted it back would confront him later. If the fish had eaten it, he would have to give up something else in return, which usually meant a sexual favor.

"But that shit only happens to punks and queers," my brother told me. "To punk ass bitches that don't know how to take care of themselves."

I could never tell Rick how scared I was to be in prison, because I didn't want him to look down on me. How could I tell him how little I could fight? He must have known how much I relied on him as a kid. I think he even resented it at times, they way he always had to stick up for me. Perhaps that's why he had that look of terror on his face the night before I came to prison. I could never tell him how cowardly I felt or about the sexual thoughts I sometimes had.

"You don't want to be a punk," Rick said. "And you *never* want to be a snitch. Punks get fucked, but snitches get killed."

When he used to write to me from inside prison, he described daily life there. He told me about the fights and stabbings and about inmates who were set on fire. He described how he made a bomb by scraping off the sulfur from books of matches into a jar. He added nuts and bolts and bits of metal that served as shrapnel. And he told me about the rapes and gang-bangs, and how a helpless newcomer was held down while several guys took turns fucking him. "The Bible says that the meek shall inherit the earth," he once wrote, "but inside these walls—they're doing their boyfriend's laundry." He said prison was a sea of restless sailors who were eager to assist the helpless land lovers gain their sea legs, as long as they were lifted high in the air.

The raw masculine barbarity of it all completely aroused my imagination. Yes, I was terrified, but at the same time fascinated. Prison sounded repulsive, yet my reactions made me wonder about my sexuality. Rick's stories gave me an adrenaline rush. My breath seemed to quicken, and my heart raced. Then came the shame and disgust—the humiliation and self-hatred that I was picturing myself having sex with a guy. I could never tell anyone what I was thinking. Why did I have to be so different? Is prison where I truly belonged?

We were in the north side card room. Chet and Taylor had brought the spud juice in a thick black plastic bag. There was a gray flannel blanket over the table. Red and Slide Step joined them a couple of minutes later. Chet dipped a Maxwell House instant coffee jar inside of the bag. The juice was a dark red color. Chet handed it to me.

"We don't use cups because the stain don't come out," Chet said, referring to the plastic tumblers everyone seemed to have.

There were prunes and orange bits at the bottom of the glass jar. The label on the jar read, GOOD TO THE LAST DROP. I took a drink and gagged, not sure I'd be able to drink more. It had a pungent odor; its taste was sharp and acidic. The guys laughed. They seemed to be studying me, acting supportive and encouraging at the same time. I enjoyed the attention more than the juice, but the warmth in my belly was inviting. The burn that went down sent coolness back up. It was like stepping into a hot bath, and the feeling you get as the chill in your body rises up through your spine.

"You eat the fruit," Taylor said, "that's the best part."

I couldn't get past the bitter taste. It was sharp and caused shivers in the back of my neck, my eyes watered. There was no way I could eat the fruit.

"Where it at? Where it at!" a short skinny black man echoed as he entered the room, giving Slide Step a high five from the side. He extended his arm, pulled it back behind him and then brought it forward, slapping his hand. He was wearing an all-white kitchen uniform.

"Hey Ed," Slide Step said, slapping him back with the same sideways motion. "Where's your goblet?"

"Right here," hoisting his instant coffee jar into the air. "Now you didn't think I'd miss a party? Did ya?"

Taylor took Ed's jar and dipped it into the bag.

"But don't give me none of that fruit." Ed grimaced. "That shit is nasty!"

He grabbed a chair and sat next to me. "You must be Tim!" He looked down at my now half-empty drink.

I smiled at him, "You don't eat the fruit, huh?"

"No way, that shit will grow hair on your ass," he said. "Ain't nothing worse."

"NASTY," Chet chided, shaking his head with a hint of Louis Armstrong in his voice, "NASTY ASSEY!"

"Well, if it's anything like the juice," I said, "I'm not sure I want any."

"Oh, he's talkin' about hair on your ass," Red quipped, "not the juice."

They all chuckled.

"Now you just leave this boy alone," Ed said, putting his arm around my chair. "This is my homeboy."

He picked up his jar and clinked it with mine. "Cheers!"

I took another swig, this time it only stung a little. Chet was sitting across from me. Slide Step was in his usual place, his back to the wall and legs crossed and propped on another chair, slowing nursing his spud juice.

"Why do they call it spud juice?" I asked. "Are there potatoes in it?"

"Nah," Chet said, "probably a long time ago. We use orange juice or grapefruit juice and whatever fruit we can get our hands on."

"But it can't have no preservatives," Taylor added.

"We add sugar and yeast," Chet continued, "and then let it cook for a couple of days. I'm not sure how they did it with potatoes."

"It's hard to get the juice anymore," Taylor explained, "since they started bringing in orange juice with preservatives and shit. So we have to rely on fruit, which there ain't a lot of around here."

Chet and Taylor had been friends for a long time. Chet said he began making spud juice in the late fifties, when he first started serving time. They considered themselves experts and called their operation The Senility Distillery.

"Had we been around during prohibition," Taylor boasted, "we'd a been O.G.s."

"What's Oh Jeeze?" I asked.

"Original Gangsters!" Chet said. "We'd a given Al Capone a run for his money."

I smiled and looked down at my drink, which I had almost finished. I was starting to feel a little warm. It had been about six weeks since I had had any alcohol to drink. It felt nice. I was relaxing, something else I hadn't been able to do for at least as long.

"In a pinch, we've used tomato puree," Taylor said, "when there's nothin' else."

"Now that's some nasty shit!" Ed chimed. "Anyone want my fruit?"

He had finished his jar, and there were a few pieces sitting at the bottom: a prune, a piece of grapefruit, and something else that looked dark and truly *nasty*.

"Let Tim try it," Red said. "He'll eat anything!"

"No, I don't want it," I said, shaking my head.

"Oh c'mon!" Ed looked over, "it's not all that bad."

"Go ahead," Chet encouraged, "it'll get you goin'."

"What the hell," I shrugged, looking around the room for a garbage can. I could always spit it out. I took the jar from Ed and lifted it to my mouth, trying to shake a piece loose without putting my lips on the rim. I wasn't sure he'd want me drinking from his jar. Some of the juice spilled on my chin.

"Here," Ed said, taking it back from me. He grabbed the prune with his fingers and lifted it to my lips. I reached for it, but he motioned my hand away with his fingers, and placed it in my mouth. The prune had absorbed the juice and was soft and swollen. I bit down on it and felt a gag rise from the base of my throat. I ran over to the butt can next to the door and spit it out. The guys were laughing.

"Don't worry," Red said. "You'll learn to swallow."

Chet and Slide Step gave him a look. I wiped my chin with my sleeve and pretended I didn't know what he meant, but I did. I didn't like Red, and I was glad Chet and Slide Step was there. Ed seemed nice too, but I began to wonder if I was being set up. I was feeling light headed.

I sat back down, and Chet explained that he liked eating the fruit, but it took some getting used to. Taylor reached over and took the jar from Ed and lifted it to his mouth, letting the remaining bits of fruit fall onto his tongue. I watched his eyes water as he chomped down on them and swallowed. He shivered and shook his head back and forth like a dog does after a bath.

"Now that's how you get a good buzz," Taylor said. "That's the Whip!"

I looked down and noticed that someone had refilled my jar. I was beginning to loosen up. I took another drink, and the acidic taste seemed to have lessened. There were no chills this time, just more warmth going down into my belly.

Chet popped some fruit into his mouth and smiled. His Adam's apple contracted as he gulped it down his throat. He winked at me, "That's the do, baby boy, that's the do."

I tried another piece of fruit, and this time I didn't gag. It was as nasty as before, but at least I got it down. My jar was getting lower, so I turned my head to see what was happening in the pool room. I was hoping they'd fill my cup again.

Were they doing this because they got a kick out of getting the kid drunk, or was something else going on? Maybe this was why Chet was being so friendly. And it's probably why I had that stifled grin on my face. A smirk from the attention I was getting. The attention that I didn't want, but really did—glad I was getting it, but ashamed of it at the same time. But what about the others? I couldn't get a read on them. Maybe they just liked the fact that I was so young, and they thought of me like a little brother. Or perhaps I reminded them of themselves when they first got here. I really enjoyed the focus and attention. I loved their smiles and the kindness they were showing me. They listened to what I had to say, and they took interest in me. Something I didn't get much of at home. It filled a void and loneliness, and it was what I had longed for. It felt real nice in spite of my surroundings.

When I turned my head back, I noticed someone had refilled my jar. I could feel my heart pounding and my breath shorten, sending a swirl of energy around my chest. My hand was shaking slightly as I lifted my drink. I swallowed a piece of fruit, and it tasted smooth. My face and taste buds were numb, but I could feel that silly smirk on my face.

Chet asked me to step into the shower room to talk. He led the way, as I felt myself stagger up the hall. I thought I knew what was happening, but my head was pretty cloudy, even more so than usual. There was a dullness that was new to me, my face was completely numb, unlike any of my previous drunk experiences. It had nothing to do with the spud juice.

I had been drinking since I was thirteen, so of course I'd had different reactions to different booze. Rum and Cokes gave me the spins, and Tequila Sunrises gave me the pukes. But the buzz before the crash was always the same feeling. I loved to watch myself when I was drunk. It was like I could get outside of myself and watch what I was thinking on a big screen. But today, my vision seemed blurrier than usual.

"So you're gay, right?" Chet asked. He had been talking to me for a while, but this was the fist thing that registered. I hadn't heard anything he had said before this.

"NO," I answered quickly, "I'm not!" At least I tried to say it quickly—instead my words came out slow and slurred. I wasn't even sure that I got the "I'm not" part of the sentence out or if I just thought I had.

"Uh-huh," he nodded. He wasn't buying it. "Then what did you think was going on? And why did you keep asking if there were any fags here?"

I couldn't say anything. There was a menacing quality to him that wasn't there before. It was as if I was talking to somebody I didn't know. And come to think of it, I really didn't know Chet.

"The picture of Bobbi last night, my classification notice, the party this morning? Did you think I was doing this because I'm a nice guy?"

"The picture? What picture? You mean that guy in woman's clothes?" There was a delay from when I said something, and when I heard myself say it. I think all that came out was a slurred "*. . . picture . . . fag.*"

"What are you talking about?"

The room began to spin. It was like everything in sight was rotating to the left, but then flipped back and turned again in the opposite direction. All I could do was hold onto the bench I was seated on and blink in disbelief.

"The classification document that I showed you last night," Chet said.

"What about it?"

"It said that I was sent here because of homosexual tendencies," Chet shouted. It was becoming clearer to me. "If you weren't gay, why'd you stick around?"

I felt trapped and cornered and didn't know how to respond. I remembered him handing me a piece of paper last night. Why didn't I read it? I looked at it a couple of times, but I was too distracted by Scatter. Did it really say he was brought here because of homosexual tendencies? Fuck! I wished I had read it. Of course Chet was being nice to me. He was interested in me! How could I have been so stupid? How could I not see what he was up to? I wished I read the clues that he'd been sending, like his friendliness, the free cigarettes and spud juice and conversations about family and looking out for each other. Until that moment, the bug in the hallway didn't register, the one that was calling him scandalous. Or what it meant when the guys kept calling him Mr. Wilson. I asked Slide Step what he meant and he said something about *Dennis the Menace* and about how Mr. Wilson was always nice to the kid. But I still didn't understand. Everybody could see what was happening but me. Or what about that picture of Bobbi—the guy in woman's clothes? How could I have been so naïve?

Red! What about Red? Was he in on it too? Why didn't I pick up on all of those nasty comments of his? How could have I been so stupid as to think that Chet was going to protect me from them. Or was this what he was trying to say? Was Chet making a play to protect me? Was he trying to become my Man?

I looked up to ask him something, but he was gone. I was sitting there alone. In fact, the shower room was empty. I started to get up, but I couldn't move. It was as if I was so exhausted I didn't have the energy to get up. The room had stopped spinning, but I still couldn't move. There was saliva hanging from my bottom lip, which I wiped on my sleeve.

Maybe Chet was right. I am gay, but I didn't want to admit it. I still wasn't sure that I was. Even if I were, I didn't want anyone to know about it. Was that why I didn't see what was coming? I did and I didn't want to admit it? I was glad to be so many miles from home, a world away from where anyone knew me. Whatever happened in there was for me alone to know about. Who I became there and what I did inside would be sealed within these walls. It would be my secret alone. I would never see these people again.

Sitting there by myself, I thought about how freeing that would be—to be able to have sex with men in an environment that permits it, someplace where in fact it's even celebrated. All of these strong, masculine men. I just wished they were younger, I wished they were my age, and then maybe I could get used to it. The only one that I'd liked so far was Scatter, and maybe

Young Blood. They were my age and both of them were beautiful. I'd love it if somehow something sexual happened with one of them. I didn't know what was happening with Scatter. That guy sitting with him the night before was mean. Maybe he was Scatter's boyfriend. He could have been offended that I asked about fags. I was confused. The booze was good, and I thought it was cool that they got me drunk. Maybe something would happen with one of these young guys. My chest and my body tingled at the thought.

I wished Chet wasn't so old. At least he was white. He seemed to have a handle on how to do time. He's got money, he's got booze, and he'd been very nice to me. Perhaps that's how it worked. He takes care of me, and I take care of him. Yeah, that's it. He takes care of me, makes sure nobody hurts me, makes sure I have plenty of booze so I can check out any time I like, makes sure I have cigarettes and candy and whatever else they sell in the commissary, and all I have to do is take care of him—though I wasn't exactly sure what "taking care of him" would entail. Chet wasn't that bad looking. If he first came here in the fifties, he must be in his late thirties. I just wished he were closer to my age.

Chet walked into the shower room and told me to follow him. I tried to tell him what I had decided, but I still couldn't get up, and now I couldn't even speak. For some reason my words were slurred worse than before. I couldn't understand a word he said. Suddenly, someone was at my side helping me to stand. The next thing I knew, I was standing in one of the dorms.

"Get on the bed," Chet ordered. My pants were gone. I didn't remember taking them off. My underwear was missing too. Chet got on top of me and pushed my face into the pillow, muffling my scream. Even with all of the spud juice that I drank, and the fruit, and the Thorazine (as I would find out later) that they spiked my drink with when I wasn't looking—wasn't enough to numb the pain of Chet thrusting himself inside me. It felt like I was being split wide open. I tried to let out a scream, but the air was sucked from my lungs by the sheer terror of what was happening.

Chet paused for a second and whispered in my ear, "Shh. It will stop hurting in a minute." But it didn't. He kept his hand on the back of my head, holding my face down as he pounded away at me, slowly at first and then with an increased rhythm. I sobbed into the pillow until he was done, and then he collapsed on top of me. The back of my neck and hair were wet with sweat. My breath slowed with his. I could hear his breathing in my ear, his heart pounding on my back. The pain had stopped, but I felt wet, like I was bleeding. But I don't think there was blood at first.

Chet ran his hand over the top of my head and then got up. I felt glued there. It was a bunk bed, and there were blankets draped on all sides, like the tents my brother and I used to make as kids. I could hear movement in the room and voices. In my shock, I couldn't make sense of anything. Someone pulled the blanket back and climbed into the bed. It was Red, and he didn't have any clothes on!

"Give me some face." He grabbed my hair and pulled my head to his crotch. He was huge, and I could barely open wide enough. "Watch your teeth," he said. He forced my mouth down on him. I didn't want to have sex—and this hardly counted as sex—but I felt like a coward. I couldn't say anything much less resist. It wouldn't have made a difference. Red weighed about 200 pounds of solid muscle. He looked like all he did was work out in the weight pit all day. His thighs were as big as my waist, and his dick was as thick as my wrist.

I couldn't breath. My nose was clogged from the spud juice or Thorazine or from my tears. He didn't care. I gasped for air and tried to time my breaths so I didn't suffocate, but then I vomited, and the spud juice and some of the fruit came up.

"Oh shit!" Red sprang from the bed. He grabbed the blanket and pulled it from under me. "Get up!" he yelled impatiently. I got off the blanket, and Red pulled it from the bed. He threw it to the floor, kicking it to the side. "Lie back down," he ordered. He was mean, and I was frozen. "Lie down," he yelled. His eyes widened as he stepped toward me. "Now turn over."

The pain was ten times what it was with Chet. I asked him to wait, and he told me to shut up. I sobbed uncontrollably. Where were the guards?

"Shut up, bitch, or I'll give you something to really cry about!" He put the pillow over my head and held it as he pounded me. My whole body felt like it was being stuffed.

"I can't breathe!" I screamed, "I can't breathe!" I struggled, but couldn't move. His weight was crushing me, and he was so strong I couldn't free myself from under his elbow that was holding the pillow down on my head.

Red stopped for a moment and lay there on top of me. I was so glad he was done, but the pain was still there. *Please pull it out*, I tried in vain to say, but couldn't mouth the words. He lifted the pillow from my face and said to me, "Are you going to stop screaming?" I couldn't answer. I started to cry again because I knew he wasn't finished. "I said, are you going to stop screaming?"

All I could do was nod my head. "All right then!" he said, and he removed the pillow and resumed humping me.

The worst of the pain had eased. Where once there had been a sharp cutting pain, now the pain was dull and pulverizing. With each thrust I could feel a deadening pressure in my stomach, about three inches above the hairline of my crotch. Could he be that big? Or was it my shit being jammed back into my intestines? I had never been fucked before, and it hurt in the worst way. More than I ever imagined. But this was violent and beyond anything I could have guessed. He didn't care that it hurt me and that I was in a lot of pain. He was enjoying the power he was exerting over me. This was what I deserved, I thought. This must be what happened to fags. This was what I got for being what I am. This was what I'd been warned about since I was a little kid. Was this what I secretly wanted?

I turned my head and opened my eyes. There was a pair of legs, crossed, sitting in the chair next to the bed. I lifted my head and saw Slide Step. He had been watching me. Was he next? Embarrassed, I turned my head around.

The pain was numbing, but my awareness had heightened. I wished I could black out and that none of this had happened.

Red continued to fuck me. How long would this agony continue? Was Slide Step next and was he as big as Red? I was drunk and hazy, and hoped I wouldn't remember anything in the morning.

Gradually the pain lessened more, and then my entire body went numb. It was like being paralyzed, and I was afraid I'd never be able to walk again. Someone threw a glass jar and it shattered next to the bed. Red stopped and lifted himself up on his arms, looking out from the blanket toward the door. I heard whispering and Red said something, but I couldn't understand it. I was in shock, and everything sounded garbled.

"Oh, GOD DAMN IT," he yelled. I heard a wet smack and pain shot down my legs as he pulled his dick out. He jumped from the bed and went over to the door. I felt like I had the runs, but there was no way I'd make it to the toilet. I tried to wiggle my toes but couldn't feel anything.

I heard arguing. At first it was muted, loud whispering, and then there was yelling and shouting. I didn't know what they were saying.

"Get up," Chet startled me. He pulled the blanket from the side of the bed and told me to put my pants on. I couldn't move.

Someone came over to help me, but I couldn't look at him. They wiped my legs with one of the blankets and then helped me put on my pants. My underwear was missing.

I don't remember much after that. The next thing I knew I was sitting in a chair back in the card room where it all began. My arms were dangling on each side. I was blankly staring at Red and Slide Step, who were standing in front of me, yelling back and forth at each other. Red was saying something about, "He's gay, he likes it" and Slide Step was screaming, "I was looking at the boy's face."

Red stormed out and retuned a few minutes later with something in his hand. It was a shank, a prison-made knife. Slide Step walked up to him, pressing his chest against Red's, "What are you gonna do with that, stab me? You've got heart nigger, go ahead—kill me!"

Chet and Taylor jumped in and soon they were screaming too. I wondered where the guards were. I looked down at my lap and saw that I was drooling again. I wanted to wipe my mouth but couldn't. Or maybe I did. Their voices faded away.

When my senses returned, I was walking very slowly and painfully down the hall. Eddie was leading me into his single-man cell, which had a bed against the wall on the left, and a desk, chair, and locker on the wall to the right. There was a small window above the headboard.

"Quick, hide down here." He lifted the blanket and motioned me underneath. It was like a hospital bed, with high posts, a large towel and blanket draped over the footboard so that the guards couldn't see underneath.

I dropped to the floor and slid under the bed. There was a blanket and a pillow laid out on the floor. I believed he was hiding me.

"Take off your pants," he said, as he slipped in behind me.

"No," I said, and started to cry.

"Oh don't worry," he said, rubbing my cheek, "I'll suck your dick." He said it as if it would comfort me. "But you can't tell nobody," he said, "No one knows I'm like that."

He yanked my pants off without much resistance, and I faded out again, but the pain and pressure of him entering me brought me back. He was humping me hard, and I couldn't breathe.

"I'm gonna pee," I wheezed. "Please, Eddie, I'm gonna pee!"

He stopped for a minute and asked if I could hold it. I couldn't so he stopped. "OK, but we're coming back," he said. As soon as I got out of his room I told him I wasn't going back there. He ignored me. "Don't worry," is all he said.

I stood in the bathroom, but I couldn't pee. I didn't know what happened. A few minutes earlier I was about to go all over, and now that I was standing at the urinal, I couldn't pee. I stepped back and went into a stall. I pulled down my pants and sat on the toilet. Someone opened the door to the bathroom and held it ajar. After a few seconds, I heard it shut, but no one had come in. I tried to shit but couldn't do that either. The door opened, and again, I couldn't hear anyone come in.

"Are you all right in there?" It was Eddie.

"Yeah, I'll be out in a minute."

After a few seconds, I heard the door shut. No one had come in again. I dropped to my knees and threw up in the toilet. I heaved into the bowl until there was nothing left, resting my head on the rim. The cold porcelain felt soothing on the side of my face and forehead. I opened my eyes and watched the small bits of orange, prunes, and grapefruit floating in the water. I reached up and pulled the handle. Now I had to pee. I closed my eyes and felt the water swirling in the bowl and my breath bouncing off the surface of the water. The room was spinning again. When I opened my eyes, I was back under Eddie's bed. I don't remember walking there. He was fucking me, and it felt like I'd never left.

"I have to pee, Eddie, please I have to pee!" This time he just kept fucking me.

"Go ahead," he said, and his thrusts became more violent. I felt like I was going to, but I couldn't. And after a few minutes more, I tried, but nothing would come out. I wanted to piss all over his blanket, into his pillow, and onto the floor. I wanted to stink his room so badly that the smell would never leave, but nothing would come out. He let out a groan, and I felt him get larger inside of me, and then he collapsed. I felt his breathing in my ear, his breath on my face, and his heart beating against my back. My shirt was soaked, as was my hair, face, legs, and hands, but I still couldn't pee.

He offered to suck me off, but I said no. I just wanted out. I wanted to throw up, but there was nothing left. I didn't know how to stop this nightmare of a movie. How could I change the channels on a program I no longer wanted to see? The Eagles' "Hotel California" was playing quietly on the radio.

When I came out of Eddie's room, a tall white guy with black hair and thick black glasses was moving quickly toward me. He had something in his hand that glittered as the light bounced off of it. Chet and Slide Step were blocking his way, but he kept staring at me, trying to get around them. Chet and Slide Step were saying to him, "He's just a kid!"

Eddie pushed me back inside the room and closed the door. There was more screaming and arguing outside the door. Eddie turned and told me to hide under the bed.

"No!" I said. "I'm not going back there."

"Just go!" He screamed. There was a look of terror in his eyes. I didn't care. I wasn't going back under that bed. He kicked the chair from the desk and told me to sit down, opening his locker to hide me from view. The shouting in the hall intensified.

"Here comes the PO-lice," he said. "Just be cool. Just be cool."

My heart was racing. "What was in that guy's hand" I asked. He looked like he wanted to kill me.

"Don't worry about it," Eddie whispered, his back to me as he looked out the window of his door. "Slide Step's taking care of it. You just be cool for a few minutes. You don't want to end up in the hole."

The arguing quieted down. There were still several voices, but the yelling stopped.

"Wait here!" he said. He stepped out, closing the door behind him.

I sat there shaking. What the fuck had just happened? Why would I go to the Hole? I didn't do anything. I couldn't even fucking pee. There was a wastebasket next to the desk. I bent over and dry heaved into it. There was nothing left.

I learned later on that the guy coming down the hall was Eddie's punk.

He was angry that I was having sex with his man. He had taped razor blades beteen each of his fingers and was coming to slice me up.

"I'll fix that little pretty boy," he said, "She'll know not to mess with my man."

"Call it," Chet said, as he flipped the pink token in the air. Red and Slide Step were standing on each side of him. We were back in the north side card room. I didn't know how much time had passed, or how long I'd been sitting there, but it was later on that same day.

"Heads," Red bellowed.

Slide Step was silent.

Chet caught the coin and flipped in onto his arm.

"Tails!"

Chet nodded to both of them and came over to me. I was sitting in the same chair as before. I had vague recollections of being led there from Eddie's room. And these were the last people in the world I wanted to be with. The spins had stopped, but my head was pounding, and my face was still numb. It was like watching a Godzilla movie where the voices were out of synch. There seemed to be a delay from when Chet said something, and when I heard him say it.

"It's settled then," Chet announced. "From now on, you belong to Slide Step."

Red walked behind him and out of the room. Even with the dullness in my brain, I could tell he was angry. Slide Step took his seat against the wall and put his legs up on a chair. I looked over at him. He crossed his arms, gave me a gentle smile and looked out into the day room.

14

Slide Step's Squeeze

*Sacred Heart Church. It was Ricky's Confirmation. I didn't under-
stand the ceremony, but I was looking forward to having waffles for
dinner. At seven years old, I hated church. It was long and boring, and
I hated all the kneeling and standing and sitting and kneeling. The best
part was afterward, when we went for a donut across the street. Eclairs
were my favorite, with their dark chocolate frosting and vanilla crème
custard on the inside.*

    *Mom couldn't make Ricky's Confirmation. She was working after-
noons, but would meet us at the Egg & I restaurant afterward, which is
how I was having waffles for dinner. It was weird going to church on a
school night.*

    *On the way from the service, Dad and Sharon talked about my mom.
They were angry with her for missing the service and didn't think she
should go to dinner since she hadn't gone to mass. "Well I'm not paying
for her dinner," Dad said, as he gazed out the window of our car, "even
if she is flat broke." Sharon said, "I don't think you should."*

    *When we arrived at the restaurant, she was waiting inside. I ran to
her and gave her a big hug. She squeezed me tight, and there were tears
in her eyes. I cried too. I always did whenever she did, I couldn't help it.
Ricky and Connie gave her a hug as well, and then we all sat down to
eat. Mom said her supervisor was doing her a favor by letting her sneak
over on her break. She was sad she had to miss Rick's service, and she told
him so several times. I didn't know what Dad saw in Sharon. Especially
when my mom was the most beautiful woman in the world. My aunts
and uncles were there too, but Mom seemed a little different. I was sitting*

next to her when the waitress came around to take our order. I asked for
an extra plate.

"Why the extra plate?" Mom asked.

"Because one's for you," I whispered.

The next morning I stepped out of 10 Building and into the sunshine. The weather was clear and sunny, and for the first time since I was attacked the day before, I felt my spirits lift. I loved the first warm days of the year and the air that's filled with the fragrance of spring. Riverside was in the country, so the outdoor air smelled fresh.

It took only a moment for the sounds of the yard and the pain in my rectum to smack my senses with the brutal reality of my surroundings. Basketballs were bouncing. Men were laughing. Radios blared from everywhere. I could hear steel hitting concrete in the weight pit off in the distance.

"That's Slide Step's kid," someone said, among a group of men standing at the foot of the stairs. He pointed at me. I smelled the pot from the joint they were passing. I lowered my eyes and hurried past, but one of them stepped from the crowd and blocked my way. "How you doing," he asked in a seductive voice.

"OK," I said, stepping around him.

They laughed as I raced off.

I decided to stroll the patchy green and filth-ridden yard. It had been exactly fifty days since I was last outside and free to walk on my own. I missed the isolation of being locked up alone in my cell in Quarantine. It seemed hard to believe that I had only been in general population for two days. So far, I'd gotten drunk, drugged, almost sliced to pieces by a jealous boyfriend, and sold—or rather won, in a coin toss. I wondered what day three would be like.

The thought of having been won in a coin toss was too much for me to take in. So whenever the memory of it would occur to me—I'd literally shake it out of my head. It was too devastating to comprehend—and since no one would ever know about it outside of here—I struggled to pretend like it had never happened.

I wanted to stay in bed all day, but I couldn't sleep. The guys in my dorm were rowdy, and then a guard came around and kicked us out. He said if we didn't have job assignments, we had to go into the day room or out in the yard until the afternoon count.

I thought about reporting the rapes, but my brother's voice rang inside my head: *Punks are fucked, but Snitches get killed.*

The twisted path that encircled the yard was made of blacktop. I wished I could walk out of there and somehow walk off what had happened to me the day before. I wanted to shake this dreadful, *Oh my God, what has happened to me?* feeling that haunted my every step. But it was too late. Everyone knew what had happened, and now everyone knew what I was—a fag. There was no going back.

"God damn!" said a black inmate, as he passed me. "That's a fine motherfucker right there."

"Mmm, Mmm," said another. "Slide Step's holdin' all the cards in this game!"

I couldn't stop replaying in my head what I could have done differently. Why did I drink? I know what happens to me when I get drunk. Hadn't Rick told me this was what happened to fish? The intake psychologist had told me point blank that I'd get fucked. But nothing could have prepared me for what happened, even if I hadn't been drinking. Still, I hated myself for falling into their trap so stupidly.

They must have known I was gay from the moment I walked on the floor—even if I wasn't sure about it myself. What if I had just said yes, when Chet first asked? Would it have turned out differently? Red must have been in on it from the very beginning, and once it started, I couldn't do anything to stop it.

Thank God Slide Step stepped in when he did. He seemed different from the others. It would have been worse if he hadn't stopped it when he did. I asked if I would have to do something for him as well, but he told me not to worry about it for now. "When you're ready," he said. "I'm willing to wait."

I was relieved, because I was sore, and there was blood when I went to the bathroom. I was afraid to ask the guards to see a doctor, because I would have to explain what had happened.

I walked past 23 Building and looked up at the Segregation unit. I could go there for protection, but I'd have to tell them why, and then I'd be locked down twenty-four hours a day. Even with special good time, I had twenty-two and half months left to go. Six hundred and eighty-four days. I'd probably go mad and kill myself. It wasn't much of an option. Nor was getting my throat slit, like that asshole psychologist had said. You either fight or submit. At least I was still alive.

It was my failure to resist being attacked that haunted me most. Why didn't I? Or scream? Or even try to say No to Red? Why did I have to be such a fucking coward? Sure I wasn't just a kid but even kids my age are known to fight back.

"But Timmy's a sissy," one of my friends once said about a fight we had with a gang of kids. He said it right in front of me, like I wasn't even there. I was too timid to stand up to him and say anything, so I just let it go. But I didn't really—his words still hurt.

I kept replaying Chet's advances over and over. I thought I knew what his intentions were, but I was taken by how friendly he was, and by the fact that he said he had a kid my age. That was probably a lie. After the coin toss, I had seen him laughing with other inmates about the rape. He was bragging and imitating how out of it I was because of the Thorazine. He seemed energized by the incident, as if it raised his standing with the other guys. The way he set me up and *turned me out*. That's what they called it when someone is raped. I "turned that boy out."

That's what happened to Bottoms, the chubby kid in my dorm. He was straight, or at least he was before he got locked up. He was turned out in the county jail, right after sentencing for stealing his dad's car. Car theft wouldn't have been enough to send him there, but he had an accident where someone died and he was convicted of felony murder. The poor kid didn't even make it to Quarantine before he was jumped and gang raped by sixteen guys, over a six-hour period. When they were done with him, the guy that set him up pimped him out for a pack of cigarettes. By the time he came there, everyone knew what happened to him, and he was forced to get a man. That's how he got the name Bottoms. It used to be Byron. There were dozens of stories just as gruesome, sometimes even worse.

I looked over at the double fence and gun towers. There was no escape. I would do what I had to survive in here. But what if my family found out? I was afraid Rick would just see the attack for what it was: I got what I deserved. It felt awful being so viciously assaulted and believing that I was responsible for it. And it felt almost worse knowing that Rick would agree with me.

Were it not for all the pain I was feeling after Chet fucked me, I might have enjoyed sucking Red's cock—at least until he made me gag and I threw up. I wished it been Scatter. He was so beautiful, and was also my age. His light brown skin. That muscular body. Those lips. I hated the way Red kept saying, "he's gay—he likes it."

Did this mean I wasn't a man anymore? I could never explain the confusion that was going on inside my head. How could I explain it? That I had felt drawn here, or that I wanted to come to prison because it was the only place in the world where I knew there were people like me? Who would believe me? After all, they would think I was crazy. Maybe I was crazy. I felt responsible for what happened. "*You made your bed,*" I heard Sharon's voice inside my head. Now I had to live with it. Was this my destiny?

I walked past 11 Building, the bug ward, and reminded myself that I had a strong mind. That I would get past this prison term. I would do whatever I had to, and I wouldn't let my fear show. At least this way, I would feel like I had control. I tried to convince myself that this is what I had wanted. Maybe not in such a violent way, but I did secretly want to have sex with a man. *Yes, this is what I had wanted.* I was glad my sexuality was finally out and that I don't have to hide anymore. I felt detached—like I was outside of myself—watching it all on TV. I would put the bad part of what happened right out of my mind, just like my mom had done with us kids: we didn't exist—it never happened—I am going on with my life as if free from the burden of responsibility. Free from worrying about what they think—because, in my mind, they never happened.

As I came around 9 Building the second time, a skinny blond queen named Cisco called out to me. I met him briefly, the day before, but I couldn't get away from him fast enough.

"Oh, Tim!" he waved wildly from the grass. He was sitting between two old white men. "Come over here, darling."

Cisco was in his late thirties, and the two men who were flanking him were each old enough to be my grandfather. Behind them, playing on a small black transistor radio was the Kendalls' "Heaven's Just A Sin Away."

"C'mon honey, come sit with Momma." He patted on the ground next to him. "You look all lost walking around the yard in a daze and all."

"I'm fine," I said. I was embarrassed by his attention. I just wanted to be alone for a while to sort things out in my head.

"I remember when I first came to paradise," he said. "You're gonna be fine, honey. A pretty young thing like you? You're gonna be just fine."

I didn't know Cisco. In spite of being embarrassed by his flamboyance, I liked how nice he was being. The first genuine expression of humanity I'd seen in prison. Maybe I could talk to him. The two older men looked on with smiles. I sat down on the grass, which was warm from the sun, but the earth beneath it was cold and damp. My state blues were already soiled.

"That's it," the old timer on the right said. "Come join us for a spell." He was holding a metal cup by the handle, and a can of Mountain Dew was resting in the grass. His teeth were yellow as was the D on his baseball cap. His face was wrinkled like a prune, and his eyes were blue and looked tired. "I'm Earl," he said, reaching out a hand.

My grandmother had died of cirrhosis of the liver, so I knew about the dark brown patches on his skin. "This here is Delmar," he pointed to his friend. "And I guess you already know our peroxide beauty."

"It's not peroxide," Cisco protested. He ran his long fingernails through his hair. "It's au naturale!"

"Of course it is sweetheart." Earl reached over and wiggled his ear. "Of course."

I didn't know why, but I felt embarrassed. I wanted to get up and distance myself from such obviously gay men, but I chose to stay.

"What are you in for?" Delmar asked.

I was getting tired of repeating myself, but it seemed to be the opening for most inmates. What are you in for? How long you got? How much money did you get? I answered while looking over at Cisco. He was leaning back, on his elbows. He took his sunglasses off and placed them on his head. There was pool chalk smeared on his eyelids.

"Well, that's not so bad," Delmar said. He reached into his pocket and brought out a metal flask. "At least you'll get out one day." He poured a clear liquid into his cup. "When I get out of here, it will be in a pine box."

"And hopefully not much longer," Earl said, stretching out his own metal cup.

"What are you drinking?" I asked, smelling a familiar chemical odor. It didn't look like the spud juice that was still clearing my head and oozing out from my pores.

"Turpentine," he said. He picked up the can of pop. "And Mountain Dew."

"It's not the best . . . " Earl said.

"But it'll do!" Delmar topped off both cups.

"Are you serious?"

"Ninety percent wood alcohol," he said. "And maybe a few other things."

I couldn't believe they were going to drink it! "Won't it poison you?"

Delmar lifted his cup. "If we're lucky. We've been down a long time, son, and we just don't care anymore. I've already got a bit of the rot gut."

"How long have you been down?"

"Well, let's see, I first came to the penitentiary in '35, and Earl here . . ."

"You've been here that long?" I interrupted.

"Not straight through, mind you, but in bits and pieces. We've been doing what's called Life on the Installment Plan."

"Well, anyway," Delmar said, "we hope it'll be over soon." He reached over and toasted his friend. "Hour by hour, we ripe and rot."

"And rot and rot," Delmar added, clinking his cup, "and therein hangs a tale."

Tilting their heads back, they quickly downed the mixture, closing their eyes and multiplying their wrinkles. I watched as they finished squinting. There were tears in their eyes as their faces relaxed. For a moment there, I could see the pain that was in their bellies. They were drunks. And I felt like I knew them well.

"Shakespeare," Delmar winked.

I didn't know what he was talking about.

Cisco was smiling up at the clear blue sky.

"Is that from an All Star Game?" I asked, pointing to Delmar's hat.

"What?"

"The Detroit Tigers hat with the red star?"

"Oh this," he grabbed his hat and looked at it. "This isn't the Tigers," he said. "Though it does look like their D. No, this is from the colored leagues in the '20s and '30s."

"The colored leagues?"

"The Detroit Stars," he said, handing me the hat. "Part of the Negro League."

"Was it separate from the majors?" I asked.

"Oh yeah. Coloreds couldn't play with whites until the 1950s," Delmar said. "That's when Jackie Robinson came in and broke the colored barrier."

"It's not the *colored* barrier," Cisco said. "It's the *color* barrier."

Cisco was from California, where they had all kinds of weird things, like hot tubs and communes and geodesic, solar-powered homes. Dad said it was the land of fruits and nuts.

Delmar took the flask and filled his cup. "They were more fun to watch than the white teams."

"And cheaper too," Earl said.

Cisco sat up on an elbow and looked at me, shaking his head. He rolled his eyes and flopped back down on the grass.

"We're runnin' low on Dew," Delmar said, shaking the empty pop can. "Cisco, why don't you be a doll and run up to the Commissary for your Poppas."

"No way," Cisco protested, "I've been there three times already."

Delmar winked at me. His face was starting to look more pickled than when I first sat down. After a minute or two of silence, Cisco got up in a huff.

"You mens!" He wiggled his ankles back and forth to get into his shoes. "A girl can't get no rest around here!"

Delmar gave Cisco a handful of tokens.

Cisco took them, looked at me with a smile and then walked off toward 9 Building. "I'm a woman," he muttered. "I ain't no mule they can just keep sending up and down the mountain all day." As he walked toward the small white building on the edge of the track, I could see a hint of green in his hair.

I couldn't help but wonder if this was how I might end up in twenty years. Using pool chalk as eye shadow and drinking paint thinner to hurry my death. I wasn't like these people. And I was determined not to become like them, either.

"Do you like baseball?" Delmar asked.

"I used to," I said, looking out across the yard. Slide Step was raking the baseball diamond. "I sort of lost interest these last few years."

"Tigers?" He asked.

"Yeah." My head still felt numb from the day before.

"Well, there hasn't been a whole lot to be excited about *lately*."

This was true. I was beginning to feel nauseous.

I remembered when I first started watching baseball and when I first fell in love with the game. It was 1968, and the Tigers had made it to the World Series. I watched them play on our old black and white TV. It was a console television that shared the cabinet with a stereo and record player that didn't work. We couldn't afford a color TV because my parents were getting a divorce.

I remembered thinking, there wasn't anything in the world that was better than baseball. The Detroit Tigers vs. The St. Louis Cardinals. They called it the Year of the Pitcher, because seven pitchers had ended the season with an ERAs below two. Dad once said, "You could be the greatest batter in the world, but it wouldn't matter. You'll always be limited by what's thrown at you."

It was the same year I moved in with Dad and Sharon. Mom said it was only temporary—until she got on her feet—and I had believed her. They split up because she had an affair with a guy name Dave. Dave was married too, but somehow he still managed to keep his family together. I couldn't understand why my dad couldn't do the same thing.

I started listening to baseball while sitting on the porch and waiting for my mom to pick me up for the weekend. I watched for her car as I listened to my small transistor radio. Sometimes Mom wouldn't call until two or three hours after she was supposed to be there. And other times, she would forget all together. The games made the time pass, and Ernie Harwell, the voice of Tiger Baseball, helped distract me from Sharon's ranting and raging about my no-good mother. She had broken my dad's heart, and he sometimes wouldn't come home for days at a time, which left Sharon even angrier. The white plastic earphones of my transistor radio were enough to escape her screaming.

When the Tigers won the World Series, they surprised everyone. They had gone into it trailing three games to one. But in the seventh inning of the seventh game, after nobody thought they could do it, the Tigers had rallied, and I was in love with baseball.

They were my only heroes that year. Even my brother Rick had run away from home. My mom, my dad, and even my big brother had all deserted me that year.

I remembered walking to school the next day and in the window of the corner drug store, seeing a big cutout of a Tiger with a dead Cardinal hanging from its mouth. It was the same drug store that called Sharon a couple of weeks later to tell her they had seen me stealing on their new close-circuit cameras they had just installed. They weren't sure what it was that I had stolen, but they clearly saw me sticking something inside of my pants. They thought it might have been a Baby Ruth bar. I swore I didn't steal a candy bar, but Sharon wouldn't believe me.

"You know," Delmar said. "Slide Step used to play in the Minors."

"Oh Yeah," Earl joined in. "He's quite the player."

I was sure they had heard what had happened to me the day before. I looked over toward the baseball field, on the opposite side of the yard. I belonged to Slide Step now, and I didn't know anything about him. He was so quiet. The way he sat back against the wall, looking at me and gently smiling.

"He played with LeFlore in Jackson," Delmar said.

"Ron LeFlore?" I asked, sitting up.

Ron LeFlore was the center fielder for the Detroit Tigers. He was considered the fastest man in baseball. Tiger manger, Billy Martin, recruited him out of Jackson Prison. It was probably the only good thing Martin did for the Tigers.

"I can't believe he knew Ron LaFlore," I said, looking back toward Slide Step. "Was he as good as him?"

"He was pretty good," Delmar said.

Earl nodded in agreement.

"No kidding," I said.

Cisco walked up with a six-pack of Mountain Dew, two packs of Pall Malls and a Hostess Twinkie. He kicked off his shoes and sat down on the grass. "I'm a bushed woman," he said. "Now don't you dare, either one of you, ask me to do nothin' else."

"Oh I've got something for you to do later," Earl said. He reached inside Cisco's overalls and grabbed his nipple. "We were just talking about fantasies before you came over here, Tim."

"Tell 'em what your fantasy is," Delmar prodded Cisco.

"OK," he said, smiling. "I want to be gangbanged by a gay motorcycle gang."

"A gay motorcycle gang?" I tried to hide my horror.

"A gay motorcycle gang," Earl echoed. He and Delmar chuckled.

"That's right honey," he said. "They have them in California." He laid back on the grass and threw his legs up in the air. "Heaven's Just a Sin Away."

Delmar poured turpentine into his cup and Earl popped open a can of pop. Still feeling nauseous, I got up and excused myself. Cisco was going home in a couple of weeks. I wished it were me, but I still had six hundred and eighty-four days to go.

I walked across the yard toward Slide Step. He raked the dirt on the infield with his back to me. The letters REC were stenciled on his dark green jacket. His shoulders were broad, and his thighs were thick and muscular. I thought about my heroes of '68. And now it was spring and the start of a new season. Perhaps it was time, once again, to take an interest in baseball.

I never told anyone what it was I had stolen from that corner drug store. It wasn't a candy bar. But what it was, I took to my new school that day and placed it on top of my desk. When the teacher came over, she picked it up and examined it.

"Is that your mother?" She asked, holding up the small, three-and-a-half-by-five-inch frame. "She's really beautiful."

"She's the most beautiful woman in the world," I said.

When I reached Slide Step, I was struck with a sudden panic. I didn't know what to say to him. With rake in hand, he looked up at me and smiled. "Hey, Squeeze!"

15

Lessons in Streetball

On a hot summer night, somewhere between the sixth and seventh grades, I grew almost six inches taller. It seemed like my body had sprouted faster than I could catch up to it. In my mind, I was still shorter than my new-found height of six foot two. My body weight wouldn't match up for several more years. It left me feeling uncoordinated, and I was constantly tripping, stumbling, and knocking things over.

"You clumsy idiot," Sharon shrieked when I spilled her coffee on the livingroom carpet. Her cup had been sitting on the floor, next to the sofa. I ran and grabbed something to clean it up, but then she screamed at me, "Not my good towels!" She stormed into the kitchen and returned with a rag. "Forget it," she said, "Just get out of here!"

Fortunately, my dad ran a carpet cleaning business on the side, so there wasn't a stain that would serve as a constant reminder of how awkward I had become.

It was also my first year in junior high school and the beginning of my problems in gym. I was always the last kid picked for teams, and the one who drew the most moans when I was finally chosen. I was as klutzy on the field, baseball diamond, and basketball court as I was in my own living room. To make matters worse, I had to shower with everyone afterward. I was nearly sixteen before I sprouted pubic hair.

I was shooting hoops by myself, when he snuck up behind me and took the ball. He did a quick lay up and tossed it back to where I was standing fifteen feet from the basket.

"What's you doin' out here?" Slide Step said playfully. "You don't know nothin' about this game."

"Sure I do," I said smiling. "Just 'cause I'm not very good—doesn't mean I don't know nothin'." I took a shot, and to my surprise it landed in the basket.

Slide Step looked up, grabbed the ball as it swished from the small chain link net, and tossed it back. I used to play Around the World in my driveway back home. We had a hoop over the garage. I took another shot, and it landed again!

"Oh, two in a row!" Slide Step said, smiling. He tossed the ball back to me. "Watch out now!" This time I missed, and he grabbed the ball and slowly bounced it as he walked behind me another six or eight feet from the basket.

He took a shot and missed, the ball hit the rim and bounced back. I grabbed it, dribbled forward and did a quick lay up. He came behind me and grabbed the ball as it dropped from the net. He passed it back. I was smiling, because the three out of four shots I just made—was about six times my normal average.

I bounced the ball forward, and he moved in to block me. That's where I usually got flustered. I could make a basket or two if I just took shots from anywhere around an imaginary arch in front of the hoop—but I didn't play well when someone was coming after me, checking and blocking. I turned my back to him and nervously leaned forward, so he couldn't take the ball. He got behind me and reached around, as I tried to go right and then left and then right again. He wasn't giving any; his hips were right on my butt.

A couple of guys going up the stairs to 10 Building stopped to watch us play. I leaned forward, backed my butt into him and then quickly turned to my left, taking a wide hook shot with my right arm. The ball swished through the net! The guys on the stairs laughed. So did Slide Step. It was a lucky shot, but I wasn't sure they knew it.

Slide Step retrieved the ball and passed it back to me. He stood just inside my imaginary arch, shadowing me as I moved right and left again. He quickly reached around and snatched the ball, bumping me in the process.

"Foul," I yelled. He took the shot and easily landed the basket, slipping around me grabbing the ball as it bounced from the net. I reached out my hands, but he ignored me. "Foul," I repeated.

"What?"

"You fouled me," I said.

He took the shot and landed it. "That wasn't a foul," he said. He looked up and smiled at the guys on the stairs. He tossed me the ball, "but you can have it, anyway."

My brother taught me to bounce the ball in between my legs to transfer it from my right to the left hand. It was the only trick I knew. I took a stride back and then bounced it perfectly between steps, smiling broadly. I was starting to feel cocky. Slide Step's eyes twinkled with delight, and the guys on the stairs laughed. A few more had joined them.

"Uh oh," Slide Step said playfully, "You better be careful, Little Squeeze, or I'm gonna have to haul my dogs out here in a second."

I jumped up in the air and pushed the ball with both hands toward the basket. The ball missed the basket entirely, and the guys behind me howled. Slide Step caught it in the air, before it ran loose in the yard.

He dribbled behind me, turned and then moved backwards toward the hoop. I tried to block him, but he just kept backing into me, like I wasn't even there. "Don't foul me," I said, but he kept on pushing. "You're fouling me," I said.

"No I'm not," and he moved right, faked left, and in a flash was behind me dumping the ball into the basket.

He came out and did it again, leaving me standing there, looking foolish. The guys laughed again and the crowd had seemed to grow. Slide Step stepped out, moved in, and easily slipped passed. This time, the ball hit the rim and bounced behind me. I went to grab it, but as I turned around, he was already on my tail and easily recovered it, grabbing it in midbounce from my feeble attempt at dribbling.

After making the basket, he let me take a shot or two, but then he started backing into me again. I tried to hold my ground, but I was no match for his weight. He stopped, turned, and bounced the ball between my legs—retrieving it behind me and then slamming it in the basket. The onlookers howled.

I stood there for a moment, staring. He came up and rubbed my head. This made everyone on the stairs laugh even more. I could feel my face getting red and I walked off, angry as hell. How could he do this to me in front of everyone like that?

No one had explained to me that Streetball had as much to do with theatrics as anything else. It wasn't winning so much as it was about humiliating your opponent.

"Oh Lord," Slide Step said, shaking his head. "Come on back, Timmy."

I wasn't having it. I marched up the stairs and the guys moved out of my way, but their amusement was only intensified. I stopped at the top landing and turned to face him. I could feel my rage boiling up from the new sneakers Slide Step had just bought me.

He looked at me and his face got serious—his eyes darting, for an instant, to the guys who were standing there. His look said, "No, don't do it!" But it was too late; the rumble was already causing my head to vibrate. I struggled for the words.

The inmates were silent.

"You . . . you . . . black bastard!"

Slide Step dropped his head, and shook it.   •

I turned and stormed into the building. I couldn't help it. It just slipped out of me. When I first said "You . . ." a hush came over the crowd of convicts standing in the gallery. And as soon as I said, "Black Bastard," there was a ricochet of "ooooohhhs" from the balcony. "Someone's got an ass whippin' coming now," I heard one of them say.

I ran up the stairs and down the hall. At the officer's station I turned left down the corridor that led to the individual cells. Mine was the last one on the left. The guards had moved me after Slide Step and Red beat up some guy who was messing with me in the dorms. I don't know how the guards knew about that—but they did. I wondered why they didn't do something, after I was raped, but there was no way I could talk to them about it.

I slammed my cell door and sat in the chair, opening the locker to block my view from the hall. I knew I was in big trouble, but I didn't care. I had disrespected him in public, and now he had to do something about it. If he didn't, his own manhood would be called into question.

There was a knock at my door. I jumped at first, but chose to ignore it. I was surprised he got up there as quickly as he did. He knocked again.

"Open the door, Tim," Slide Step said. "I know you're in there."

"No," I said.

"Open the door!"

"No!"

"C'mon," his voice softened. "Let me in."

I knew not to challenge his authority, especially in front of the other inmates.

"C'mon Timmy—open the damn door."

"Uh uh," I said. "You're gonna hit me." I started to cry.

"I'm not going to hit you, just open the door." He sounded sincere, but I didn't trust him. "C'mon, Timmy. Have I ever hit you?"

I was afraid to let him in, but I didn't know what else to do. I would have to come out sooner or later, so I opened the door.

He rushed in, pinning me back against the chair. The locker slammed into the wall and made a huge bang that echoed up the hall. Terrified, I let out a breathless whimper, but before I knew it, he stuck his tongue deep inside my mouth. He was kissing me, passionately, as the tears continued down my face. We climbed under the bed, to hide from view of a passing guard, and Slide Step fucked me for the first time.

16

Blemished Masculinities

Her name was Beth and she was two grades ahead of me—I in the seventh and she in the ninth. The kids called her Pizza Face.

When it first happened, I didn't have time to think. Three or four girls had her pinned against the lockers. "Break it, Break it, Break it," they taunted. They were trying to get her to pop a zit, the size of a boil, on her cheek. The others were cheering them on.

I felt sorry for her, so I pushed the girl closest to me. "Why don't you leave her alone?"

The girls backed down and retreated up the hall. Beth looked up at me and smiled. Embarrassed, I shied away. We only had five minutes in between classes and what I needed from my locker (which was next to hers) could wait.

That afternoon and for several days following, she greeted me with the same fluttering eyes, I started to regret helping her and was embarrassed by the teasing I was getting from the guys.

Finally, I told her, "Beat it, Pizza Face."

I can still see that look on Beth's face, which said I'd done something worse than anything those girls could have ever done. And every pimple I have gotten since has reminded me of her.

We were sitting alone at the back of the day room. Most everyone else had gone to chow. The midday news was on TV. President Carter was trying to end a thirty-year war between Israel and Egypt by inviting both sides to Camp David. The last remaining inmate got up to leave.

"Now if they at war," he said. "Why would a motherfucker want to go camping?"

Slide Step looked over at me and shrugged. He was sitting sideways, next to me, in the orange rocker. When the man walked out Slide Step placed both of his hands on top of mine. It was the first time I noticed how different he was when no one else was around.

"Can you handle my having feelings for you?"

"What?" I said. I felt myself blush.

He was smiling, but his eyes were serious, which made me feel even sillier.

"What do you mean?" I repeated. I thought he might be playing with me.

"I mean, just that. Can you handle my having feelings for you?"

I didn't know what to say, but I enjoyed the way his hands felt resting on mine. They felt warm and comforting, like Slide Step had been to me.

"I'm talking about caring for you," he said.

Unsure of myself, I started to laugh. "I thought we were talking about: I take care of you and you take care of me. That's the deal, isn't it?"

"No, that's not what I'm talking about. I want to know if you can handle feelings."

I looked up at the ceiling and then away. I was immature for my age, but it still never occurred to me that love was a possibility between two men. I grew up in the suburbs, in a working-class neighborhood, where I didn't see many blacks—much less queers. And I was still struggling to come to terms with all that had happened to me since I got here.

When I was younger, I attended Catholic School, at least until Sharon took a belt to one of the nuns who used one on her son—Sharon's Irish/German temper getting the best of her. After that, we were kicked out of the school, as well as the Parish, which was fine with me because it meant I didn't have to be told how wicked and vile my sexual thoughts were. And if my thoughts were so unnatural, how could there be *feelings*?

"Is that possible?" I asked.

He dropped his head and sighed. "Oh yes." He said it as if they were already there. He looked up and smiled. He wasn't making fun of me.

I had heard that when men went to prison for a long time, their boys often became their wives, so I guessed it made sense that these guys would develop feelings too, but I wouldn't know what that felt like. I had never been in love before.

I smiled at him with a goofy grin. "I guess so, sure."

He studied me and shook his head. "Nah. I don't think you can."

His right fingers were caressing the top of my hand. He dropped his head and let out a long-winded, high-pitched "woo." The sound echoed off the walls of the empty room. The guards, as usual, were tucked away in their station on the other side.

Slide Step got up and tussled my hair. "We'll see, little squeeze. We'll see."

He walked out of the room and up the hall toward his cell. His head was down and slowly shaking. There was a playfulness in his swagger, a slow deliberate rhythm, as he twirled his key on a long string back and forth around his finger. That walk was how he got his name, and I stared after him as he disappeared, wondering what he meant by having feelings for me.

Anita Bryant came on the TV, the beauty queen-turned-spokeswoman for the orange juice industry. She was accusing gays of recruiting children into being homosexual and the news was covering a boycott of orange juice. A few months earlier, someone had pushed a pie in her face. I remembered it because it was a banana cream pie, which was my favorite. The news showed a bumper sticker that read: Kill a Queer for Christ.

I thought about my dad and wondered if he would be more upset because Slide Step was black, or that I was a fag. But it's not like he would ever know about it. He hadn't come to visit me, and I had been away for a couple of months by then. I hadn't heard from anyone, and I was feeling abandoned and alone.

Always seeking attention was the frequent note on my report cards from school. I craved it because I wasn't getting any at home. At least that's what a guidance counselor once said. I needed someone to notice me, to pay attention, and to let me know that I mattered. I wanted to be taken care of, looked after, and for someone to make me feel safe. I wanted to stop the world from spinning and told I was OK. I would have given anything to bask in the glory of someone's affection, to see their face light up when I walked into a room. Even at age seventeen, I still wanted someone to be proud of me, to want to be with me, and I desperately wanted somewhere to belong, to feel like I was finally home. But Slide Step was a man, a black man, and this was prison.

An inmate named Manley walked into the room and told me that Slide Step had asked him to look after me—to make sure I didn't get into any trouble. I'm sure he was more concerned about others than he was about me. Manley was a heavy-set black man, but manly he wasn't. He was in his thirties and weighed about two hundred and fifty pounds. He was wearing kitchen whites, which helped explain his weight. He was good natured and jovial, with a pockmarked face. He offered me a cigarette and then tossed me a pack.

"Let's hit the commissary, kid. Slide Step says you need a few things."

At first, I wondered if Slide Step wanted me to do something with him, but later on he told that I was too old for Manley. "Too old?" I was the youngest boy at Riverside.

"He likes 'em much younger than you," was all Slide Step said. "But don't worry, he's harmless. I just don't want you walking around by yourself, until it's well known that you're riding with me."

The grapevine would spread word quickly, but Slide Step wasn't taking chances. As my man, he was responsible for my safety, and he had already sent one guy to the infirmary.

"As soon as everyone sees you two walkin' the yard together," Manley said, "They'll know what time it is. If anyone tries to press you, just tell Slide Step, and he'll take care of it. But don't worry, nobody's gonna fuck with you, because if they did, it'd be the same as if they were fucking with Slide Step."

Slide Step, I'd learn, was well respected, and everything in prison was about respect. You either had it or you didn't, and even when you did, it was frequently tested. There was a pecking order in prison, and inmates were constantly checking to see where they fit in. The boys were given the same level of respect as their man, and the man was obligated to protect them. The price for this protection meant that the boy gave up his independence (if he ever had it in the first place). Among other things, he no longer had control over his own body, which meant he had to put out sexually. But considering the alternative, it seemed the least damaging way to survive. "At least you only have to do it with one," Manley said, "rather than with anyone who can catch you."

This was true. It definitely could have been worse for me. Manley said that some men shared their boys with friends while others made them turn tricks by forcing them into prostitution. Over at the Reformatory there were boys who were owned by entire gangs, and they were forced to have to service the whole lot of them. "The man calls the shots," he said, "and the boys are expected to obey."

The quality of a boy's life was dependent on his man. So who your man was made all the difference. It seemed to go beyond sex, as if some of them took as much pleasure in dominating another. Perhaps it was their way of dealing with the frustrations of being locked up and told what to do all the time by the guards. Some men made their boys do all sorts of things. Back when I was staying in the dorm, Bottoms had to do his man's laundry and make his bed in the morning and anything else his man didn't feel like doing himself.

"Some men beat their boys," Manley said, as we arrived at the commissary. "While others, like Slide Step, spoil them." To the right of the commissary door, a price list was taped to the wall. An inmate clerk filled orders from the goods stocked on the shelves. Manley pulled a stack of tokens from his pocket and winked at me. "Your man is also responsible for commissary. So whatever you need, Slide Step's got you covered."

The commissary goods included soaps, shampoos, toothpaste, and deodorants. Cosmetics, as the inmates referred to them, along with cigarettes and candy and canned goods for cooking on the hotplates up in the units. Spam, chili, roast beef, and Vienna sausages. "Zoos Zoos and Wham Whams," Manley said. "Stock up baby boy, your cupboards are bare."

I thought about what he said, about the quality of a boy's life, and thought about how long it had been since I really was just a boy playing with toys. But it had been a toy that got me here—the plastic gun I had found in a field and a pretty girl inside the Photo Mat. Had it only been a year since I first learned to drive?

Slide Step was kind to me. He smiled a lot, and he always had a twinkle in his eye. At least he did for me, but mostly he was gentle—especially when he fucked me. I didn't like getting fucked, because it hurt. More than hurt, it felt like I was being cracked open, busting apart at the seams. It felt like I was being crushed, and it sent a wave of pain through my body. But soon the pain lessened and was replaced by a deadening, pulsating ache. Slide Step went slow and easy, rotating my hips until I was able to relax. He kissed the back of my head and ran his lips along the side of my neck—his warm breath in my ear relieving the panic. It was never enjoyable, but it wasn't terrible either. I was grateful he was so gentle.

Slide Step was a powerful man, athletic and strong. He also ran the drug trade inside the prison, as his mother did on the outside. I heard that she was a large distributor who the other cons talked about. Slide Step had the juice, the power, and his hand in a lot of things. I just wished he wasn't so old. At thirty, he was nearly twice my age.

Scatter Brain came up behind me and tugged at my hair. It was long and curly, like Peter Frampton's (my favorite singer).

"Homeboy!" Scatter said, smiling.

"Hey," I smiled back.

If only Slide Step was seventeen like Scatter and me.

Manley and I returned up the stairs, each of us carrying a box full of goods. "You need to be careful, Tim, because Slide Step is responsible for whatever you get into."

"What do you mean?" I asked.

"Well, you're a pretty motherfucker, for one thing. And a lot of these guys are going to come at you."

I stopped and looked at him. "I thought Slide Step was going to protect me?"

"He is. I'm not talking about that." Manley put his hand on my shoulder. "They'll come at you from the side, on the down low, to see if you'll slip up and do something with them." Meaning, would I cheat on my man. Manley stopped to look at me. "It could be a problem because it would be a *disrespect* to Slide Step."

I must have looked hurt, because he backed off right away. He said that it would be easy for me—being a fish—for someone to trick me into a compromising situation. Then Slide Step would have to straighten them out. He didn't want to see Slide Step get fronted off like that. It would be better if I stayed close until I learned the ropes, so no one would do anything that would get them thrown in the hole.

Manley told me about a guy who knew his boy was fucking around on him, and he didn't do anything about it. "The nigger was from Saginaw," Manley said as an aside, meaning that if he wasn't from Detroit, he wasn't a real man no-how.

"So the next thing you know, he fucked around and lost his boy."

"How?"

"The guy just told the boy he couldn't talk to his old man anymore."

"So what'd the old man do?"

"Nothing," Manley said. "Which became a problem for him, because by doing nothing, he was showing himself as a punk. He ended up having to lock up, by going into protective custody."

"Why?"

"It was either that or *get a man*. Because once someone shows himself as a punk, it's all over," Manley said. "Some guys are doing shit under the covers." In other words, getting fucked or sucking dick without anyone knowing about it, but as soon as someone finds out, they pull his "ho' card." A ho' being a whore, and ho' card meaning they were *laying that way*.

"Only a man can have a boy," Manley said. "And once a man finds out someone is a punk, she'll have to get a man, because she can't walk the yard alone."

I asked him why he called them *she*, and he said that a lot of men liked their boys to act and look like girls. Like Cisco, who wore pool chalk on her eyelids and grew long hair and nails. Prison was divided between the men on one side and the punks, drag queens, and boys on the other.

A lot of the boys were straight before they got there, but once they were turned out, they were no longer considered that way.

"Shit," Bottoms said one night in the dorm. "I'm going out of this motherfucker the same way I got here. I'm going right back to my woman."

"Oh, you think you're gonna be a man?" an inmate asked. "Bitch, you ain't no man! You weren't no man in here, and you damn sure ain't gonna be one out on the street. If I ever see your punk ass out in the world, I'm going right up to you and smacking you—pulling your ho' card right out in front of your woman. And then I'm taking her!"

"That's right bitch," another said. "You just ought to get off that bunk right now and do your man's laundry."

Black, who was his man, just laughed. He treated Bottoms like he was nothing, and the others felt free to do the same. If they crossed a line, Black would let them know about it, but he hardly ever showed Bottoms any mercy. "What the fuck would you do with a woman anyhow," Black said. "Bump pussies?"

Bottoms got quiet while the others laughed. He tried to hide what he was feeling, but the color in his cheeks gave him away. I thought about Beth (Pizza Face), and I wanted to do something, but there was nothing I could do. Speaking up would have turned their attention on me, so I just lay there on my bunk fingering a zit on the side of my face. I didn't want to get Slide Step involved in something that wasn't any of my business. It was the kind of thing that Manley had been warning me against.

I felt sorry for Bottoms, because of how he became a punk. And because of how he struggled to accept his circumstances. He confided in me once that he used to think he was straight, but then a few times—while he was being fucked—his dick got hard by itself. "I even came once," he said, "without touching myself. So I figured that maybe it was a sign that I'm really gay." If Bottoms could have talked to the prison doctor, he might have been told that his involuntary ejaculations had something to do with the involuntary massage of his prostrate—but Bottoms remained convinced that it was his own fault.

I heard Red say once, "The tip of my dick can't tell the diff. It's hips, lips or fingertips," he said. "'Cause when I close my eyes, it's all good." But for some men who were uncomfortable with the notion of having sex with other men, the more their boys looked like women the better. Some made them even change their names. One boy, who was named Bobby, became Barbi, while others were forced to dye their underwear red (using hot Kool-Aid) because their man wanted to see them in panties. The men generally wore boxer shorts. While the white fitted briefs, because of how they hugged the ass—were preferred for the boys. The inmates called them *Come-Fuck-Me's.*

I didn't care what happened to me, I was not going to change my name and become like one of those queens. They made me feel ashamed of what I was becoming in there, and the further away from them I got—the better.

I thought about Cisco and how helpful she was the day after my rape, as I walked the yard in a daze. I didn't feel threatened by her, nor by the two old timers that were with her. They were small and weak, and I could have easily defended myself. And because California was a queen, I felt superior to her, so I was willing to make an exception. So I swallowed my pride to talk to her. Especially since she was leaving in a couple of weeks.

Manley explained "swapping up," which was when two boys got together to take care of each other sexually (since a man wasn't going to be any help in that area). "But clear it with Slide Step first," he said, "because you don't want to start any problems."

It wasn't going to be a problem, because none of the "boys" appealed to me. The drag queens were too swishy for me, and I didn't care for the few boys I'd met. It was all a bit overwhelming.

Except for Manley and Red, the rest of the men in Slide Step's circle all had boys. Chet's boy was away at court but was due back later that week, and I had almost met Eddie's, the day he came after me with the razor blades that were taped between his fingers.

Taylor's boy, Paul, was eighteen. He was slender and short, about 5 feet 6 inches, with long red hair, which he kept pulled back in a ponytail. Taylor called him Green Eyes. When I first met Paul, he was distant and cold, and I was convinced he didn't like me, but Slide Step said it was because I was prettier than him and he didn't like the competition.

I blushed when Slide Step said it.

"You know you're a bad motherfucker, right?"

I didn't, but I did like hearing it. I never heard that back home. The girls in my neighborhood liked me, but not like that. "You're the sweetest boy we know," Tammy and Carol said, as they kissed me on the cheek and ran off with the bullies.

"Well you are," Slide Step said. "You're the baddest motherfucker in here. And you've got quite a few of these motherfuckers jealous."

I wouldn't have been able to admit it, but I was beginning to enjoy the attention. I felt my step lighten, just a little bit higher. I raised my eyes from blacktop and saw that people were watching as Slide Step and I circled the yard. He didn't say anything for a while. We just walked and I felt less self-conscious the second time around.

"You know," he said. "You'd make a good drug dealer some day."

"How's that?"

"Because you don't use," he said. "Most guys who get high, end up using their profits, and then you can't trust 'em."

Slide Step didn't do drugs either, except for an occasional joint or little spud juice every now and then. He seemed smarter than the others and I was beginning to trust him.

"Maybe you can work for me some day," he said.

"Really?"

He nodded. "But after we both get out of here." Slide Step's sentence was a lot longer than mine. He was serving a fifteen-to-twenty-five-year sentence for assault.

His gaze became serious as he stared off across the yard. His eyes gleamed with all their power, but underneath his cool icy stare seemed to be a lonely man who wanted to reach out and connect with someone. Yet prison was hardly the place where you could let your guard down easily.

A few days later, Slide Step and I were talking when Red walked up to us. I asked Red if he could give Slide Step and me a minute alone.

"What!" Red shouted. "What did you say?"

Suddenly, Slide Step was standing between us and then marched me up the hall. I didn't know what I had done.

"Bitch!" Red shouted. "You don't be asking me nothing. Who the fuck do you think you are?"

"Hold up, Red!" Slide Step said. He had an embarrassed look on his face, but I couldn't tell which one of us had embarrassed him.

"That's your man's job, Bitch. You don't ask a Man nothing!" Red said.

Slide Step walked me into the shower room and sighed. "Let me handle this."

He explained that Red was still pissed he couldn't have me. I couldn't help thinking how differently my life would've been had Red won the coin toss. He treated people like shit. I was afraid of him because he was short-tempered and mean, and from what I gathered from Slide Step, he didn't treat his boys much differently.

"The last one locked up for protection," he said. "Red chased him across the yard."

"Why?"

"Because Red was smacking him around."

"Why would he do that?"

"Because that's Red," was all Slide Step would say at first. The two of them had been friends forever, Red having worked for Slide Step's mom. He and Slide Step also served their first bit together.

"Red wanted to brand him," Slide Step said, "but the boy wasn't having it. So he broke loose and ran screaming, buck naked, across the yard to the Control Center."

"Brand him?"

"Red was going to tattoo RED'S PUSSY across his ass."

The boy was Grasshopper, my friend from Quarantine. "He'll be all right," Slide Step said. "He's been transferred to H-ward, the protection unit over at M-R."

Grasshopper had arrived at Riverside a couple of weeks before I did, but by the time I got there he was already gone. They held a similar reception for him as they had for me. I asked Slide Step if Red won the coin toss that time, but he didn't answer me. He just looked at me for an uncomfortable moment, and then he tussled my hair. "I wouldn't know, Squeeze, I wasn't around when it happened."

"How can you be friends with him?"

He shrugged. "We grew up together."

I was quiet. I didn't know what else to say. Slide Step just stared off.

"We're very different," he said, "but if I need him, I know he's got my back."

I wondered what would happen to me if something bad happened to Slide Step. One thing was certain; I'd run to the Control Center as well. Slide Step said that Red had another boy, for a long time, and that he was crazy about Red. He must have treated him differently, I said, but Slide Step told me Red always treated his boys the same. He treated his women the same way too. I couldn't understand how someone would be loyal to a man who was mean and abusive. Not even in prison, where there's little choice. It didn't make sense to me.

Drugs were smuggled into prison by way of rubber balloons. They were double wrapped if it was heroine or cocaine, and the inmates would swallow them in the visiting room. The next day, they'd shit the balloons out and clean them up before opening them.

Manley said, "You can get just about any drug you want in prison; heroine, cocaine, reefer, or speed. Whatever it is you need."

121

"What if the balloon breaks?" I asked.

Manley smiled. "Well then you go out happy," he said.

Slide Step was quiet. We were lying on the grass talking.

"The drugs in prison are always the best," Manley said.

"How come?"

"Because they have to be," Slide Step said. "There's nowhere to hide."

"You can run, but you can't hide," Manley chimed. "You can't be selling no shit."

Every now and then a balloon would break, and someone would get rushed to the infirmary, but it didn't happen that often.

"How do they get it into the visiting room?" I asked.

"The women smuggle it inside their pussies," Manley said.

"Mmm, Mmm," Chet walked up. "Finger licking good."

Manley said, "I don't be eatin' no pussy, now."

"That's why you been eating them little boys," Red snapped.

"Now how the fuck are you going to play me?" Manley said.

Slide Step raised his hand before Manley could get up.

"That's all right, Drag," Red said. "He ain't gonna do nothing." He was staring at Manley with a sadistic grin, happy to have gotten a rise out of him.

"That mouth of yours is gonna need a tampon in a minute," Manley said. "You keep talkin' out the side of your neck."

Slide Step was silent, but I could detect a slight grin.

"They'll be a long, white-ass string hanging out that motherfucker," Manley said. He shook his head back and forth, as if wiggling an imaginary string.

The three of them laughed.

Red said, "Well if you're feeling like a frog—Jump! Motherfucker."

"It's true," Manley said. "A real nigger ain't eatin' no pussy, now."

"But them drippings sure does make them balloons slide down," Chet said. They all nodded.

In addition to running the drugs, Slide Step also ran the rec department, sat on the inmate benefit council, and had a hand in a couple of card games. He had the juice, he had the money, and he knew how to serve his time comfortably.

I was out of my prison blues within a matter of days. Convicts were constantly stopping by us with pants, shirts, shoes, watches, and other items for sale from the outside world. "Here," Slide Step would say. "Go check these out, Squeeze." And off I'd go into one of the dorms to try them on. We were allowed street clothes, but they had to be shipped from the outside or purchased from one of the catalogs—JC Penney or Sears. The money would be taken from an inmate's account.

When I first arrived, the resident unit counselor said I should hold off on having my clothes shipped, since I'd be going back to court in a few weeks. That meant I would have to go through Quarantine all over again. They'd ship everything back home as I went through the bubble, but Slide Step wasn't going to have his prize boy looking like a scrub, so he had me out of my state blues nearly as quick as that coin dropped into Chet's hand.

One day, while I was getting my split-ends clipped in the barbershop opposite the guards' station, Big Cat the barber stepped out and whispered something into Slide Step's ear. When Big Cat returned, he announced that I was getting a facial. When he finished cutting my hair, he pulled a lever on the chair and reclined it, and began pouring hot water over some hand towels. For the next couple of weeks, every afternoon at three, I reported to Big Cat for a hot towel and mudpack facial. The results were amazing. My face began to clear up. Now, I was starting to look, act, and feel like a bad motherfucker.

17

What's in a Name, Anyway?

"You're a sissy," my brother Rick sneered.

I don't remember why he'd said it, but it was as if he had kicked me square in the stomach.

Our parents were separating, so we had just moved into Grandpa's house on Cook Street and we were starting a new school the next day. It wasn't any wonder why, when my kindergarten teacher told me that I had to walk with the safety girls—that I didn't want to go. The Safety Girls were the ones who wore the orange safety belts, and helped the kids cross the street.

"No way," I said. "I'm not walking with girls."

But Miss Greenport insisted. "You have to," she said, "at least until you cross Telegraph Road." It was a large intersection with four lanes of traffic.

"I hate girls," I said.

"I'm sorry, Timmy, but there aren't any other boys that go that way."

"No," I said, defiantly, "And you can't make me."

"Oh yes I can," she said.

"Well, if you try and make me, I'll break your glasses."

Well she did, and so did I. Before she could say another word, I jumped up in the air and snatched them off her face. When we heard them crunch under foot, we both froze in place with our mouths wide open.

I was not going to be called a sissy.

Inmate movies were shown every Wednesday and Saturday night. The gymnasium was converted into a theater with rows of folding chairs that were stored on stage, behind a red velvet curtain that looked as old as the River-side complex.

The Inmate Benefit Council, the majority of which was black, selected the films. Slide Step chaired the committee of six black and two white inmates. The movies included *Shaft, Superfly, Foxy Brown,* and *The Black Lolita.* I'd never heard of these titles and was amazed at how many had the word black in it, like *Blacula, Blackenstein, Black Belt Jones,* and *Black the Ripper.* Occasionally, the warden would make them order something that appealed to whites, so they'd invariably pick some low budget flick that was either about CB radios or some outlaw trucker with a sidekick chimpanzee.

Every now and then, they chose a movie that pleased everyone, like *The Sting* or *The Godfather* or some other film about gangsters and con artists—men getting over in some form or another. And everyone liked a good comedy like *Cotton Comes to Harlem* or a disaster film like *The Towering Inferno.*

During the movies you could usually see someone giving his man head, especially if they had been separated into different housing units. They would have to find some other places to hook up, and the movies were dark and convenient.

Occasionally, some boy would end up blowing several guys in a row. It was done as punishment if someone was caught cheating; or it could be his man was just sharing him; or perhaps he was being made to hustle by turning tricks at $5 a pop. It was hard to focus on the movie when you could hear the heavy breathing and slurping behind you.

I looked up at Slide Step and curled my face. "I'd *never* do that."

"You better not." He grinned.

I hit his arm.

Slide Step looked over his shoulder at Bottoms, who was bobbing his way down the line. "That boy's been banged more times than an old screen door," he said.

"In a wind storm," someone next to us added.

Slide Step said it was the usually the bucket heads that did that sort of thing, meaning the punks and ugly boys or the nasty queens.

I felt sorry for Bottoms.

"In Jackson," Slide Step said. "They hooked up in church."

"In church?" I couldn't imagine anything more sacrilegious.

"Square business. They'd meet up in the balcony." Slide Step smiled and turned to watch the movie.

The film that night was *The Mack*, starring Max Julien and Richard Pryor. It was about an ex-con named Goldie, who, in an early scene, told his mother he had to go out and fight The Man the only way he knew how. So he became a Mack, a big city pimp, complete with a hat and velvet cape. He drove a Cadillac and carried a gold-tipped cane.

You could always tell what the inmates thought of a movie because they talked throughout it. They would yell up at the screen, as if they were home in their own living rooms. "Kill that peckerwood," someone screamed, or if they didn't like a character—"Aw, motherfucker! You ain't shit."

Entertainment was important to convicts. It broke up the monotony of being confined, but if it wasn't happening, they were quick to make it up on their own. Like when a character came on the screen with an obvious flaw that was similar to one of the inmates. Someone would yell, "Look at Dexter up there, y'all, with his big old nasty fangs."

In *The Mack,* when Goldie and his brother killed two white cops who earlier had killed their mother, the auditorium went crazy. Mothers were sacred to inmates so it was like lighting had hit one of the gun towers. "Man, don't nobody want to fuck with a motherfucker's momma," someone in the front of the auditorium said.

For the most part, the guards left us alone. I think they understood that movies not only killed time, but they helped us burn off some of our hostilities.

Slide Step said *The Mack* showed what it was really like on the street. I was fascinated by the whole concept. Why did a girl need a pimp anyway, and how did they get her to have sex and turn over all her money? Slide Step pointed out Silk Daddy to me, a convict who was serving time for pandering (the legal name for pimping).

Silk Daddy, at forty, was older than most of the others there. His well-trimmed mustache was sprinkled with a few gray hairs. He had dark brown skin that glistened and a short-length afro that was perfectly shaped by the pick he kept in his front shirt pocket. I was standing maybe three feet away, but I could still smell the scent of cocoa butter.

"How do you get them to do it?" I asked.

"Well now," he said, "let's kick it around and see." He took a Kool cigarette from his pack by neatly unfolding the silver tabs and then replacing the foil so that it looked like it wasn't opened. "But before I answer that for you, let me ask you a few things first." He took out a lighter and lit the cigarette. "You like to have sex, don't you?"

At that point, no, I didn't, but he didn't give me a chance to answer.

"Of course you do, Baby, everybody do." He blew smoke in my direction. "It's one of the most enjoyable things we Homo sapiens like to do."

I smiled, because I knew what the word meant, but wondered if he had a double meaning in mind.

"And," he said, pausing to take another drag from his cigarette. "It's one of the few things *The Man* can't stop us from doing. Even in here. So what's the one commodity you can give up, but you still gets to keep?"

He stared at me with a dazzle in his eyes, as if he were getting high on the sound of his own words. "Sex," he said. "Now ain't that a wonderful thing? It's the only thing in the world you can sell and still maintain ownership of. Can you dig what I'm sayin'? You're doing it any way. So it's like getting paid for what you like to do. So you get to give it up, you get to keep it, you enjoy doing it—no, make that *love* doing it—and you get paid for it all at the same time. Now what could be more beautiful than that?"

Wow, I thought, it did make a lot of sense.

"Thanks, Silk Daddy."

"All right now," he chuckled. "Be sure to tell Slide Step I said hello."

As I ran down the stairs to catch up with Slide Step, Silk Daddy's "girls" were standing at the bottom of the landing. They were two black queens, Pootie and Miss Pepper, and they were made up as usual with red-colored lips and shirts tied at the mid-drift. Pootie had long braded hair and Miss Pepper's, which was shorter, looked nappy and tussled. It was probably from all the fun they were having getting paid during the film. Pootie's pockets were packed full of tokens, and the others teased as they walked past.

"Who would like to pay my price," Miss Pepper sang. "For a trip to paradise?"

I smiled as I went by and Miss Pepper nodded at me. Pootie blew me a kiss.

I was starting to feel less threatened by them, especially since Slide Step reassured me that I didn't have to act or dress like them. I guess on some level, I was still feeling a little ashamed of who it was I was becoming in there, but it was also confusing, because it also felt liberating somehow. I was enjoying the attention, and I was free to become whoever it was I wanted to be, and Slide Step would make sure that nothing else bad ever happened to me. So as long as no one back home found out about it—Why not?

Behind me, I heard Peterson the rookie guard come down the stairs. "Let's go ladies," he said to the queens. "The show's over."

Peterson was in his twenties and he easily blushed, so the queens loved to fuck with him. "Hey Petey," Pootie said. "You know what they say—a little time in the hole ain't such a bad thing, if you know what I'm sayin'."

"That's right," Miss Pepper added. "You just might *get off* with a little good behavior." Pootie stuck her butt out and rolled her hips.

When Peterson turned red, the two queens screamed.

My world was looking a lot different than the one I grew up in. So much was being thrown at me, that it seemed hard to believe I had only been in here a couple of months. I was getting quite an education—meeting pimps and pushers, real-life con men, and racketeers. I wanted to learn from them, as much as I could, so that my time inside would be productive. That way, when I got out, I could make up for the time I had wasted inside.

I would finish high school, as soon as I got back from court, and I might even take some college courses, which were offered at night. I would be the first person in my family who went to college (my dad never completed the sixth grade). I wanted to be smarter by the time I got out. I might even get me some ho's out there, so I could do some pimping. But then Red said that only "a man" could be a pimp.

I was starting to piece things together, but figuring out my identity was more difficult than I first realized. I knew I belonged to Slide Step and that my place in the pecking order was tied to him. But how could I be myself, if I didn't know what that was? I wasn't like the punks, and I wasn't like the queens. The queens were easy, because they were so far out there, but I wasn't like the punks either, and it left me confused about who or what I was.

Was I really gay? Did I actually feel the way I did the night before I came to prison, or was it just a trick I was playing on myself to make what was happening to me in there easier to take? In the past, if I lied to myself long enough some-times I would start to believe it—pushing the truth so far from the surface that I began to doubt its existence. How much of what I had been thinking was just normal adolescent questioning? I didn't know anymore.

Allegedly, punks were fucking because they were weak. "He's fucking because he's a punk," I'd heard inmates say. Bottoms was a punk, turned-out when he first got to jail, and it was clear by the way everyone treated him. So was he fucking because he was a punk, or was he a punk because he was fucking? It was like the chicken and the egg.

When Taylor's boy, Paul, first arrived, they wanted to call him Miss Holly because of the combination of his red hair and green eyes. But Paul wasn't having it. He was gay and proud of it, but he wasn't a girl, and had no desire to be thought of as one.

At the time, I couldn't imagine anyone being proud of being gay, though I admired him for it and wished I had his courage. "I don't play that," he was quick to say. "Like it or not, I've got a dick and I'm not about to trade it in for a pussy."

Taylor, his man, was crazy about him. He would just chuckle. "Hey, I'll tell you what—my baby don't take shit from nobody, and that's just the way it is."

At five foot six and weighing less than 140 pounds, there wasn't much Paul could do on his own, but Taylor had his back, and that meant a lot. Paul just had to be careful not to disrespect anyone, because then Taylor would have to defend him. Although he was only eighteen, Paul knew how to handle himself. He had come to prison when he was sixteen, and before that, he spent time in juvenile hall. I liked Paul, but he never let his guard down when he was around me. We would become close, later on, when we were both at another prison, but for the time being—for reasons I wouldn't know until much later on—he seemed indifferent to me.

Since there was a distinction between being a man and being gay, I decided to tell myself I was gay before I got there. It was a way to feel better about the situation. I'm not sure this was clear to me then, but it was easier to tell myself I was gay than being completely powerless. I wasn't fucking because I was a punk—a sissy coward; I was fucking because I wanted to. At least this line of thinking allowed me to hold onto some degree of dignity.

Yet even with Slide Step's gentle ways, I didn't like being penetrated by a man. It was painful, and I wanted to get it over with as fast I could.

It's not like Slide Step was unattractive. He was rugged and muscular, and I loved the way he smiled at me. It was like a kid's grin, with a half-open gape, that held onto just a hint of wonder. But Slide Step was a man, a grown man, and I was still a boy.

Now Scatter Brain—he was a different matter. He was eighteen and smooth, and he excited me whenever he came around. My hands would shake, and I would have to look away, because I was afraid he might guess what I was thinking. When I smiled at him, he would smile back, but in a reserved way. I saw him coming out of the shower once, and I turned and left the room quickly. I wished I had grabbed a peek, but the thought of getting caught was too much for me. I remembered Bottom's having to blow an entire row of guys, because Black had caught him cheating.

I caught just a flash of Scatter's pubic hair against the backdrop of his chocolate skin. His muscles were well defined, and his stomach was ripped. For the first time, I was starting to notice the variations of black skin tones. There was milk chocolate and dark chocolate and myriad shades in between. Scatter's complexion was like coffee with cream—Mocha. It was tight and smooth with a silky sheen, especially where it curved at the muscles. He had a slight mustache, which looked like satin, the way it framed his upper lip. Outside of prison, he could have been a model or actor the way he seemed so perfect to me.

Yet Scatter was straight, and though he did give me every indication that he wanted to have sex—I knew he was off limits to me, unless I cleared it with Slide Step first.

"I think I'd like to try something with a younger guy," I told Slide Step.

He seemed to take it pretty well, at first, though he didn't actually say much other than nod. I chickened out and didn't press the issue.

Manley had already told me that it would be OK if I had sex with another boy—as long as Slide Step knew about it ahead of time, but that I could forget about doing anything with "a man" (i.e., a straight man). It took a while to understand this distinction, but doing it with another boy wasn't a threat to the man—like having sex with another man would be. They considered us almost lesbians—if two boys got together to do something.

As long as I kept trying to please Slide Step, he kept showering me with attention, which made me want to work harder at pleasing him. And he always told me afterward, how good I was. "That's the whip there," he said once, placing his finger on my bottom lip. "Where'd you learn how to do that?"

I was embarrassed and shrugged, not knowing what to say. I'm sure I wasn't all that good, but he always encouraged me. I preferred going down on him, because it didn't hurt like getting fucked and because he would allow me to stop, just beforehand, so I wouldn't throw up. When he fucked me, he took his time and went easy. He even tried to jerk me off once, to see if that would help relax me, but he said I could never say anything about that, because it might be taken the wrong way.

I was always surprised by the different sides of himself he showed when we were alone. He'd share personal things with me, and he liked to cuddle on the floor underneath his bed, which was where we had to have sex without being seen by the guards. I was always eager to hurry out so I could shower or brush my teeth, but Slide Step liked to lie there and talk. Manley or Red were often somewhere up the hall keeping an eye out for us.

Sexual Misconduct or Two-in-a-Room were major infractions that could land us as much as a week in the hole. Slide Step said the guards rarely enforced it, because they understood that a man has his needs, and it helped keep violence down. I suspected it had more to do with how understaffed Riverside was.

Slide Step could make his voice rumble, getting low and raspy, and he would sometimes imitate Barry White in my ear so that it vibrated and tickled. He would overpower me and I'd lose my breath from laughing. He also made his voice squeak, like when he said *Hey, Squeeze!* in his high-pitched wheeze.

If Riverside housed protection cases, I wondered why Slide Step was there. "We pulled some strings," was all he would say. He didn't say who the "We" was, and I didn't think to ask. "Everyone wants to come here," he said, "because it's so open."

After a while, it didn't feel like a prison at all, at least for me it didn't. It was like a playground, where I could do what I wanted—and Slide Step made sure nothing would happen to me.

Manley acted like a big kid and we spent a lot of time together when I wasn't with Slide Step. Sometimes, he chased me around, especially when he found out I was ticklish. He wouldn't stop chasing me, and when I ran into a dorm I wasn't suppose to be in, a guard almost wrote me up for being out of place.

Slide Step got mad at Manley and told him to stop. "You knuckleheads are gonna get thrown in the hole," he said, but as soon as Slide Step left Manley did it again.

When I asked Manley what he was in for, all he said was "I'm innocent." He wouldn't tell me anything else, but it was only rapists and child molesters (and sometimes murderers) who claimed they were innocent to other cons. To the rest of the world, everyone was innocent, but to each other—they mostly bragged about what they had done. And about all the other things they never got caught for. Everyone in there, it seemed, had fancy cars and big homes, diamond rings, and plenty of ho's.

"Pimpin' ho's and slammin' Cadillac doors," was a common expression, but you had to say it with a cat in your walk—swinging your arm with one hand and holding your crotch in the other. Manley tried to teach me how to do it, but he gave up after a couple of tries. "Forget it, white boy, you're just too damn white."

I started to notice that you could tell who was streetwise, or conwise, by the way they carried themselves. I watched how they walked, the way they looked at you, and by how they pronounced certain words and phrases. Respect was determined, to some degree, by how long you had been doing time, so everything you did was telling.

I asked Slide Step why respect was such a big deal and how it related to teasing. It seemed a blurry line. It was, he said, and depended on who was doing it, because everyone is always watching what others are doing. "As they see one do," he said, "another will do. And then someone else will come along and want to try something larger. I try and avoid it," he said, "because I don't want to have to kill one of these knuckleheads over some silly bullshit."

I also liked the attention I got from convicts other than Slide Step. Everywhere I went it seemed, inmates smiled or said hello to me. Or they'd nod their heads slightly, and I could feel their gaze on me long after I looked away. Their voices would soften and their edgy shells would melt away—especially if no one else was around. I felt almost seduced by it, but I knew pretty quickly that most of them wanted to do something more than just kick it with me—especially if it was out of earshot of Slide Step.

Manley said I needed to be careful, but it was more complicated than that. He said he couldn't really explain it.

"They knocked off all of his bitches," Red said one afternoon. We were lying on the grass while he and Slide Step were talking about some pimp they knew on the street.

"Why would they kill his bitches?" I asked.

"Stay out of grown people's business," Red said to me.

Slide Step looked over at me and explained that *knocked-off* meant when one pimp took another pimp's woman. "It comes from the expression, when somebody comes knocking," he said. "If she chooses another man, the pimp has to either accept it or he throws down over it," meaning he'd have to fight it out.

"Pimps usually let it go," Slide Step said, "accepting it as a weakness in his game."

"Why would she do that to her man?" I asked.

"Hos are weak-minded," Red said. "And always *suspectable* to another player's mind fuck."

"Susceptible," I corrected him, without thinking.

"Whatever," Red said. He gave me a dirty look.

"So how you handle that," Red said, "is you don't allow your bitches to talk to another man."

Red knew a lot about prostitutes because of his mother, Slide Step would tell me later, when we were back under his bed after having sex. "She was murdered when Red was ten. Probably by a pimp she tried to rip off."

That was when Slide Step's mom took Red in.

Slide Step and Red's mothers had grown up together in Detroit's Brewster Projects. They even worked together until Red's mom got strung out on heroin and turned to prostitution. That was how Red was born.

"A trick baby," I said. I remembered the term from the Donald Goines book about black gangsters I read while in Quarantine. Slide Step told me I could never let Red hear me say that.

"He's got a crazy temper," he said.

It was Red's temper that got Slide Step his first prison term, he told me. They worked for Slide Step's mom and were supposed to pick up a package from a guy that owed her some money. "Red went crazy," Slide Step said, "when the man called Red a trick baby."

They had served ten years for aggravated assault, while the other guy lost his teeth, his right eye, and suffered severe nerve damage. Looking at Slide Step, I got a glimpse of how he felt about Red. He was like a brother to him.

Slide Step's mom never came to visit him, and I could see how much this hurt him. "We have an understanding," he said. "She won't come to a penitentiary because she thinks it'll jinx her business. So she does what she can, from where's she at." She meant everything to Slide Step, and I could see in his eyes how much he missed her.

Later that day, as I came in from the yard, Slide Step stopped me in the hall. "I want you to take your shower now."

"OK," I shrugged, but he seemed a little odd.

When I entered the shower room, Slide Step had Manley posted at the door. There was a shower room on both the north and south sides. As you entered, there was a row of sinks beneath a large mirror and a changing area with a long wooded bench on the opposite end. The showers, which were out of sight from the door, were in an open area with a half dozen spigots or so that came out from the wall.

When I stepped into the showers, there was a white man waiting for me. He was tall, in his early twenties with jet-black hair. He was heavier than me, but not very muscular, and his chest was hairy. His dick was standing straight up, and if it wasn't quite obvious what I was there to do, he came over and placed his hand on my shoulder.

18

Careful What You Ask For

"You kids can have either a hamburger or a cheeseburger," Dad said.

"I want a Big Mac," I said.

He shook his head. "I don't have the money. Hamburger or cheese-burger."

"But I want a Big Mac."

"Gimme a cheeseburger," Bobby said.

"Me too," Billy seconded.

"Can I have a Filet-O-Fish?" Connie asked. "It's the same price."

"I want a Big Mac," I repeated.

"God damn it, Timmy!" Dad said. It didn't take much to get him mad, but even at eight years old, I knew how to wear him down.

"I want a Big Mac or nothin'," I said.

"Well, you little bastard," Sharon said. "You're gonna get nothing."

"I'll get him a hamburger," Dad said.

"I said I want a Big Mac," I raised my voice, "or NOTHIN'!"

And that's exactly what I got. I glared at Sharon from the backseat of the car, as her son ate my hamburger and his kid brother munched my fries.

My sister, Connie, watching them gloat, whispered, "You can't be so stubborn. You'll never get what you want that way."

As Peterson made his rounds for the 4:30 count, he stopped in front of my cell. "I thought I'd seen something," he mumbled, shuffling through the stack of mail in his hand. He looked at my name on the door. "Nope. Sorry." He moved on.

My hopes had been raised then dropped. I lay back on my bed, wishing he hadn't stopped. The split second of hope and the disappointment that followed was worse than not expecting anything. When I was back in Quarantine, I used to stand at the bars and watch as the guard made his way around the tier handing out mail, but nothing ever came for me.

Recognizing the importance of maintaining family connections, the prison provided inmates with three stamped envelops a month. More could be purchased from the inmate store. I wrote home to Dad and Sharon, my brother and to my mom, though I knew she'd never answer. I even wrote to my ex-girlfriend once, but I hadn't heard from her either. We broke up right before I went in.

When I first got to Riverside, I called home once, but Sharon was just leaving to do her grocery shopping. She accepted the charges, but told me, "Don't call here that much." She was worried about the phone bill. It was the first time I'd called from prison, but I knew she'd be that way. Dad, as usual, wasn't home. "Let us know when you go to court," she said. "We'll try to get up and see you when you're in the county."

Money was always tight at home, and Sharon was good at managing it; but it couldn't cost that much for me to call.

I tried to phone my brother, Rick, but his line had been disconnected. He probably forgot to pay the bill again. Or maybe he changed the number so I couldn't call *collect*. Rick was turning out to be a big disappointment.

After count, I skipped dinner and sat on the back porch of the north side dayroom. It wasn't mandatory that everyone go to chow, and I wasn't hungry.

"There you are!" Slide Step said. "I've been looking all over for you."

I turned and peered out the block-shaped frames of the veranda's steel cage. The rolls of razor wire atop the thirty-foot fence were glistening in the sunset.

"What's the matter?" he asked.

I shrugged.

"Why are you out here, by yourself?"

He grabbed one of the heavy wood rockers from against the wall and slid it over to where I was sitting with my legs propped on the parapet wall. I was just starting to believe he cared about me, though I still had doubts I could have feelings for a man. Now, after what he had just pulled with the white guy in the shower, I knew I couldn't trust him.

He sat down, sideways in his chair, facing me. His right arm nestled between his side and the back of the chair. He squeezed my shoulder. "Talk to me."

I nudged his hand away. Out of the corner of my eye, I could see his face drop, but I didn't want to look at him directly. He sat there, quietly and stared at me.

"Why did you make me do that?" I asked. "It's not like you needed the money." Between his drug dealing and gambling, and whatever else he had a hand in, I couldn't understand why he'd force me to turn a trick.

"What are you talking about?"

"That guy in the shower," I said.

"I did that for you!"

I wasn't expecting that out of him. I knew I was young, a new fish and all, but I wasn't that naïve to believe him.

"Square Business, Squeeze."

I looked at him.

"You said you wanted to try it with a younger guy."

When Slide Step told me I was better than the others—it made me feel special. Even if the feeling lasted only a few moments, it filled an emptiness I felt inside. In the movie *The Mack*, the prize of Goldie's stable was a young white woman. Was this all I was to him? One of the ways pimps got their women to do what they wanted was to spend a lot of time with them, making them feel special and getting them to fall in love—and then BAM: "You have to trust me, Baby. We're gonna build a beautiful life together, but you have to do as I say—even if you don't understand it at first."

"What?" Slide Step asked. "You didn't like him?"

"Hell no," I said. I couldn't believe he'd think I'd enjoy a man like that. "He was chubby and hairy," I said. "He was like a big flabby fur ball."

"A dick is a dick," I heard an inmate say once, which of course wasn't true, but to someone like Slide Step it probably seemed that way. He wasn't exactly the Crypt Keeper, but at twenty-five, he was closer to Slide Step's age than he was to mine.

I studied Slide Step. He held my gaze silently, rubbing my shoulder occasionally with his right hand. He looked disappointed.

"I'm sorry," he said. "I thought you would've been happy."

I took a deep breath and let out a sigh. The razor wire had stopped glistening. The cornfields, beyond the fence, had been freshly plowed. It was early May, and they were ready for seeding. The blue water tower in the distance was fading in the sky.

"Parsell," the Guard called out. "You've got mail." He handed me the letter. "News from home."

I took the letter from him. It had already been opened. "Did you read it?" I asked, suspicious of the slight grin on his face. He shrugged and walked away.

"It's from Claudia, my ex-girlfriend," I said to Slide Step.

"Girlfriend?"

I wanted to wait until I was alone to read it, but couldn't with Slide Step there.

"Did she send a picture?" he asked.

"No." I said, for which I was grateful. She was slightly overweight and not that attractive. We were better friends than we were boyfriend and girlfriend. The relationship was more on her insistence than it was on mine. She needed a date for the prom, and I didn't have one. After that, everyone just assumed we were a couple, and it developed from there.

"Out there tryin' to be a man, huh?" Slide Step said.

I swatted him on the arm.

The letter was six weeks old and had been forwarded from Jackson to Riverside.

> *Dear Tim:*
>
> *I debated writing you, especially after the way things turned out, and the way you treated me those last few days, but I thought you should know I'm pregnant.*

I stopped reading. "Oh my God!"

"What?

"She's pregnant!"

"By who?"

I looked at him, but ignored his comment.

> *I don't know what to do. My parents will kill me when they find out.*

Her father never liked me. He considered me from the wrong kind of family. And her mom didn't trust me—not since that time she watched me wrestling with Claudia's younger brother in the back yard. I was sixteen, and John was fifteen, but he already had a slight mustache and when his shirt came up while I pinned him down, the muscles in his stomach were rippled. I looked up and saw Claudia's mom staring at me from the kitchen window. She ordered John to come into the house.

If it were up to me, I never would have slept with her, but she was pretty insistent about that as well. I did it for her, as much to prove to my classmates that I wasn't a fag.

"It could be a good thing that's she pregnant," Slide Step said.

"How so?"

"When you go back to court for sentencing," he said. "The judge might cut you some slack if you tell him you've got a kid on the way."

"Does that make you a grandfather?" I asked.

This time, Slide Step swatted me.

I didn't know what to think. I couldn't imagine being a father. And now especially, what kind of example would I be—a prison punk for a dad. She didn't say what she was going to do. I'd thought for sure, her parents had thrown away my letter before she got a chance to read it.

"You never told me you slept with girls," Slide Step said.

"You never asked," I said. "I told you I'd never slept with a man."

It occurred to me that other than Slide Step, I had no one to confide in. The next closest person was Manley, but he was more like a babysitter, and his loyalty was to Slide Step. So I didn't have anyone I could be open with. Cisco had just been released, and was probably already in search of his gay motorcycle gangbang. No wonder he was called a horny bitch.

I was horny too. It seemed like all I ever thought about was sex. I was seventeen, so if the wind blew slightly, in any direction, my dick got hard. Though it was sex with someone my own age that I was thinking about.

I was constantly ignoring or turning down offers from older convicts that wanted to sneak off somewhere and do something. I wondered how I would feel if I were in a prison with men my own age. Then maybe I wouldn't mind being pimped. It might even be fun, like Silk Daddy said, doing what I like to do and getting paid for it all at the same time. But that was just fantasy stuff that went on inside my head. The only sex I'd had in here was with those I was forced into having it with—and it wouldn't be until I was with someone I liked that I'd know for certain if I was really gay or not. Maybe these homosexual feelings were just a phase I was going through.

When Manley told me about swapping up, having sex with other boys, he referred to it as "bumping pussies." "I don't have a pussy," I told him as I laughed and grabbed my crotch and shook it at him.

"That's OK," he said. "Then you can just rub your big clits together."

I chased him up the hallway, laughing the whole way.

Swapping up with other boys didn't interest me. If I had a type other than someone my own age, it was not a boy or queen. I liked men, masculine men, but other than Scatter Brain, I hadn't seen anyone who aroused me.

Manley said, "I think you'll like Chet's boy, Brett. He's away at court, now, but he's due back any day now. If you like him, ask Slide Step's permission."

"I don't think so," I said.

When Slide Step set me up with Josh, he was able to do so because Josh was white. But since Scatter was black, it was a lot more complicated. Doing something with Scatter would have raised the issue of disrespect to Slide Step, and it potentially could have created an opening for my being knocked off by Scatter.

The men in prison seemed to live by the same rules that pimps did out on the street. If a boy or queen agreed to go along with another man, it was up to the two men to settle it.

Scatter, I'm sure, wasn't interested in knocking off a boy. He didn't have the juice or the power to own one, but he flirted with me every chance he got, which made me blush like a schoolgirl with a crush. I hated that about myself but I couldn't help it. Whenever he tapped his foot, I turned as red as a taillight.

I wrote to Claudia that night and asked her what she had decided to do.

Did she tell her parents? Could she get an abortion? Her parents were strict, and I was glad I wasn't there when they found out—maybe the only time I was relieved to be in prison. I didn't know what to do, but felt like I needed to say something. "I'm sorry," I wrote. "I should've used a rubber."

The first time we had sex was in the back of her dad's Ford Pinto. It was at the drive-in movies in Wayne where she worked in the concession stand. We backed the car into the last lane, dropped the seats and lifted the hatch back. Everyone else parked in the back row was doing the same thing, which had nothing to do with watching the movie.

After we necked for a while, I tried to yawn and act like I was tired, but she said, "Uh, uh," and pulled me back down on top of her. I had to go through with it.

I ended up watching *Jaws* thirteen times that month. Each night I would slip under the fence, drive her car from the back of the concession stand and wait for her in the back row to get off work. To keep from getting bored, I memorized every line in the film. "Uh, oh. We're gonna need a bigger boat," I said, when Jaws leapt from the water.

While my crush for Scatter continued, Miss Pepper seemed to develop a thing for me. She began to smile and stare, and for a queen, could get fairly aggressive. "Now don't start dropping your cookies, honey. I'm just admiring your beauty," she said one day in the bathroom.

"Drop my cookies?" It was a weird expression, but Miss Pepper was good at spicing up her conversation with made up words and twisted phrases. "What are cookies?"

"Them pretty little dimples of yours."

"I didn't know I had dimples," I said. I looked at myself in the shower room mirror.

"Well don't be droppin' your face and hiding the cookie jar, little boy. I ain't gonna bite."

"Thanks." I smiled, out of embarrassment, but I didn't want to encourage her. "I have to go," I said.

"Well one of these days, honey, you're gonna have to shit or get off the dime."

"You're mixing your metaphors," I said, remembering my fifth period English class.

"Now don't be talkin' out the side of your neck, honey. You know Miss Thing don't be doin' no orgies."

She made me laugh.

Later that evening, while brushing my teeth before bed, I stared at myself in the mirror again. I wasn't sure what dimples were exactly, but I was pretty sure I didn't have them. My face was looking clearer. Big Cat's facials were working.

Miss Pepper's feminine features and mannerisms didn't do it for me. Since I liked macho men, I could have sworn, I heard my cookies when they hit the floor when Chet's boy, Brett, returned from court. His blond hair, blue eyes, and rugged good looks of a high school varsity team quarterback completely dazzled me.

19

Taken by Surprise

It's not like there was anything in particular I had done wrong, but I just came to associate parent/teacher conferences with punishment and pain. Most kids looked forward to it, because it meant a half-day off from school, but my parents usually came out of the meetings angry and ready to punish me.

It was after one of these conferences that I learned I was being held back a grade. Because of my behavior, they said. I was still with my mom then, but now I was living with Dad and Sharon.

It was Dad's turn to go that day. "Wait in the car," he said to me.

Would I be grounded again? And for how long? Maybe he'd just hit me and leave it at that.

When Dad returned to the car, he didn't say a word to me. I sat there silently, as we made the thirty-minute drive downtown. I didn't want to ask, in the hopes that by the time we got to wherever we were going, he would forget about whatever it was that was said.

"Hungry?" he asked.

"Not really." When we arrived at Hudson's Department Store, he took me inside and up the escalator to the old-fashioned soda fountain, where he ordered us each a Saunder's hot fudge cream puff.

To this day, I have no idea what the teacher said. I never had the courage to ask.

Peterson came by with the mail, but as usual didn't stop. It had been two weeks since I mailed my letter to Claudia. I was leaving for court at the end of the week and prayed that she'd respond before then. I was finally being sentenced for the Photo Mat.

"The guys don't think you're coming back," Slide Step said.

I had taken a plea bargain, so I was expecting to receive two and a half years, matching the time I was serving for the hotel.

"You'll go through Quarantine again," he said. "And then probably to a camp."

"I don't want to go to a camp," I said. "I want to come back here." Slide Step had been making my time there as comfortable as possible. And other than having to have sex with him, I felt safe and I was enjoying his company. Considering what had happened when I first got here, it was the last place I wanted to be—but there was an emotional pull that was developing because I was getting the attention here that I wasn't getting at home.

He frowned at me with sadness. "I don't think they'll give you a choice. You won't have enough time to serve to come back here."

"I'm coming back," I said, stubbornly.

Slide Step didn't look convinced. "Black and a few of the others asked me if they could have you before you go."

"What does that mean?" I stared at him.

Since I wasn't coming back, they thought Slide Step wouldn't mind if they pulled a gangbang on me before I left. "I told them to go fuck themselves," he said.

"Thanks."

Slide Step seemed as incensed about the situation as I was. I realized how lucky I was to have him as my man. Red would have let them do whatever they wanted.

Slide Step not only protected me, but whatever I wanted, he got it for · me. Yet the one thing I thought I had really wanted, I couldn't have.

Brett was young and handsome and, much like the varsity team—he was untouchable and out of my league. Forget it. It was never going to happen. Neither Brett nor Chet seemed open to his being with anyone else, even if it were another boy.

Since having sex was so common in there—I wanted to at least once have sex with someone I might enjoy. Not being able to have him was tearing me apart inside. I couldn't stop looking at him—my eyes devoured every detail about him. Brett seemed flawless. When he smiled, his teeth were perfectly straight. He was built like a gymnast with his lean and muscular body. Most men didn't allow their boys to lift weights, but Chet didn't care, so Brett spent his time on the yard toning his body. The tiny frays on his jeans mimicked his laid-back nature.

My obsession became so obvious that it started to become a joke. *Uh oh, looks like Timmy's lost his voice again.*

"If you keep that up," Taylor said. "We're gonna start callin' you Scarlet the way you're turning red all the time."

Brett soon became aware of my interest, and I don't think he liked it. He acted as if he didn't care for the sexual stuff that went on there, not even among boys. He avoided being gang raped, by cutting a deal with Chet, but he never hid his contempt for it. He was serving a fifteen to thirty for sales and possession of drugs, so being locked up in solitary for that long wasn't much of an option.

At least Chet had a small dick. Brett was lucky he wasn't with Red.

Most of the time, Brett wouldn't even look at me, at least not when Chet was around. But then *that* gave me a glimmer of hope!

One afternoon, while I was walking the yard looking for Brett, Josh said without even asking who I was looking for, "He's over in the school house." He pointed to the small white building on the northeast corner of the yard. I walked over and found him standing at the window on the second floor. He smiled and waved.

I lit up with excitement, waving back, but then he glanced over my shoulder and mouthed something to someone behind me. I turned around and saw Chet coming up the walk. When I looked back—Brett was gone. I didn't know if he disappeared because of Chet, or if he was even waving at me in the first place.

"Where's your man at?" Chet asked. He looked right through me as he walked past.

"10 Building," I said.

He was acting strange. Not his usual phony self—pretending to be friendly and nice. I hoped he didn't think I was trying to steal Brett. But why would he? It's not like I could. I ran to catch up to him, thinking I could reassure him. "So how's it going?"

He looked over at me, but didn't respond.

I learned to watch the eyes. To look at them and listen to what they told me. I was starting to hear what they had to say. Were they dangerous or lonely? Were they lying or just looking to get laid? The eyes would tell me.

I had been avoiding Chet, ever since he set me up when I arrived. And when I couldn't avoid him, I gave him back what he showed me; a false front. I wanted to get with Brett, and because he was Brett's man, the only way two boys could do that was if both of their men agreed.

"Listen Tim, I'm really busy," he said. "So how about doing me a favor, huh?"

"Sure, Chet. What is it?"

"Put an egg in your shoe and beat it."

I hated Chet. I hated everything about him. He was as fake as his fucking teeth. They were cheap too—the kind that caused a slight whistle whenever he spoke. When he took them out at night, he looked more like his true nature: an ugly redneck with a sunken jaw.

When I told Slide Step what happened, he said things between Chet and him had been heating up since Chet and Taylor seemed to be trying to pull a fast one on Slide Step. With his mom providing the supply, they worked for Slide Step. But now they had other plans in play that they were trying to hide from him. "These motherfuckers must think I'm a sucker," Slide Step said. We were under his bed when he told me about it, but all I could think about was how any fallout would affect my chances with Brett.

"I know how to handle it," he said. "They're not crossing me out. They'll have to leave this motherfucker first."

Slide Step was upset as I'd ever seen him. But my not being able to get together with Brett made me as angry as Slide Step was for being double-crossed.

"Listen, I want you to stay clear of them, until Red and I take care of this thing."

I looked at him and nodded. Did that mean Brett as well, but I didn't want to ask, leaving open the possibility of hooking up with Brett.

"And Brett, too," he added.

My face dropped.

Slide Step looked at me and smiled. "You are *so* readable."

"I am not!"

"Like a bookie reads a racing form." Slide Step started to tickle me. "I got your number!"

"You do not," I laughed.

He drove his scruffy chin into my neck. "Oh, yes I do."

I was amazed at how quickly he went from rage to playfulness, as if one didn't affect the other.

"Quit it," I said, but I couldn't stop laughing.

Would I ever be able to have sex with someone I wanted?

The next day, I stepped away from a card game on the yard, and went to use the bathroom in the basement of 10 Building. It was next to an open area where they held AA meetings once a week. I was standing at the urinal when I heard the door open behind me.

"Homeboy," Scatter said, smiling. "What are you doin' down here?"

"Hey," I said, feeling a slight quiver in my voice. We were alone, and I was surprised to see him. Had he followed me?

He smiled and stared as we both peed. "So what's happening?" He asked.

"Nothin'," I said, looking straight ahead. I could see him, out of the corner of my eye, but I was afraid to turn my head.

He twisted to see if the stall was empty, and I snuck a quick peek.

Oh my God! I zipped up my fly without shaking and quickly moved for the door. I felt my underwear getting wet. "I've gotta go," I said.

"Wait!" he whispered.

I held the door open with my hand. The light from the stairwell illuminated the empty area between the bathroom and the outside door. There was no one around.

"What?" I asked.

He had a mischievous look on his face—as if he were about to do something wrong, and was gleeful about it.

"C'mere," he said.

Slide Step was tied up in the card game. It was his table that day, which meant he got a cut from every hand. Plus he was dealing and slipping the hole card to the bottom of the deck like he practiced the day before, which meant he was cheating. Though you couldn't tell. At least I couldn't, and I was watching carefully. He probably had the sucker's money piling up so high by now, that he wasn't paying attention to where I was. And Red and Manley were there too, covering his back.

"What do you want to talk about?" I said. My throat felt dry.

He slowly stepped back from the urinal. I looked down at him and swallowed. I couldn't believe how fast my heart was beating. A bead of sweat skittered down the side of my body. I was about to do something, that up until that moment; I had only been forced to do.

I let go of the door.

When we finished having sex, Scatter told me to go back first and he would wait. No one could see us coming out together or I'd be in big trouble. On my way up the stairs, I had to stop twice—to adjust my pants. I was still sporting the residue of my excitement and the boxer shorts didn't provide the same support as my old BVD *come-fuck-me's*. Since Scatter was straight, I would have to take care of myself later. I put my hand in the pocket and held onto my erection as I hustled passed the crowd that was standing around Slide Step's card game.

Red stared at me with his usual glare. He nodded, as if to say something— but what? Slide Step and the others were preoccupied with the cards. I worried about what Red might guess.

I went into 10 Building and up the stairs to take a shower. I couldn't stop thinking about Red. What if he saw Scatter follow me down into the basement of 10 Building? And no matter how long Scatter waited, Red would see him when he came back out. It would look even worse, and Red would surely tell Slide Step.

I turned on the showers and stepped under the hot water. What would Slide Step do if he found out? I was leaving for court in two days, so maybe it would blow over by then. As I soaped up, my thoughts drifted back to Scatter. I couldn't believe that we got together. Scatter was fucking amazing. I had given him a blowjob, and yes, I was definitely gay.

I was alone in the shower, so I finished myself off and couldn't stop smiling.

I went back to my room in time for the 4:30 count. I fell asleep, thinking about how much fun I had had. It was as if I'd been asleep my whole life and now I was suddenly awake. Alive and awake and in this place—for the moment at least, everything felt soft and kind and warm and delicious.

After count, Slide Step pounded on my door and startled me awake.

"What are you doing?"

"Nothing," I said. "Taking a nap."

"Are you all right?" He frowned.

"Yeah, I'm fine."

"C'mon. It's chow time."

I put on my shoes and scrambled to catch up with him. He was walking with his head down, and he didn't look happy. My heart was pounding. Finally he spoke.

"What'd you do?" he asked.

"Huh?"

"This afternoon?"

I looked at him. His was looking down as he walked, but was listening.

"Nothing."

He didn't respond.

"How'd you do," I asked. "At the card game?"

"Not well. I lost."

He placed his hand on my back and led me through the door.

When we entered the chow hall, I grabbed two trays and handed him one. Scatter was sitting down already, laughing and talking with others at his table. He didn't look up. Red was sitting in the far corner, talking with Chet and Taylor.

"Listen," Slide Step said. "I want you to stay close to me tonight." He was staring at Red, who gave Slide Step a nod.

The food was liver and beets and banana cream pie for dessert. The cook's idea of pie was whipped cream and pudding on a layer of half-cooked dough.

"Looks like another night for a cook-up," Slide Step said. "C'mon, we'll get Manley to put it together."

The cook-up was canned roast beef and chili, with Cheez Whiz heated on the hot plate and spread onto whole-wheat bread. It was delicious with mustard and chips on the side, but we were out of chips. "Get them from Steppenwolf," Slide Step told Manley.

The inmate store was open only during certain hours, but there was always one or two cons who ran an inmate store. The mark-up was 30 to 50 percent, but if you needed credit—it was two for one. "Hey, if you don't like my price," the convict running the store would say, "then you can wait for draw day." Inmates could withdraw money from their inmate accounts twice a month—on the 1st and the 15th of each month—and they were limited to thirty dollars. Other money could come from inmate visits, where visitors could bring you an additional fifteen dollars a visit.

Manley came back with the chips, and told us that Bottoms was blowing a bunch of guys in the bathroom again. "Got caught cheating on his man," he said. Black was teaching him a lesson, by making him blow several guys in a row. I looked at Slide Step, who was on the other side of the room. He was staring at me. Suddenly, I wasn't hungry.

As pure fantasy, the idea of having to do a bunch of guys might seem like fun to some—but in reality—the guys in there were mostly creeps. And some of them didn't even shower every day.

Slide Step nodded at me to take the chair next to him, in front of the TV. I went over and sat down. "You all right?" he asked. "You seem kind of funny."

I said that I was OK.

A black inmate, I didn't know, stood in the doorway to the dayroom and nodded to Slide Step. He nodded back. They weren't saying hello.

"What was that?" I asked.

"Don't worry about it," he said, his eyes were fixed on the TV, "it's nothing."

I took a bite of my sandwich, but I didn't want another bite.

Red, Chet, and Taylor walked through the day room and headed out to the back porch. Red looked at Slide Step and nodded. It was the same kind of exchange as the guy who had stood at the door.

Slide Step looked down at my plate. "You're not hungry?"

I shook my head.

"Scatter," he shouted toward the pool room.

"Yo!" Scatter yelled back.

"You want my boy's spread?"

Scatter came out smiling, holding a stick. "Cool! Good looking out."

"I'm not feeling well," I said.

"You don't look good," Slide Step said. "Why don't you go lay down for a while?"

"OK." I got up and went down to my cell.

I never was very good at getting away with anything.

I went down to my room, but it was too early to sleep. My head was swirling with questions. Did Slide Step know, and how did he find out? Did Red say something? Or what about Scatter? He promised he wouldn't say a word, but what if Slide Step asked him directly? And how could I trust him, anyway, since he'd already got what he wanted?

I thought about Bottoms being punished for cheating. Old Iron Jaws, someone called him, because you'd need iron jaws to do that many guys. I would kill myself before I let someone make me do that, yet somehow I don't think Bottoms minded it. On draw days, I had seen guys lined up in the hallway, as Bottoms did what he seemed to like to do and was getting paid for it all at the same time. I remembered him coming out of the bathroom smiling, with his pockets jingling with tokens. Except that when he was done, he had to give the money to Black.

When Bottoms yelled up the hall for Black, a guy who was sitting down next to him in a chair looked up. "Bitch! Don't be spittin' them dead babies out your mouth while you're standing over me!"

Slide Step never would have made me do something like that, even if I was caught cheating on him. I had never thought about it before, but I was curious as to why Bottoms was named that in the first place—since he should have been named something closer to Head or Lips. Slide Step said that only Black tapped that ass, meaning, he would pimp out Bottom's face, but he saved his ass for himself.

I was surprised at how casually Black had asked Slide Step if he and the others could fuck me before I left for court. If was like he was pointing to Slide Step's tray and saying, "Are you finished with your dessert?"

I would have asked to be locked up, in solitary confinement, if I thought the gang was going to come after me. But that was assuming I could see it coming before it went down. And of course, that also assumed that the guards would let me. Bottoms said that when he once tried to get into lock-up, the guards told him that if he didn't like fucking no more, then he should go back out on the yard and fight like a man. They weren't going to take up space in segregation for a punk who was having marital problems. Bottoms told me that the worst thing about it was how they told him. "They said it with the door wide open, so that everyone in the dayroom could hear."

I wasn't sure I believed Bottoms story. There weren't that many guards at Riverside, but I had never seen them act that mean to anyone.

What if Black and the others got me before I saw it coming? Or what if they drugged me, like Chet had done, by slipping me Thorazine? I thought about locking myself up, while I still had a chance, but if they wouldn't let me, I'd have some explaining to do.

I wished I had someone to talk to, but my dad used to say that you could tell a lot about someone by the company they kept. I avoided the punks, like Bottoms, because I didn't want to be compared with them. And on the other side, I didn't trust the drag queens because they gossiped too much.

I was surprised how quickly I forgot about Brett, the stuck-up prick who wouldn't even look at me. Scatter was breathtaking, the way he held my head in his powerful grip and gently stroked my face. I turned toward the wall, knowing all the trouble that he'd already caused me. I placed my hand inside of my pants and pulled to relieve the tension. The light from the hall cast a silhouette on the wall in the shape of my secret lover. The excitement of it, and the danger of being caught, turned me on even more.

When the guards cleared the 9:30 count, we had an hour and half before we had to return to our cells for the night. In the shower room, I squeezed toothpaste from a tube while Miss Pepper stared at me from three sinks away. I tried to ignore her, but her focus on me was intense. It was as if she was sending energy rays that were burning my face. I struggled to stifle a grin, because she was making me feel kind of silly. I didn't want to encourage her more, so I stuffed the toothbrush in my mouth and started to brush.

Chet came in and placed his cosmetic bag on the sink next to mine. He hung his blue robe on the hook and stared at himself in the mirror, picking at something in his fake teeth. Slide Step told me to steer clear of him, so I ignored him.

"So what's up with you and Scatter?" he asked without looking at me.

I hesitated for a second, but then tried to hide my reaction.

"What do you mean?" I said with my mouth full of toothpaste.

"I noticed you two are getting tight. That's all."

I spit in the sink. "We're homeboys," I said.

Chet gleamed at me for a moment, and then stared back at himself in the mirror. He took a plastic denture cup from his bag and filled it with water.

"So what's going on with you and Slide Step?" I asked.

"You have to ask your man," he glared. "But basically, it's none of your business."

I cupped my hands under the water and rinsed. "Fine," I said. I regretted having engaged with him in the first place, but he had rattled me by asking about Scatter.

"What's happening with Brett?" I asked.

He ignored me at first, placing his teeth in the soapy dish. "Why? Do you want to swap up with him?"

"Nope."

"Are you sure? 'Cause I can set it up, if you want." He stepped closer to me. I knew he was just taunting me. He had no intention of setting it up.

"But you'll have to do me a favor, first." He rubbed my ass.

"Stop it," I said, slapping his hand away.

"Or what?" He grabbed my ass again and squeezed. "You'll tell Slide Step?"

I wrestled with his hand. "Don't think I won't, Chet."

"Go ahead, and tell him what? I wouldn't let you swap with my boy and you're so desperate that you'll do just about anyone?"

"I don't know what you're talking about." He twisted my fingers and was bending it backwards. "Stop it!"

"Are you all right over there?" Miss Pepper asked.

"Stay out of my business," Chet said.

"Oh, I'll get in your business," Miss Pepper said. "Don't even try it with me, Chet, because you're all up in Slide Step's business now."

"Yo!" Someone in the doorway yelled. "Y'all need to hurry up. The line is halfway up to the control center."

There was usually a wait to get to the sinks at night.

"Just be careful," Chet said, letting my fingers go.

"Be careful of what?"

"Just be careful, that's all." He grabbed his toiletry kit and robe and headed to the showers. "You're not the only one who's got something to tell."

"What does that mean?"

His slippers sounded like sandpaper as he crossed the floor.

Miss Pepper came over and asked if I was OK.

"Thanks," I nodded. "I just wish he'd go off and die somewhere."

"Like a mangy-ass, no-good-dawg," Pepper sneered.

"And he can take his pretty little white boy with him," I added.

Miss Pepper looked at Chet's teeth that he had left soaking in a tray at the base of the mirror. She smiled and gave me a devilish look.

When I came out into the hall, I ran into Slide Step and nearly dropped my bag. "There you are!" he said. "I've been looking for you."

"I was just brushing my teeth and about to go to bed." I explained, nervously.

"C'mon back down and see me. I need to talk to you."

"OK," I studied him for some kind of a clue as to what he was thinking. "Can we talk in the morning?"

"Are you OK? You seem kind of nervous."

"Nervous!" Red said, passing us in the hall. "The boy is shaking like Don Knotts."

"I'm not feeling very well, but I'm sure I'll be fine in the morning."

"OK," Slide Step said. "But we need to talk first thing in the morning."

"OK," I said. "Good night."

I scurried away, with a small trail of water dripping from my bag. I made a quick pit stop in the bathroom and went down to the last stall. I had been avoiding that one, nearly since I first got there. It was the stall where I sat on the floor and hugged the bowl, resting my head on the rim, watching the fruit from the spud juice floating on the surface of the water. But this time, it was Chet's teeth in the toilet, resting at the bottom. I pulled the handle and smiled as I watched his dentures whoosh away.

A few minutes later, when the guards flashed the lights for nightly lock-down, I heard yelling from the end of the hall. I ignored it at first, but then there was laughter, which made whoever was screaming even madder.

"Whoever took 'em, you dirty cocksuckers, you better put them back 'cause someone's about to leave this motherfucker tonight."

The angrier Chet became, the funnier the situation was to us inmates.

"Damn, Dawg!" an inmate called out. "Someone got your teeth? That's fucked up. How you supposed to eat?"

I lay on my bed and smiled, listening as the guards chased Chet down to his cell. Sleep for me, came fast and sweet.

The next morning, Slide Step knocked on my door. "C'mon Squeeze. We need to talk." He waited in the doorway as I got dressed. It was unusual for him. He normally waited for me at the end of the hall, since he could be given a ticket for being out of place.

"Is everything all right?"

"Just hurry up," he said.

He said nothing more until we got out to the back porch. He told me to keep an eye out, while he pulled the bench away from the wall and removed a loose brick.

"Did you take Chet's teeth?" he asked.

I looked at him for a second. "Is that what this is about?"

He shook his head, no.

Concealed in the wall was a steel shank, which had been sharpened in the metal shop. It looked like an ice pick, with a handle that had been made from a ball of masking tape. Slide Step explained that because of its shape, the puncture wounds from the shank couldn't heal.

"Listen, I want you to go out in the yard until I tell you it's safe."

"What's going on?" I asked.

"Me and Red have to go take care of this thing with Chet and Taylor."

Slide Step wasn't about to let a move on his drug trade go unchallenged, no matter who was involved. I was nervous for him, especially after he had pulled out his shank, but somehow I felt confident that he and Red could handle it. Or maybe I was just relieved that what was about to go down had nothing to do with me.

I stood there frozen and stared at him.

"Don't worry Squeeze, they're not gonna do nothin'. I'm taking this just in case. Nobody wants to die up in here today."

I headed toward the yard as Slide Step had told me, so I wasn't around when whatever went down happened. "If you see Chet coming, I want you to go the other way."

I nodded.

"Are you sure you didn't take his teeth?"

I looked at him without answering at first. "My dad once told me, to never trust a guy who'll tell on himself. Because if he does that—he'll tell on anybody."

Slide Step looked at me and slowly smiled. "You silly ass knucklehead."

"I don't know what you're talking about." I smiled back.

"Listen, we need to talk about something else as well, but it can wait."

I looked at him and nodded. "Be careful."

When I got down to the yard, I saw Brett standing over by 9 Building. I wanted to join him, but I had to respect what Slide Step said. What was about to happen was serious, and I wondered what would happen if Chet was seriously injured and had to leave Riverside. Would Slide Step take control of his boy?

Whatever happened, it didn't mean that Scatter and I were in the clear. I was troubled by Chet's asking me about Scatter. He must have been tipped off somehow.

The emergency siren began blaring, and guards ran across the yard to 10 Building. My heart started to race. Suddenly it dawned on me: What would become of me if Slide Step got hurt? Who would protect me?

"Return to your housing units," the voice over the speaker ordered, above the roar of the siren. "All inmates, return immediately to your housing units."

When I got upstairs, a guard at the top of the landing was sending everyone to the north side. Guards searched inmates as we passed through the corridor.

At the end of the hall I saw a stretcher and a couple of medics through the guard's station. We were sent to our cells and locked in.

Looking out the window of my cell, I saw more guards running into the building. Chet and Taylor were being escorted across the yard in handcuffs. A few minutes later, I saw Manley and Red being taken as well. But where was Slide Step?

I watched the yard while we waited for the guards to clear us from lockdown. There weren't toilets in the single cells and the guards told us to hold it until we were released. "Just piss out the window," my neighbor B.C. yelled.

I thought about it, but we were on the second floor and the inmates below wouldn't have appreciated it. I was in enough trouble already.

B.C. was an overweight Mexican who had a crucifix tattooed on his belly. He had it done when he was young, but now that he was fat, it looked more like Buddha on a cross.

From the vantage point of our windows, we could see the south wing of the building. Inmates hollered back and forth in an effort to piece together what had happened. Someone said they saw Peterson, being escorted across the yard in handcuffs.

"Peterson?" I yelled. "The guard?"

"He was dirty," an inmate shouted. "He was caught moving drugs. Chet and Taylor snitched him out!"

"Snitched him out? Why would they do that?"

"I dunno. Maybe they thought they'd get an early release out of it."

"I knew them bitches were snitching," someone yelled.

"Does anyone know what happened to Slide Step?" I asked.

"I ain't hip," B.C. said, "but I saw two of his crew being taken to the hole."

"What about the medic? Do you know what the stretcher was for?"

"Sure don't," he said, "but it looks like that guard is about to become one of us."

"How so?"

"Heroin," he said. He pronounced it Hair O' Wine. "He'll catch a case and they'll probably give him prison time."

"They won't just fire him?"

"They don't fuck around with smack," he said. "Mandatory minimums and shit."

"Fuck 'em," another inmate shouted. "He should've known not to trust those two ho's from the get go."

"Chet and Taylor are the ones that snitched on those guys at Jackson, back in '75," someone else said. "For smuggling guns into the prison."

"Guns?"

"You didn't know about that?" B.C. said. "That's why they're at Riverside. They turned on a guard and two civilians who helped—thinking they'd get an early parole."

"How'd they get the guns in?"

"Laundry baskets," he said. "There were some cons in on it too. They were planning an escape from the North Side of Jackson. Every one of 'em caught a case over it." Meaning, they were prosecuted for a new crime. "Except for Chet and Taylor."

Inmates talked about catching a case like it was the flu.

"Shit, there's a bunch of people like to see those two motherfuckers dead."

"It wouldn't be a bad thing," I said, thinking about what Chet had done to me.

"I heard that," B.C. chuckled. "I definitely heard that."

I smiled, picturing Chet's teeth floating in a cesspool.

It was hard to believe I had been there only three months. I'd been through so much. Remembering that Riverside was a close-custody prison for protection cases, I wanted to ask B.C. if he knew why Slide Step was there, but I didn't want to know. Slide Step was different from the others, and that's all I needed to know.

I couldn't bring myself to tell Slide Step I didn't want to come back here. My lawyer said after I'm sentenced for the Photo Mat, I'd probably go to minimum-security. To a camp, where I wouldn't need a Man to protect me, since everyone there would be short—within a year or so from parole. But I wasn't out yet. I still had the rest of the day, and night, ahead of me.

If something bad had happened to Slide Step, I decided I'd lock up for protection or even do something that would get me thrown in the hole. If Slide Step wasn't in the infirmary, maybe I could holler to him from our cells in solitary.

Just as I was about to piss in my cup, the guards yelled "Clear!" and released us from the cells.

Some inmates kept jars in their rooms, and I'd see them in the mornings carrying their piss to the toilets. I thought it was disgusting. I'd rather go down to the bathroom in the middle of the night than smell stale piss in my room. When I came out of the head, Slide Step was waiting for me in the hall.

"Slide Step!"

"Hey, Squeeze." He smiled at me, though his eyes looked sad and tired.

"I'm so happy to see you," I said. "I thought you got hurt or something. There was a stretcher and medics, and I saw Chet and Taylor and Red and Manley taken to the hole. When the sirens went off, I got scared, and I asked about you but nobody knew where you were and . . ." I managed to stop and catch my breath for a second, as I noticed others looking on. "I'm just glad you're all right—that's all."

"C'mon," he said. He put his hand on my back and walked me into the day room. Although his demeanor appeared serious, there was a touch of gentleness in the way he looked at me. We went out to the back porch again, past the loose brick in the wall where he'd gotten out his shank earlier in the day.

Slide Step was able to escape the round up, because someone had tipped him off before the guards made their move and starting searching everyone. The medics on the floor, was just a decoy. Manley and Red were caught with shanks.

"Yo, Sims," he said to a con smoking a cigarette on the bench. "How about givin' me and my boy a little privacy, huh?"

"Sure, Slide Step, whatever." He tossed his cigarette in the can and left.

"What's up?" I asked, trying to sound calm. The smoke from the cigarette continued to smolder in the can. Before Slide Step answered, a guard came to take him to the Control Center. "Inspector wants to see you," he said. Slide Step looked at him and nodded. "I'll be back," he said to me. "They probably want to find out if I know something. Hang out in the dayroom till I get back."

"Is everything OK?"

"Just hang loose," he said, "We'll hook up later." He gave me a sly glance that indicated sex. It was a look in his eye, a raised eyebrow, and his nostrils slightly flared. He gave me a wink.

I sat in the day room, as instructed, but a dumb soap opera was on TV. When I was a boy, my mom stood behind the ironing board and sniffled at her stories. I never knew why she cried, but it always made me sad. I looked over at the poolroom. Brett was sitting alone, starring out the window.

"You all right?" I asked.

He nodded.

I racked the balls and chalked my stick. "Sorry to hear about Chet," I lied.

He didn't respond.

I broke the balls with a loud crack.

"It's not Chet I'm worried about," he said.

"Do you want to play?" I asked, offering him my stick.

He shook his head, no. His blond hair almost glowed in the light.

I felt sorry for Brett, not sure what would happen to him now. Chet and Taylor were being held in Administrative Segregation, indefinitely, for their own protection. Word was out that they were snitches, so they weren't coming back to general population. Brett would need a new man. I even felt a tinge of guilt about the mean thoughts I'd had about Brett. It's not like he had any more control around here than I did. I leaned over and banked a ball in the side pocket.

"Nice shot."

"Thanks." I smiled.

He looked at me for a long moment.

"I can talk to Slide Step, if you'd like," I said, trying to reconcile any ill feelings between us. He shrugged and returned his gaze out the window. "Are you sure you don't want to play?"

He shook his head again. "Thanks, though."

When Slide Step returned, we went immediately to his room and under the bed. Since I was leaving the next day, I knew he wanted me, but this time was different. Sex with him was still an obligation, but at least lately he had jerked me off while he fucked me, which helped ease the pain—or at least helped take my mind off getting fucked. But this time, he didn't touch my dick, and I was afraid to ask why.

Each thrust seemed to have an edge of desperation to it. It was as if he held on, for as long as he could, to make each small movement last forever. He kissed my neck, and sniffed my hair. My sweat mixed with his and hung in the air. As always, he was gentle. His lips and scratchy stubble, felt warm on the side of my face.

When he was done, I laid there looking deeply at him while he stared back at me. There was a wide range of expression in his eyes. They glittered, like the time he looked up at me from the baseball diamond and called me Squeeze for the first time. They were intense, like when he chased me to my room and slammed me against the locker and then stuck his tongue down my throat. I remembered how I first struggled uncomfortably as the object of his stare. I didn't understand what he was asking for, when he talked about his feelings for me. Though I still wasn't sure, I knew he kept me safe and that nothing bad ever happened to me under his watchful eye. At least not yet, anyway. Did he know about Scatter? I couldn't tell. His eyes were shining on me now, as we spent these last few moments together.

"I know I'll be back," I said. "You'll see."

In spite of everything I'd told to myself earlier about not wanting to come back. In that moment—I really did. I felt cared about, and maybe I was feeling grateful to him.

His expression looked sad again, and I wished I could do something to ease him.

"You know I'm gonna miss you," he said.

I didn't know what to say. His mood suddenly felt heavy.

"Did you hear what I said?"

I nodded, but I wanted to check out, because I still didn't know how to handle his feelings. Goodbyes were never easy for me, especially after my mom left us behind. I think Slide Step may have felt the same way since his mom essentially did the same thing to him—even though he never told me this directly. There was a tenderness we both felt, but some things could never be expressed in prison—no matter what was going on.

I wasn't always a quick read of people, and I was still operating from the haze of my youth, but the danger of prison was teaching me to pay close attention to subtleties. I usually captured certain gestures in people and then recorded it in my head. I would study them, become aware of their moods and expressions—mostly to see if there was danger—but then I'd slip away again. I'd go off into my thoughts and fantasies, to my own world where things were different. But even then, on some level, part of me was still paying attention. I'd pick up on what was said, or not said, even though I wasn't thinking about it at the time. I'd record it, like on an eight-track tape, and then listen to the threads later on, when I thought it was safe. But something sad was registering in Slide Step's eyes, and maybe it was because I was leaving, and they were right—I wasn't coming back here. I wondered what Slide Step would do after I was gone, and that's when the idea came to me: What about Brett?

"What about Brett?" Slide Step said.

"Well, I was thinking that maybe you and he could get together. Who knows if Chet will ever get out of the hole, and Brett's going to need somebody to protect him."

"I can't believe you're talking to me about hooking up with Brett," Slide Step said. "Isn't Brett your boy?"

I smiled and looked down.

"You seemed to have gotten over him pretty fast. What happened?"

"Nothing."

"C'mon. You were so gah-gah over him for the longest time. It became a joke. And now you're completely over him? That's not the Timmy I know."

I grinned, not knowing what to say. "It's just that I saw him in the pool-room today and he looked pretty lost, that's all. What's he gonna do now that Chet's gone?"

"Someone will pick him up. That's for sure."

"Is Red coming back?"

"You'd want to see him go to Red? You must *really* be over him!"

"No! I'd hate to see Red get him. Are you kidding?"

"So you do still care about him? Uh, huh. There's my Timmy!"

He started tickling me.

"Stop it," I laughed, struggling to catch my breath. "I do not. It's just that I'm thinking about you too and what would happen if I don't come back here."

Slide Step leaned back on his side and gently took hold of a lock of my hair. "I'm going to miss you. That's what would happen to me."

"Won't you need another boy?"

"I'm gonna miss you," he repeated, tugging on my hair.

"Me too," I said, but I was focusing on another thought.

"No you're not. You're gonna be with you."

"Ha ha," I mocked. "I'll miss you too, but that's not my point. I'm gonna be back here, anyway, so it doesn't matter. I'm thinking about you, so why not take Brett, so you'll have someone to keep you company until

I'm back? Manley said I'd have to go through Quarantine again, so it could take a couple of months."

My feelings about Brett keeping Slide Step company had as much to do with my feelings for Brett as well as Slide Step. Slide Step had been good to me so I knew he would be gentle with Brett too. It also made me happy to know that the two of them were together. Slide Step wouldn't be alone, and Brett would be safe.

Slide Step stared at me, shaking his head. "I don't believe you, sometimes."

"What? I don't want you be alone, that's all."

He shook his head and smiled, and the sadness returned to his eyes.

I was washing my hands at the sink, when someone came up from behind and playfully covered my eyes. Startled at first, I realized quickly they were friendly hands.

"Hey, Pepper."

"So how do you suppose Mr. Efferdent is doing right now?"

"Mr. Tidy Bowl, is more like it," I said. "How are you?"

"A lot better than Chet. That's for sure. He's probably tryin' to get his gums around that sorry ass pork chop they served for lunch right now."

"In the hole," I grinned.

"A pig in the poke," Pepper smiled back.

I dried my hands and was about to leave when Pepper stopped me.

"So what's this scandal I hear about you and Scatter?"

"Huh?"

"Oh, c'mon, Mr. Innocent Blue Eyes. Momma wasn't born yesterday."

"How'd you know?"

"I didn't," she said, "until just now."

She smiled. "I heard Chet ask you about it the other night."

I felt my eyes widen.

"Relax, I ain't gonna say nothing."

She looked down at my crotch, and then back up again.

"Do you think Slide Step knows?" I asked.

"I dunno." She looked down, again.

"I can't, Pepper," I said. "I'm in enough trouble, already."

"Relax, honey. That man ain't gonna do nothin' to you. Don't you know how crazy he is about you?"

"Thanks," I said, putting my hand on her shoulder. "I hope you're right."

As I turned to walk out, I noticed Black sitting on the bench by the shower. He must have heard the whole thing.

After the last count, I grabbed my plastic mug from the back of my locker when a con banged on my door.

"Slide Step wants you to come take a shower," he said.

"I already took one."

"He wants you to take another."

"Why?"

"He says grab your robe and come now."

He walked off, but I could see Slide Step talking to someone at the end of the corridor. The guard, behind him, stepped out and locked the office door. "I already took a shower," I yelled after the con.

"He said come anyway."

Slide Step waved at me then disappeared before I could protest further.

I grabbed my towel and toiletry kit and headed down the hall. It didn't make sense. He knew I'd already showered, after we'd had sex earlier. When I got to the end of the hall, he was gone and the guard's station was empty. They must have off making their rounds. To my left, I noticed Pepper and another inmate sitting together just inside the dayroom. They both stopped talking and looked up at me.

I went down the other hall and slowly opened the shower room door.

Slide Step was sitting on the bench, on the far side of the room. Was this my punishment for what I'd done? I stepped into the room and someone closed the door behind me. Slide Step told him to keep an eye out. It was Scatter! I froze in place and looked at Slide Step.

"I have a surprise for you," he said.

I turned around, and Scatter smiled.

I was terrified and confused.

"Go on," Scatter said. He nodded toward Slide Step.

"C'mere," Slide Step said.

I hesitated.

"C'mere!"

I saw a shadow from around the corner of the wall, and I heard voices, but the echoes inside the shower room prevented me from knowing whether the voices came from inside or out.

My mind raced as I walked toward Slide Step—thoughts of Black, Scatter, and Pepper. How Slide Step hadn't touch me earlier. He had a smirk on his face as I got closer and cleared the opening to where the showers were. Out of the corner of my eye, I felt a figure standing in front of me, but I was afraid to look.

"Go take a shower," Slide Step ordered.

I turned, quickly, to see who was there. The shower blasted hot water and filled the area with steam. Out from the shadows walked Brett smiling.

I looked back at Slide Step.

"Go for it, Squeeze!" he said.

20

Compromising Choices

It was a normal weekend in early November, and Dad showed up just like he'd said.

"I don't care," Mom said. "You can't have them."

"You've done this before, God damn it, and you're not doing this to me again." He raised his hand, as if to slap her, backing her into the kitchen table. "Get in the car, kids!"

Rick was already there. Connie stood at the back door.

"Daaaaaad!" I screamed in protest.

"I said, 'Get in the car!'"

"Don't you dare," Mom shouted.

"God damn it! 'Get-In-The-Car!'"

Connie obeyed. I dropped my GI Joe doll and ran toward my room, so I didn't see him slap her. Please Daddy, *I thought,* Don't make me choose.

I walked into the County Jail with a "cat in my stride" —the slow rhythmic swagger that I learned from Scatter—it was supposed to communicate that I was street-wise or institutionalized to lessen the odds that I would become a target. Slide Step warned me that because the county jail was so transient, it could be more dangerous than prison.

I had been in the bullpens all that day, shuffled from one to the next, as they sorted and shifted through hundreds of prisoners.

A deputy walked past the bullpens calling my name, "Parsell!"

"Yeah?" I stepped over several bodies to get to the front of the cell.

He held my wrist to the bars to confirm my name on the plastic hospital-style bracelet they put on me when I arrived. "Open Four," he yelled. "You have a visitor."

I stood there stunned for a moment, but then smiled as the gate lurched open under the noisy hum of the electric motors. It must be my brother, I thought.

We walked past the showers and through the Intake area where my fingerprints had been taken, just a few months earlier. So much had happened to me since then, that it seemed like a different life to me now. A flash went off in the adjoining room, and I remembered dropping the letter board when they first took my mug shot.

Three inmates were standing at the rear of the elevator. The familiar WAYNE COUNTY JAIL was stenciled on the back of their dark gray clothes.

"Step in and face the wall," the deputy said, as he slid the accordion gate closed on the elevator.

We were taken up several floors and into a hall where small windows lined a wall. "Fifteen minutes," the deputy said.

I saw my brother Rick waiting on the other side of the window.

"Hey!" Because of the echoes off concrete and steel, I had to shout into the small intercom at the base of the window and then hold my ear to the speaker to listen.

Rick's wife Belinda, who was straining to see behind him, cried as soon as she saw me. She was probably the only person in my family who cried about my situation. I imagined how much she'd sob if she knew the full details of my time at Riverside.

"Hey little brother! How you doing?"

It was good to see him, but I was angry he hadn't come earlier. "How are you?"

"Better than you!" He grinned.

"Fuck you," I shot back, and we both smiled.

Belinda tried to squeeze in, but Rick wouldn't let her. "In a minute," he said impatiently. He gave me a tired look that told me they still weren't getting along.

"How's the food?"

"Couldn't be better. I'll send you a doggy bag."

There was so much I wanted to tell him—about Slide Step and Brett, Riverside, and Chet and how I got revenge by flushing his teeth down the toilet, but then I realized I couldn't tell him any of it.

"Have you turned queer yet?" He asked, jokingly

"Fuck you." I said and stuck out my chest.

"Good Boy!"

I was better than ever at masking my true feelings. "And I've got *your* boy," I said, grabbing my crotch and shaking it, "hanging right here."

"Now don't start turning nigger on me."

I winced and looked around quickly.

The jail was in the middle of Detroit, and I was relieved that nobody heard him. He shrugged it off. It was easy for him, on that side of the wall, where there were mostly mothers and girlfriends. There was nothing but men on my side.

One thing was clear, I could never tell Rick about Slide Step.

He looked different to me, but I wasn't sure why. It was the first time I noticed we were splitting apart. But there was also something else there, but I wasn't sure what. His hazel eyes reminded me of Grasshopper's, and his hair red was like Chet's—though he didn't look like either of them. In a couple of months I would turn eighteen; and in October he would be twenty-three, yet he didn't seem that much older than me now, or as smart and tough or as good looking as he'd always appeared to me. He probably acted like Chet, when he was in here.

When he stepped back from the window, his wife Belinda came into view. She had stopped crying, and her mascara lined her cheeks. She started to say something, but then stopped abruptly. "Your face has cleared up!"

She stared at me with a baffled look, as if struggling to make sense of how my complexion would be clearer now that I was in prison. My heart sank when I remembered guys in high school say that all you needed for your pimples to go away—was to get laid.

Rick moved back into view. "Dad says he'll try to be at court tomorrow. He's not sure he can get off work."

I said it didn't matter. "How's Dad doing?" I asked.

"OK. He quit drinking."

"Uh-huh. How long this time?"

"You're probably too young to remember, but he wasn't always like that."

"I know," I cut him off, "before Mom ran off and left us."

Rick was one to talk. Belinda was nothing but white trash, though she did seem genuinely upset about my being in here. Everyone in the family hated her. Dad said she was OK—to use as a landing pad for when Rick first got out of prison, but that he was stupid for marrying her. She already had two kids at the time, and Rick thought the new one on they way might have been his. Nobody else did.

It was typical of him to take Dad's side. Up until then, Mom was the only issue that separated us. I loved Dad, too, but I also remained loyal to Mom. Even when they all ganged up on her, and said she was no good for leaving us, I would drown out their words in my head. They didn't understand. She had to leave to save herself, she once told me. I just wished she had kept her promise and had come back for me.

Rick and I stared at each other, neither of us knowing what to say.

"Are you sure you're all right?"

I nodded. "Why haven't you visited?"

"I couldn't get off work." He looked at me sheepishly. "I've been flat broke."

I wanted to ask why he hadn't written or sent me his new phone number, but I couldn't bring myself to say it. So I put that out of my mind too. He was here, now, and that's all that mattered.

"Hey! I almost forgot. I bought a new truck."

"That's great," I said, sounding a bit distracted. It wasn't lost on me that he had just told me that he was flat broke. I let it pass. I had to shut down to survive in there. So I tucked all my feelings away. I couldn't think about it, because that might lead to true feelings something, and you couldn't afford feelings inside. If you do that long enough you start to get good at it after a while. Then you get so used to disappointment that you become grateful for even the tiniest crumb. Still I was glad he came. I missed him.

"Time's up!" the deputy said.

He'd only just got there. It hardly seemed like fifteen minutes.

I sat in the bullpen waiting for Classification. I thought about Brett and how Slide Step had set me up with him before I left. It was pretty brave of Slide

Step to do that—given all the checks and challenges that go on with "manhood" in prison. Inmates viewed kindness as a weakness—so for Slide Step to be that generous with me could have brought unnecessary heat on him. Yet even still, he wielded a lot of power and since most inmates viewed two "boys" getting together as lesbian sex—it wasn't a threat to Slide Step's manhood.

I'm not sure if Slide Step knew about Scatter and me, because he didn't mention it. And neither did I. *Never trust a guy who'll tell on himself.* I couldn't wait to get back there, now, especially after what Slide Step had done for me. I wanted to write him and thank him again. But that was Slide Step. He always seemed to look out for me, and he took as much joy in seeing me happy, as I took in having sex with Brett. And I couldn't wait to do something with Brett again, but I'd have to wait for a pre-sentence investigation report, before the judge could sentence me for the Photo Mat.

The pre-sentence investigations were completed by the Probation Department, and I would be stuck in the county jail until it was completed.

Inmates loved to talk about how they knew the system inside and out. Even when they didn't know, they talked like they did—so you had to be careful about what and who you listened to. "Fuck all that mumbo jumbo you hear when you first get there," I said to a con in the bullpen. "However much time you've got—that's where they're sending you."

"Were you in Gladiator School?" a young white inmate asked.

For the moment, I was the only one in the bullpen who had been to prison, so having all this knowledge made me feel important. I enjoyed the power it gave me.

"Not at M-R," I said, "but I was at Riverside."

"Is it better?"

"I heard they have a lot of fags there," another con said.

"I wouldn't know." I looked at him. "They never bothered me."

"I'm supposed to go to a camp," the young white inmate said. He had just been sentenced and was on his way to Jackson. "But I still have a couple of cases pending."

"What for?" I asked.

"Burglary."

"You'll be all right," I lied. Burglary carried up to fifteen years, which meant they would have to treat him like he had been given the maximum sentence, until he went back to court. That's what happened to me. Though I didn't have the heart to tell him otherwise. He looked younger than me and a lot greener. "Just don't take no shit from nobody, that's all. And whatever you do, don't listen to what that psychologist might tell you in Quarantine." I wished there was more I could have told him, but given my experience—he was in for a rough ride.

I was glad there was nobody there from Riverside, who could pull my ho' card. And so far, at least, I had been kept in relatively tame bullpens.

When they called me in for classification, the deputy asked if I was a homosexual. I was expecting the question, because the other cons told me it would be coming. I was quick to say no. I didn't want it on my record, and I damn sure didn't want to be placed in isolation. The cellblock where they kept the queens was locked down twenty-three hours a day. At least in the other wings, you were let out of your cell during the day into the common area in front of the cells, and some wings had TVs. It helped pass the time.

The deputy said that because I was coming from the state system, I was no longer eligible for the Romper Room—where they kept the nonviolent, first-time offenders.

"Have a seat in the next pen," the deputy said. "We'll take you up in a little bit."

When I entered the bullpen, it was quieter than usual. I could sense tension in the air. I sat on the bench, along the sidewall, and then I noticed it. It was a small pool of blood, in the middle of the floor, with a broken tooth. The smell hit at about the same time, causing my stomach to turn.

"What happened," I said to the guy next to me.

"Some motherfucker came in here for killing his momma."

"His momma?"

"Can you imagine? It's Mother's Day weekend, and this stupid motherfucker comes in here and tells us he just killed his momma."

"I wondered what she did to him," I said.

"Boy! Are you crazy?" The black con looked at me. "It don't matter what she did. You don't come up in here and tell a motherfucker you just killed your momma."

"And it's Mother's Day," another inmate repeated.

"They would've killed that motherfucker if the deputies hadn't dragged his punk ass out of here."

Looking at the blood and broken tooth, I wondered if I'd made the right choice.

21

What's My Lie?

Television game show host Bob Barker had already moved on to The Price Is Right. *I remembered him from a few years earlier on* Truth or Consequences. *It was a program where the contestants were asked a difficult or sometimes even a trick question. If they answered incorrectly, or didn't respond quickly enough Beulah the Bell would buzz, and Bob Barker would say, "Oh, I'm sorry, you failed to answer the question truthfully and now you must face the consequences."*

In 1978, Detroit Recorders Court had a backlog of over 5,000 criminal cases. The Michigan Supreme Court appointed a receiver who instructed judges to plea-bargain their caseloads. But Judge Geraldine Bledsoe Ford didn't believe in bargaining with criminals. She stuck with the old format of doling out justice that seemed to "fit the crime." Mean Geraldine, the newspapers called her, Short on Bail/Long on Time.

The inmates had other names for her, but mostly they feared her.

"Shit, that bitch gives out time like its water," one of the cons in the bullpen said. "She told this one motherfucker, who was being sentenced for armed robbery, 'Young Man, do you see that clock on the wall?'"

"Yes ma'am."

"What time does it say?"

"Well it's 10:20, Judge."

"Well that's how much time you got, ten to twenty."

The inmates laughed—at least everyone who didn't have her as their judge.

Newspapers reported that attorneys and defendants alike would let out a gasp at arraignment hearings when they heard they'd been assigned to her court. One inmate claimed she told him to look out the window. "Young man, do you see a tree out there?"

"No, Judge. I don't see a tree at all."

"Well, there will be—by the time you're let out again."

Others claimed she kept a coffee can filled with coins and at sentencing time she'd reach in and grab a handful, doling out a year for each one as she counted them out aloud "One, two, three . . ."

"That bitch has got some pretty big hands too," another con said.

When she refused to plea bargain, the state tried to reassign her to a lower court, but then there were literally protests in the street. She was the grand-daughter of a slave, her father was a civil rights activist, and she was the first black woman in the state to become a judge.

"You'd think she'd cut the brothers some slack," the guy next to me said.

"Shit! She's whiter than that white boy," the other nodded at me. I didn't know what he meant at first, but he didn't need to point, since I was the only "white boy" in the bullpen.

It's not like I wasn't aware of it, but this was the first time someone had commented on it in front of me. I lowered my eyes in silence. It wasn't the only difference —the other difference was easier to hide, and I had hoped that no one would figure it out.

I lied when the Intake deputy asked if I was homosexual. I didn't want to be placed in the lavender tank with a bunch of queens. Miss Pepper said it was like being in placed in Administrative Segregation—the hole. And the longer I waited in the bullpens, the more I began to wonder if saying I wasn't gay was even a lie at all, especially since the only sex with men I had had was forced. The fact that I enjoyed it with Scatter and Brett was a secret I wasn't about to share. And once I got out of there—I wouldn't even admit it to myself. Miss Pepper had warned me. "Once it's on your record, honey. It's there for keeps."

I started to wonder whether I could keep up my self-denial any longer, especially given how much I enjoyed what I did with Scatter and Brett. It was pretty clear to me now what I was—and now that I had a taste of it—it awak-ened an appetite I couldn't ignore. I shifted in my seat on the bench, and had to cover my crotch from view. Those thoughts would have to wait, until it was safe again. I wished I could have taken Slide Step with me to the county jail. There were twenty-eight of us inside the fifteen by twenty-foot holding tank which was probably built for no more than a dozen men. There was a concrete bench along each sidewall and an open toilet and sink in the rear. Two of the four lights were out, so it was dark toward the back of the cell. We had to take turns stretching out on the floor to sleep, but there wasn't any order to it. You waited for someone to sit up or move and then you slowly had to slither into place. Some shifted more cautiously than others, depending on their size and shape.

It was Sunday afternoon, and I'd been there since I arrived on Friday. I stayed near the front of the cell, where there was more light and it was easier to breathe. The inmates' clothes had absorbed the pool of blood that had been in the middle of the floor—from the guy that had killed his mother—and his tooth was probably embedded in the bottom of someone's shoe. The stench was overwhelming. The toilet had backed up again, and the deputies were slow in coming around. We heard them laughing down the hall and knew it was because we had to piss in the sink and hold our dumps until they were good and goddamn ready to bring us a plunger.

The bars felt cool on the side of my face, as I sat on the floor and leaned against them. I had a headache from lack of sleep, the smell of body odor, and from holding my shit since I first arrived. It had nothing to do with the toilet; I was hoping to wait until I got up to a single cell.

I tried to take my mind off the situation by reflecting on different times. I remembered the locker room at my high school, the musky smell of sweaty boys and stinky feet mixed with the clink of a closing padlock and of the hollow crashing of a locker door. I recalled the softer sound of a sneaker's squeaking on the court, and of the sharp shrill of a whistle echoing in the gym and the rhythmic thump of a basketballs. But none of that worked, because all the sounds and smells of jail kept bringing me back. The clamor and noise of jail or prison was unlike anywhere else in the world. A drunk on the other side of Intake had been shouting for over an hour—something about Castro and Cuba and the CIA. The others finally gave up on yelling at him to shut up.

A deputy with a clipboard came to the front of the cell and shouted, "Open Five." He rattled off several names, ordering us out. "Turn around and face the wall." Nine of us were being taken upstairs to single cells. The guy standing next to me said, "They don't be releasin' nobody on Saturday and Sundays, so there wasn't no reason we had to stay in that fuckin' bullpen all weekend."

"You're right," the deputy said. He placed the inmate back inside the pen. "Close up Five," he yelled behind.

"What?" the inmate pleaded. "I didn't mean nothin' by it."

"You can just wait," the deputy said, "and maybe by next Sunday we'll have a cell for you."

A few minutes later, as we got on the elevator, we could still hear him screaming. "Aw, c'mon Dep, I was just kiddin' around. OK, OK, but can I please have a plunger?"

I didn't remember it being so dark upstairs, but then everything from my first time through felt hazy to me. I was terrified when I first got here, not knowing what to expect—so I went in with blinders on—trying to block out as much as I could and hoping I'd come out the other side OK. But I was lucky back then, because the deputies had placed me inside a cellblock with other nonviolent, first-time offenders.

This time, they put me in a cellblock for inmates who had been found guilty and were either awaiting sentencing or being transferred to the state prison system. There were twelve cells along the right, with a set of showers on the far end. The open area, to the left, was about fifteen feet wide and spanned the length of the cellblock. Two built-in tables with a metal bench were situated on each end. Because of the layout, the deputies weren't able to see inside a cell unless they stood in front of it. We were locked into our cells at night, but were let out during the day and free to move about within the confines of the common area.

Four inmates looked up from a card came as I walked past carrying my bedroll. I noticed three more talking in a cell. I was also carrying the carton of cigarettes I brought in with me.

"Hey, Slim, got a smoke?"

Several jumped up optimistically.

"Sure," I said. "Just let me get settled in my house, first."

The racial mix wasn't as lopsided as it had been in the bullpen. I spotted at least three other whites and two of them were young like me.

"Good lookin' out," one of the blacks said, as I handed out a few cigarettes. "The commissary doesn't come till Tuesday, so its tighter than a motherfucker in here."

I had to be careful, because I couldn't replace them when the commissary cart came around. I should have asked Rick to put money in my account, but he probably would've whined to me about being broke again.

The others seemed friendly, except for one—a black guy, who kept staring as if sizing me up. He slid off the bench and swaggered over, carrying his stocky frame with an edge that said he was almost too comfortable in there. Since everyone had a cigarette, the air was clouded with smoke.

He was in his mid-twenties or so, and older than most of us there. I was in my cell, making my bed, as he watched from the doorway. "Are you back on a writ?" he asked.

A *writ of habeas corpus* was the legal term for bringing an inmate from prison back to Court. In Latin, it means "you are to have the body."

I guessed he could tell by my state shoes, that I was coming from the prison system. "Riverside," I said.

"They got a lot of fags there?"

"I wouldn't know." I shrugged, trying to sound indifferent. He was making me nervous, especially the way he glared at me with his steady gaze. There was scar just below his right eye that extended diagonally across his cheek, and another on the left of his neck. My bed was almost finished, but I continued messing with it nervously. "You?"

He reached in the cell and handed me his prisoner ID card.

I looked at it and handed it back. It was from the Michigan Reformatory. His name was Nate.

"Did you notice where it's from?"

"Yeah." I looked at him. I wasn't' sure what he expected me to do. He thought I should be impressed because he was at Gladiator School. Or perhaps intimidated.

"You back on writ too?"

"Yeah, I've got a murder charge pending," he said. "And you?"

"Armed robbery," I said. My voice cracked, and I cleared my throat, pretending like I had something stuck in it. "I go for sentencing tomorrow."

"You had your PSI done yet?"

"PSI?"

"Pre-sentence Investigation," he said. "The Probation Department has to do the PSI before the judge can sentence you."

"They did one the first time," I said, "when I was sentenced on my other case."

"I don't think so." He shook his head. "They need to do one for each case."

For a second, I felt a little dizzy. "How long does that take?"

"It depends, the motherfuckers are all backed up. But then there's the hundred and eighty day rule. How long has it been since you got busted?"

The hundred and eighty day rule was a well-known law. It referred to your right for a fair and speedy trial. In Michigan, it meant they had to have you to court by 180 days. If not, theoretically, your case could be thrown out. "But if you cop a plea," he said, "they'll rarely do that. So chances are, what will happen to you tomorrow is they'll go for a postponement until your PSI is complete." I wondered why he was being so talkative, and I started to notice a few more nicks and scars on his body. He seemed to enjoy the uncomfortable look on my face. He looked as if he'd been through quite a few fights. He was muscular, so I doubt he lost very many. "I've been here for three and half weeks," he said, "and I'm still waiting."

Three weeks! I'd go mad. There was no fucking way I could stay in there for that long. "Why don't they send you back to M-R?"

"Because probation officers can't travel outside of the county. And so it looks like you're stuck here with me, pretty boy, until they get off their asses and do it."

I hoped he was wrong, but he wasn't. The next day, the judge postponed my sentencing until the Probation Department could complete a PSI. My lawyer agreed to the continuance, and the judge ordered the Probation Department to move post-haste. My sentencing was rescheduled for three weeks time.

When I got back up to the cellblock, Nate was waiting with a smile and a sneer. "What'd I tell ya? Your ass is up here with me baby boy."

I didn't like how he said it, but I ignored him and went into my cell. My cigarettes were gone.

"Who took my cigarettes?" I yelled out. No one answered.

I stuck my head out. "Who took them?" A couple of guys looked up from a card game, but no one said anything. I looked the other way. Nate came out of his cell.

"Somebody took your shit?"

"Yeah!"

"That's fucked up. Just now?"

"That's right. And it's pretty fucked up too. I'd been sharing with these motherfuckers, and they turn around and take my shit!"

"I got your back," he said.

I looked at him, not liking the sound of that.

"Don't worry. I'll get 'em back." But I was more afraid of what that would cost me. He cut me off before I could say anything. "Don't worry. You'll get your shit."

Maybe I could split them with him.

The guys at the card game were grinning. I didn't like the looks of that either.

Sure enough, about an hour later, Nate came into my cell with four of the six missing packs. I'd gone through four already, giving them away or lending them out to guys who would pay me back on Tuesday.

"Where'd you find them?"

"Don't worry about it." He sat down on my bed. "I run things around here."

I handed him two packs. "Here, I really appreciate it."

"Nah, that's all right. I've got some."

I thought he said he didn't have any cigarettes, but I was happy to have gotten some of them back. I opened the pack and lit one. He leaned back and watched me.

"So who took them?"

He waved his hand, dismissing me. "I don't snitch."

"Snitch? I thought that only applied to the police."

"You don't snitch, do you?"

"No."

"Good." He tapped the inside of his thigh with his thumb. "That's good."

"It depends," I said quickly.

"On what?"

"Exactly," I said.

He smiled, and so did I, but I don't think he was amused. He looked at me silently for a moment. At first, I wasn't sure the conversation was going where I thought it was. And then, I wasn't sure if he was testing me, or serious—but now I didn't like the look in his eye or the way his scars were frozen.

"You'd snitch?"

"Yeah," I said slowly. I knew that snitches were killed, but I was afraid that if I told him no, he would take that as an invitation to make the next move. So I was bluffing, and hoped that he was, too.

He shook his head. "You'd actually snitch?"

"Yeah." My hand started to shake.

He tensed up like he was going to hit me.

I looked at him, not knowing what to say. He was sitting on the side of the bed closest to the doorway. I tried to get up, but he moved forward, so I sat back down.

"You know what happens to snitches, right?"

I didn't answer at first. "I'm not a fag."

"Who's talkin' about fags?"

"Well then what are you talkin' about?"

"I'm talkin' about snitchin'."

"Well then, no. I'm not a snitch."

"But you'd snitch if I took that?" He looked down at my ass.

"You're damn right."

He got up and walked out, stopping in front of my cell. "You know where I'm from, right?"

I nodded.

"Boy, if we were at Gladiator School right now—I would have snatched that pussy from your ass two days ago, you snitch ass bitch."

22

What's Under the Covers?

"It's only been a handful of years since the race riots left Detroit smol-dering," the reporter from Eyewitness News *said. "But in this over-whelmingly white high school of 1200 kids, they've elected a black class president from among their only twelve black students."*

Everyone in the auditorium had applauded when Kevin Pregister told the student body, "Don't vote for me because I'm black—Vote for me because I'm the best man for the job."

My parents still had a sign in the living room window that read: THIS FAMILY WILL NOT BE BUSSED.

Kevin was from Inkster, the town next to ours, where they had extended the school district by two blocks.

Yet for all our talk about unity, inside the lunchroom, everyone stuck to their place. The jocks were in one corner, the nerds in another. The popular crowd, the socialites, formed an orbit around the varsity teams, with the club kids straddling the middle—Chess, Science, and Math on one side and Drama and Yearbook on the other. The burnouts were out back, behind the school, sneaking a cigarette or smoking pot. There were a few floaters, kids like me, who didn't seem to fit anywhere else, but we had to be careful, or we'd get lumped with the losers and labeled as geeks. The only exceptions were the couples, but then everyone mostly dated their own: The Jocks with The Socks and The Nerds with The Turds.

I tried to blend wherever I could, slipping from one group to another. I rode the bus with the burnouts and ate lunch with the clubs. It seemed my whole destiny would be determined by whatever group accepted me.

My guidance counselor said it didn't matter, which was easy for him to say, since his life was practically over to my thinking.

If a kid sat where he didn't belong; or if someone tried to climb too high—he kids at the top were never shy about smacking him back into place.

The bars closed with a clang, sending vibrations through my body. The ting in the pipes seemed to grow louder as the sounds of shouting slowly decreased. My senses were on high alert, which made it difficult to sleep. I couldn't stop thinking about Nate.

He wasn't that tall, but he was solid and, worse, mean. His anger scared me more than anything else about him. He was like Red, only quieter and more intense. I hoped he believed me when I said I would snitch and that the threat of it would be enough to keep him from hurting me. I hadn't been there long enough to tell what the others might do to back him up.

The next morning, the windows along the wall of the catwalk were open. I heard the screeching cries of a lunatic from outside. Every morning, I was told, for the past several years, a woman stood in front of the jail and yelled obscenities because her husband had been killed inside. Yet nobody knew why or how he died.

"The Goon Squad got him," an inmate said, referring to a group of large deputies who were called whenever there was a disturbance. No one fucked with the Goon Squad.

Whatever it was that actually killed him didn't matter. There was genuine agony in her voice. Perhaps she was just crazy. The accusations she hurled at the jail sounded as delusional as the stories that were sometimes told in there.

Even in the early morning, with the windows open, it was hot inside my cell. My sheets were soaked, and beads of sweat trickled down my neck. I vaguely remembered waking in the middle of the night, but I wasn't sure. I was on the floor, and halfway to my feet, moving toward the front of the cell—like I'd been sleepwalking. I remembered screaming something, but maybe it was just a dream.

After breakfast, Nate stopped in front of my cell. "Who's Slide Step?" he asked.

"Huh?" I stared at him in disbelief.

"You called out his name last night."

"I don't know what you're talking about."

He stared back and nodded. There seemed to be fire in his eyes, which surprised me. His eyes had been deadpan since I arrived.

At breakfast earlier, Nate stood behind one of the white guys and asked, "Will you buck for your food?"

"What?" he said. The expression on his face looked as dumbfounded as his voice.

"You heard me. Will you buck for your food?"

"Buck?"

"Buck, motherfucker," said the loud mouth sitting next to him. "It means fight!"

The white guy didn't answer at first, as if pondering a choice, his face turned red. It was one of the few times I ever noticed silence in the cellblock. Even the noise outside had disappeared. "Well, yeah," he said slowly, "if I had to."

"OK," Nate said, and nodded.

The white boy sat down.

Without a word, or the slightest hint of emotion, Nate whacked him with his metal tray, knocking him off the bench. Blood trickled from the side of his ear and mouth as he lay on the floor.

Nate reached over, picked up the guy's food and calmly walked to the other table.

"Yo!" the loud one said, covering his mouth with a fist. "That shit's fucked up." He laughed as he said it. "My man here, says, 'Will you buck for your food?' and then BOP! Hits the motherfucker on the head."

Two more blacks joined in laugher, giving each other high fives. "Hey Nate! That's fucked up!" They continued to laugh.

The white boys were silent. There were four of us, in total.

The guy picked himself up from the floor and slowly walked back to his cell.

I started to notice how most inmates, when something bad happened, would either get excited, as if entertained by it, or—like the white guys— took this glazed expression, as if the situation were hopeless. But Nate was different. He was above it all. He was unruffled by whatever went on.

Now he was in front of my cell, with that glint in his eyes, but then it seemed to dissolve as quickly as it had appeared. "Do you know Shorty?" he asked.

"Who?"

"His real name's Cromwell. He's my cousin, supposed to be at Riverside."

I shook my head. I didn't know him.

"Then I'll have to call my auntie," he said. "See what I can find out about you."

My heart fell when he said this, and Nate seemed to catch it in my face.

"Yeah," he said. "I'm gonna have to do some checking on you."

He went back to his cell.

I wasn't sure if he was bluffing or not, but he acted like he knew something.

I wanted to take a shower, because it had been so hot, but there was no way I was going to take a chance leaving my cell. Not with the threat Nate had just made. Instead, I'd take a birdbath in my sink that evening, after they closed us into our cells.

"Hey deputy," the white boy who had been knocked to the ground shouted, when the guards came back for the tray.

"Man, what's you want, honky," Loud Mouth said to him from the table. He was playing cards with the others who had been laughing that morning. "Hey, Dep! Hey, Dep!" he said mocking the inmate. "Hey is for horses Motherfucker. You better carry your snitch ass self back to your cell."

"Can I—Can I make a phone call?" the white guy asked.

I stood in the doorway of my cell, as I watched an inmate in an orange jumpsuit grabbed the trays and then the deputy shut the door.

"Can I make a phone call," Loud Mouth repeated. He slapped a card down on the table, before picking it up with the three others that were lying face up. "Go Big or Stay at Home!" he said, slamming down the Ace of Spades. "Trump, motherfucker!"

For the second time that day, the white guy slinked off to his cell.

I was hoping he'd snitch for me, and that Nate would be taken to the hole. But as I'd find out later, Nate and Loud Mouth were part of the same street gang, so even if the white guy had snitched and was moved to another cellblock, his life would be at risk by the other gang members. I went back inside my cell and picked up *The Executioner's Song* by Norman Mailer, which I had traded for a pack of cigarettes.

I didn't know what I'd do if Nate asked me the same thing. Will you Buck? You're damned if you answered yes and you're fucked if you said no. I could see where things were going, and I wondered if that's what I needed to do? Perhaps I could compromise and avoid being beaten up.

It felt horrible not having Slide Step there to protect me. After my first day at Riverside, Slide Step's protection had been as steady as the drone of an electric fan, but now that it was silent—I was starting to sweat again.

Nate was standing outside my open cell, staring at me. His right hand was resting just inside his waistband. He caught me looking, so I raised my book quickly until he walked away.

Maybe I was getting nervous for nothing, but I was determined to protect myself from a repeat of what happened to me at Riverside. About two minutes later he came back and entered my cell. He came in, uninvited, and sat on the bed.

All of the doors in the cellblock were opened at the same time. It wasn't possible to lock one, and open another. When the guards pulled the lever at the end of the block, they either all opened or were all closed at the same time.

"What's up," I said, trying my best to sound calm.

"You."

I ignored him and tried to keep reading. Someone started past the cell but then stopped and retreated. I looked over at Nate. I wasn't sure, but he may have signaled them somehow, because the expression on his face changed suddenly. He looked at me with an embarrassed smile.

I got up from the bed, but he propped his foot against the doorway blocking my exit. "What?" he said. "I'm just sitting here."

"What do you want?"

"Nothing." His tone was reassuring, but his face suggested otherwise. "I just want to kick it with you." He nodded toward the bed. "Sit down, I'm not going to let nothing happen."

"That's all right," I said. "I'll stand."

I could see he had a hard-on inside his pants, and he caught me looking at it.

My throat felt dry, and my heart raced. My hands started to shake and my legs felt wobbly. I had flashbacks of Riverside, and I didn't want a repeat of what went on there. But it also felt hopeless, trying to resist.

He pulled down his waistband and released his dick.

For a split second, the sight of his dick excited me, but this was not sex—and I didn't have a choice in the matter. I got down on my knees and took him inside my mouth, hoping it would be enough to keep him from raping me. But I could see quickly, he wasn't going to stop there.

"C'mon," Nate said. "Let me fuck you."

"No," I said. "I don't like it."

"C'mon, I'll go real slow."

"Just let me do this," I begged. At least sucking him off didn't hurt *physically*.

"I'm keeping these motherfuckers off of you, boy. So you've gots to give that up."

"Please, Nate. I don't like it. I'll do this, but can't you just leave that alone?"

He reached over and felt my ass.

The others were on the far side of the cellblock, hanging out in the first cell or two, or playing cards at the front table. Nate said no one knew what was happening, but it didn't matter. "I run this," he said. "Now let me hit that ass."

He smacked me on the head.

It could have been meant as a playful tap, or maybe not. I wasn't sure. I was getting the impression that if I didn't go along with it, he was going to take it anyway he liked.

"OK," I said, "but promise you'll go easy."

"Now that's what I'm talkin' about," he said. He pulled off his pants.

He started fucking me and the smell in the air was unmistakable. Vaseline mixed with shit. There was no way the others wouldn't pick up on it and know what was happening. Nate had said he would keep it a secret, but suddenly someone was standing outside the cell. And he didn't keep his other promise either. He was fucking me hard, and it was hurting badly.

"Please Nate," I begged. "Go easy."

He didn't. He just kept fucking me. I put my head down into the mattress and tried to block out what was happening, but the pain was too intense for me to leave the moment. I could see stars and shades of red and white and black. I clenched my jaw and stared into the darkness of my soul. I never should have sucked his dick. What was I thinking?

Nate grabbed a clump of my hair and yanked my head back. Loud Mouth was standing in front of me with his pants down to his ankles.

"No," I screamed.

Nate slapped me hard in the face, and Loud Mouth laughed.

He stuffed his cock in my mouth, while one of them said, "Shut up, bitch," but I couldn't tell which of them said it. I thought about biting off Loud Mouth's dick, but I was too frightened to fight back. There were a dozen others in the rest of the cellblock who might join in.

"Parsell," a voice shouted from the end of the hall.

Nate and Loud Mouth stopped when they heard the bolt of the cellblock door slide open. "Parsell," the deputy repeated, "Let's go! You've got an attorney visit."

When Nate got off me, he had shit all over his lap, which made me glad. The fucker deserved it. I tugged at my pants that were under his feet. He scrambled to put on his own.

"He'll be right there," Loud Mouth shouted. "He just got out of the shower."

I wished I could've shit all over him as well. The smell was suffocating.

"Hey," Nate whispered. "Don't you fuckin' snitch on us, bitch. 'Cause we'll get your ass," he said.

"Isn't that what you just did?" I felt the rage boiling up from the bottom of my soul. "You . . . You . . . fuckin' nigger."

Nate looked at me for a second, and laughed. "You fucking nigger," he mocked. "Go ahead, bitch, and snitch. Then I'll kill your motherfuckin' ass." He started toward me and I ran from the cell.

He was part of a gang, and its members were spread out all over the jail, so I knew I couldn't snitch on him—not if I wanted to stay alive. I also knew I was wrong for calling him a nigger, but it was all I could think of that could possibly hurt him. I wanted to hit him with the only thing I knew I could hit him with. And that's what he was to me. A big, black ass, motherfuckin' nigger, and if I had a gun—I would have killed him.

23

Help Ain't Gonna Come Runnin' No Time Soon

Mom said that in 1953, when she first went down to Fort Campbell, Kentucky, to be with Dad in the army, there were separate bathrooms for blacks. "I'd never seen nothin' like it," she said. "Your dad showed me separate drinking fountains and how they weren't allowed to eat in certain restaurants. NO COLOREDS, the signs read, or WHITES ONLY. I just thought that was wrong. Now everybody knows there's a difference between blacks and niggers."

Grandpa O'Rourke, who'd come for Sunday dinner, said, "I ain't got nothin' against 'em. I just don't want to live with 'em, that's all."

Mom said, "Well, I know plenty of white people that are niggers, too."

Were it not for Slide Step, it would have been easy for me to lump all black prisoners in together, but Slide Step *was* different. And I knew that if he had been at the County Jail, he would have killed them both.

The deputy walked ahead briskly, without looking back. He pointed only once in the direction we were headed, as we entered a series of long corridors. There was an odd stillness in the hall—a quietness that seldom entered in the cellblocks—except when the deputies first pulled back the bolt on the heavy steel door.

The tinkling of keys, dangling from his belt, lingered in my ear, along with the thud of his heavy footsteps. I struggled to keep up. I felt dizzy, out of breath and ready to hurl. The fluorescent lights overhead gave off a halo as we passed under each one. A guard at the end of a hall flung his keys to the deputy who was escorting me.

The metallic jangling and clink-clank-rumble of tumblers turning opened the door with a loud screech. I winced at the sound. My senses were beyond overload. It was all I could do to grab hold of something to focus on. Yet, no matter what came to mind, I couldn't drown out the harsh sights and sounds around me.

The deputy leaned on the edge of the open door and tapped his key on the surface. He faced the other way, as if to avoid eye contact or the smell of my body.

"Where'd the sergeant go?" he asked the other deputy.

I stepped inside and couldn't hear the response as he slammed the door and locked it.

As it turned out, this was not an attorney visit after all. It was the Probation Officer who sat at a small table attached to the wall. He was there to complete the Pre-Sentence Investigation Report.

"Give a yell when you're ready," the deputy said to him through a small opening in the door. His footsteps faded up the hall, followed by the sound of a crashing gate.

The probation officer was a large man, with clammy white hands, who appeared unusually chipper. He held mine for an awkward moment as we shook. "Your hands are soft," he said.

I sat down, and he grabbed my right hand again, facing it palm-side up.

Inside the cramped space, there were two stools on each side of the table. The man was so large, his body spilled over the stool.

"No calluses at all," he said. "That's amazing." He rubbed my fingers with both thumbs. "Do you do any manual labor?"

"No." I took my hand back and placed it under the table.

There was a kindness in his voice that I wasn't expecting.

"Hey! What's this?" he said, looking at me as I started to shake.

I was still trying to process what had just happened with Nate and Loud Mouth. As if I were trying to deny it—but couldn't. I wanted to run, but my feet wouldn't move, so all I could do was sit there and tremble.

"Are you OK?"

I nodded.

"Are you sure?"

I shrugged. At least the first time it happened, I was drunk and drugged with Thorazine, so I didn't have to feel everything.

He sat silently, and I couldn't speak.

"Kind of rough in here, huh?"

I nodded, beginning to cry.

He handed me his handkerchief.

I couldn't believe I was crying in front of him, but I couldn't help it.

"Do you want to talk about it?"

I shook my head.

"Well, you don't have to," he said.

He pulled out a pack of cigarettes from his shirt pocket and offered me one.

"Thanks," I managed to say, but my voice was choked.

The side of my face hurt from when Nate smacked me, and the blood in my mouth tasted like metal. He lit my cigarette and put the pack away. I had left mine in my cell, which I was sure were already stolen. "You're not having one?" I asked.

"I don't smoke." He smiled, gently. "I keep them handy, because I know what a commodity they are in here." He reached in his pocket and placed the pack on the table. "Keep 'em. I have more in the car."

All I could do was nod.

He let me finish my cigarette before he spoke again.

For a moment, I started to blame myself again—like what had happened was my fault, but this time it was different.

There was no way to avoid being attacked. It was like what had happened that morning, when Nate asked the guy with the food tray if he would buck for his food. He was damned if he did, and fucked if he didn't. At least I wasn't beaten up, but it felt like they had taken more than sex from me. It was as if Nate and Loud Mouth reached in and stole something more. I couldn't explain it. And no matter what, I couldn't say anything about it. Not then, and probably not ever. Not if I wanted to stay alive.

"You're up for sentencing on Tuesday," he said, "and I have to get this report to the judge." He tapped the blue file on the table with his pen.

I nodded. I was grateful that he'd given me time to pull myself together.

"So what did you rob?"

"A Photo Mat."

"A Photo Mat? Why did you do that?"

"For fun." I shrugged.

He chuckled. "Was it worth it?"

"No."

I still couldn't look at him, and I wondered if he could smell what was soiling the inside of my pants. I couldn't tell if the smell was real or imagined, but I was sure I would never forget it. And the pain down there was unbearable. I shifted in my seat.

"Well, if I ever got caught for some of the things I did when I was your age," he said. "I would be in here, too."

Judging by how large he was, I doubted he'd have the same problems. I wondered if the rest of him was as wet and clammy as his hands, but I appreciated how nice he was being. "When will I be sentenced?" I asked.

"Next Tuesday."

"That's right. You said that, didn't you?"

"I see you're serving time for larceny. You stole something from a hotel?"

"I use to work there," I said. "Some friends and I would sneak there at night to find an empty room to sleep in."

"Why didn't you go home?"

"Because if we woke our parents up—they'd beat us for coming home late."

"So what happened when you didn't come home?"

"They wouldn't notice, mostly."

"Have you been here in the county jail the whole time?"

"Riverside," I said.

"Riverside. Isn't that maximum security?"

"I had to go there until I got sentenced for the Photo Mat."

"Why did they send you to Riverside?"

"Because Armed Robbery carries up to life, and until I was sentenced, they had to treat me like I had been given life."

"Did you plea bargain?"

"My lawyer said I'd get two and half years. It's supposed to run concurrent with the time for the hotel."

"We'll that's not too bad. You'll be home in no time."

"No time soon," I said.

"How was Riverside?"

I shrugged.

"Anyone give you a hard time?"

Again, I shrugged. In spite of how nice he was being, there was no way I could say anything. If I snitched, my life would be worthless. Then I thought about the look on Nate's face when I told him that I would.

"Do you think I could be moved to another cellblock?" I asked.

"Why? Is someone bothering you?"

I didn't respond.

"Did you ask the deputies?"

I shook my head.

"Well, I doubt they'll listen to me any more than they would to you. Why don't you ask them?"

I couldn't answer him. I remembered reading about a prison riot in New Mexico, where the inmates broke into the protective custody wing using blowtorches they'd taken from the machine shop. Once inside, they turned the blowtorches on the faces of all the snitches. I'd also heard that if you asked to be moved, you had to tell the deputies who it was that was bothering you, and it was doubtful that the deputies would protect me.

"What made you do it?" He asked.

"What?"

"The robbery of the Photo Mat. You knew you were being placed on probation for the hotel thing, so why risk going to jail?"

"I didn't think I would get caught," I said.

"But still, why risk prison?"

"I didn't think they would send me to prison."

I thought of telling him that I robbed the Photo Mat before the hotel and that I got caught for it later, but it didn't matter now. "DeHoCo maybe," I said, referring to the Detroit House of Detention, "but I never thought I'd go to prison."

"Yeah, its kind of hard to believe with you being so young and good looking."

I moved to the other stool. It was cramped inside the cell, and I thought I felt his knee lean against mine.

"Do you see a lot of action in here?"

"Huh?"

He looked embarrassed. "I mean fights, bloodshed. You know, violence."

I shrugged. It seemed strange coming from him.

"A little," I said. I pulled another cigarette from the pack.

He struck a match and cupped it with his hands. I leaned forward and lit it.

He blew out the flame and held the match between us as we watched the blue and gray smoke rise slowly from the tip. "You have blues eyes," he said. "It almost matches."

His kneecap touched the inside of my thigh again, but this time it stayed there.

I jumped up and looked at him. "Are you finished?"

His eyes darted between the small opening in the door and me.

"Sit down," he said. "I have a few more questions."

"That's all right. I'll stand."

"Sit down, cowboy." He glared. "I'm the one in charge here."

I sat back down, and he finished the interviewed.

He didn't bother me again, but his whole demeanor had changed. He picked up the cigarettes from the table and placed them back inside his pocket.

When the deputy came to take me back to my cell, I asked him if I could be moved. "Why?" he asked.

I didn't answer at first.

He unhooked his keys and opened the sliding gate at the end of the hall.

"Because some guys are pressing me," I said. I stepped past him and waited as he closed the gate.

"Who?" He asked.

I said nothing.

"You have to tell me who, if you want to be moved."

He continued up the hall.

I struggled to catch up with him. I thought about telling him what had just happened with the probation officer, but I doubted he would believe me.

"I can't," I said. "They'll kill me if I say something."

He shook his head, but then stopped suddenly to look at me. "How old are you?"

"Seventeen."

His face softened, but then he let out a sigh.

I stood in front of him, shaking.

"Let me get the sergeant," he said, sounding exasperated.

I thought about Coach Kelly and how he yelled when I missed too many baskets, or passed the ball by accident to the opposing team. He'd blow his whistle and shake his head. "Hug the bench," he'd say to me, as he looked down at his clipboard and waited for everyone to notice. "What a dork," one of the kids on the sideline would say.

When the deputy opened the holding cell door and told me to have a seat on the floor, I thought about gym class and how the guys used to call him Coach *Nelly,* because of the way he came into the locker room to see who was undressed with their dick hanging out—jotting it down on that fucking clipboard of his—those of us who had showered from those who had not. But looking back on it, I would have given anything to be there again, to have the chance to shower with boys my own age in high school where the worse that could happened was someone called you a fag.

The deputy turned the key in the lock and then tapped it against the bars. He asked if I had anything in my cell that I needed.

"No," I said.

I was too afraid to go back for my cigarettes, where Nate and Loud Mouth were waiting for me.

"Are you sure?"

"My smokes," I said. "But I don't want to go back there."

"I'll get 'em," he said. But when he returned, I wasn't surprised to hear him say they weren't there.

As he walked away, I watched his keys dangling from the side of his belt. The simplicity of those small metal objects—just beyond my reach—that fit inside the locks and turned the cylinders to freedom and safety and to the outside world. If he'd just tossed me his keys—I'd never be back here again.

When I was kid, my brother Rick tried to teach me how to pick a lock. He said I had to feel and listen for the sound of the tumblers triggering inside. "It's like having sex," he said. "You stick your little pin inside the slot and jiggle it around until you feel the cylinder release." But his analogy was lost on me.

I just wanted to get to a shower. I wanted to wash away what had happened earlier. The smell of shit lingered in the air, but I still couldn't tell if it was real or remembered. Perhaps the preoccupation was just another attempt to escape what had happened. My head pounded with a band of pressure and I felt nauseous.

From inside the holding cell, I felt the rumbling vibration and clatter-clack-clack of the approaching meal cart. "That's him there," one of the inmates said to another, pushing the cart past. He nodded toward me, but the deputy wouldn't allow them to stop.

"I hope they put her up on my block," the inmate said.

I was hoping no one would find out about me and thus increase the chance of it happening again, but the inmates who delivered the meals were also the guys who carried the information. All food came from the same kitchen. So the food carts, as they rumbled past, were the lines of communication to every corner of the jail.

I started to feel there was nothing I could do to avoid what was happening or what might happen again. Sitting on the floor and waiting on the sergeant to decide what to do with me, I wanted to sleep forever, to lie down and not wake up again. But I couldn't bring myself to close my eyes. I'd never be able to close them again it seemed. All I could do was sit there and think. Inside the cell was a mop bucket, which I threw up in twice.

Where was the fucking key that would keep me safe?

24

You Never Know Where It's Coming From

"I fucking hate you," I screamed at Sharon through the torn screen door.

The temperature was in the single digits, and no one had bothered to put in the storm windows. It was just as well, they would have shattered, given how hard I'd slammed the door. I was thirteen and vowed never to come back again.

There was snow coming down, and the wind chill made it feel even colder. With nowhere to go, I wandered the streets all night, ducking in and out of convenience stores and twenty-four-hour supermarkets to keep warm.

Early the next morning, crossing the parking lot of Farmer Jack's, I felt someone following me. When I turned around, my dad was about fifteen feet behind. Though he looked relieved, his eyes were tired and sad—like he had been up all night, and I could tell that he hadn't been drinking.

He didn't say much, but what he did say were the kindest words he'd ever spoken to me. "C'mon home, Son."

"I have to say, this court is extremely disturbed by some of the statements made by the defendant, as indicated in the Pre-sentence Investigation Report." The judge looked down at me, over the rim of his black-framed glasses. "Would you care to explain?"

"I'm not sure what you mean, Your Honor?"

My attorney shrugged. He looked as puzzled as me.

"Well, for someone so young," the judge said. "I find it troubling that your level of calculation and knowledge of the system would be so advanced."

"I'm sorry Judge, but I still don't understand?"

"Did you tell the Pre-sentence Investigator that you figured on probation?"

"Huh?"

"It says here, you didn't believe you'd get caught, but even if you were, you'd probably get probation." He held the report up. "You were expecting a free ride, it says."

"That's not what I said, Judge." I turned to my attorney for help, which wasn't coming. I'd met him only two minutes before the sentencing hearing began. I'd have had better luck with the other lawyer, from the Public Defender's Office, but he was tied up in another court. This lawyer just stared at me with an embarrassed grin.

"Did you make that statement?" The judge asked.

"No. Well, sort of . . . It's not exactly what I said."

"Well, I'm *sort of* disturbed by your calculative savvy," he said. "Counselors?" He motioned the two lawyers to the side of his bench.

That fat fuck of a probation officer! He must've misrepresented what I'd said to him, right before he started rubbing his knee along the inside of my thigh. But how could I say that? He was the adult and I was a kid—a criminal with no credibility.

I turned to the back of the courtroom. My dad and Sharon sat in the last row. Sharon seemed to be frowning at the judge while my dad glanced up and nodded at me.

I shrugged and raised my hands in the air.

The lawyers came back to the front of the bench, and the judge asked if I had anything to say before he passed final sentence.

I opened my mouth to speak, but nothing would come out. I wanted to explain what I'd said to that probation officer, and what happened right afterward, but it seemed hopeless. I wanted to say what a horrible mistake I'd made, that it started as a joke, a stupid opening line to the pretty girl inside, and that it wasn't until she handed me the money and smiled that I grabbed it and ran. I wanted to tell him how sorry I was and how I'd give anything to go back to the Photo Mat and undo that impulsive moment. Or explain to the judge, how some people were strong enough for prison, while others—like me—were not. But all that came out was, "No, Your Honor."

The courtroom was still in the silence that followed. Only then did I realize my whole life was in the hands of that judge and how powerless I was to say or do anything.

"Very well," he said. "Having accepted your plea of Guilty to Armed Robbery, and having reviewed all the circumstances in this case, including assessment of the Pre-sentence Investigation documents as prepared by the Department of Probation, this court will follow the recommendation of the Probation Department and remand you to the State Department of Corrections for a term of not less than four and a half years and no more than fifteen years to be served in the state penitentiary." He smacked his gavel and handed my file to the clerk.

My attorney whispered something about violent crimes and capital offenses and judges having latitude in sentencing, but I didn't hear him.

"Wait a minute!" I screamed. "What happened to the two and half years?"

"Bailiff," the judge called out. He looked down over his glasses at the two sheriff deputies who quickly handcuffed me.

"I'll come see you in lock-up," my good-for-nothing lawyer said. "There was nothing I could do. Armed robbery carries up to a life sentence, and the Probation Department . . ."

I cut him off. "Can I see my parents?" It was all too much to absorb. I just wanted to talk to my parents.

"Your Honor?" the lawyer asked. "May the defendant speak to his parents?"

"That's up to the deputies," he said. "Next case!"

When we stepped from the courtroom, the sheriff deputies gave me a few minutes with Dad and Sharon. I stood in the corridor, my hands cuffed in front of me, while the two deputies waited nearby.

"How're you doing?" Sharon asked. Her voice was kind, and there were tears in her eyes. "You look awful."

"I'm all right," I lied.

"What the hell was that all about?" Sharon asked. "I thought you were supposed to get two and half years?"

"That's what I thought." I was too embarrassed to tell her what happened with the probation officer, and she probably wouldn't have believed me either.

"Where's that other attorney? The one who told you to plead guilty?"

"He couldn't make it. So the public defender sent this one." My handcuffs clinked as I motioned toward the courtroom.

"That's a crock of shit," she said.

Up the hallway, outside the heavy doors that led to the courtroom, was a high-backed wooden bench. A man in a suit talked softly to a family waiting to go inside.

"How're you?" I asked Dad. As usual he was starring off into space.

"Huh?" His blue eyes were clear but glistening with tears. "I need a cigarette," he said.

"I'm gonna go down and wait on that lawyer," Sharon said. She walked toward the people sitting on the bench.

It was the first time I'd noticed how short they both were. Though Dad was slightly taller than Sharon, neither of them came up past my chin.

"So what does this mean?" he asked.

"It means I have four and half years."

"Jesus Christ!" He almost shouted.

The deputies glanced up from across the hall.

"With good time, I'll be out in three."

"Jesus Chrr-rist." He repeated, giving Christ an extra syllable.

He seemed more upset than I was, and I felt like I needed to comfort him.

"I'll get through it, Dad."

He kept looking at me, but the glaze returned to his eyes—that far off look that told me he'd disappeared into himself again. I was sorry I'd hurt him.

I didn't have to worry about Sharon. For all my complaints about her growing up, she was as tough and mean as any of those judges. She paced the courtroom doors, waiting to see that attorney. I remembered the third grade nun, that took a belt to her son, and then Sharon went up and took her own belt off and used it on the benevolent sister. She had that same look in her eye, now, and she did back then.

"She don't take shit from nobody," her son Bobby would say. But even with all her might, she wasn't strong enough to take me home and out of this mess I'd gotten myself into.

As the sheriff deputies led me away, I heard Sharon attack the lawyer.

"What the hell was that all about? He was supposed to only get two and half years!"

The lawyer spoke in a hushed tone, so I couldn't hear what he said, but then Sharon screamed; "Now that's a crock of shit! I know what he said, God damn it. *I was there!*"

Later that day, Dad came back to visit me at the county jail. He was alone and looked as forlorn as he did earlier, yet he did his best to hide it behind a smile. His black hair was slicked back, like he'd worn it in the fifties, though his sideburns were shorter and starting to gray. He never was much for showing emotion, especially if he wasn't drinking.

"Where's Sharon?" I asked.

"She's at home."

We stared at each other uncomfortably, neither of us knowing what to say.

"Well, tell her I said thanks for going after that lawyer for me."

Dad nodded. "There wasn't much she could do. That lawyer said the judge could give you whatever he wanted, since armed robbery carries up to life."

I didn't want to think about it anymore.

"Still not drinking?" I asked.

"Nope." He shook his head with a half-smile, but there was lack of pride in it. "Quit last year."

My brother Rick said he had stopped right after I got into trouble, though we doubted that had anything to do with it.

"Just got tired of it," Dad said. "And anyway, Sharon's pretty happy about it."

"I'm sure she is," I said, dryly. Sharon had a long history of battling alcoholism, but not her own. Both her parents died from it, and her first husband had been a drunk. We she first started dating my dad, she worked in a hospital for alcoholics as a nurse's aide.

Dad knew how I felt about Sharon, almost from the beginning. Dad also had a stepmother who hated him. It was amazing to me that he'd allow the same situation to happen between his wife and his kids that Grandpa let happen to him.

But at least Sharon stuck up for me that day, and even if it hadn't done any good—she had tried. I wished she were there with Dad so I could thank her. It meant a lot to me.

Dad went on to tell me that Rick and my stepbrother Bobby were now getting into trouble together. Bobby was seventeen and Sharon's oldest boy.

"A detective came around wanting to talk to Bobby," he said.

"What about?"

"Well, he and the *other one* got mixed up in a robbery," Dad said.

We had to be careful about what we said because the sheriff deputies sometimes monitored the speaker boxes we were forced to yell through.

"Do they know about the 'other one'?" I asked.

Dad shook his head. We were talking about my brother Rick.

"The police want Bobby to come down and do a line up."

From what Dad was saying, I was able to piece together that Rick and Bobby had robbed an old couple, in their trailer, who'd advertised the sale of a diamond ring in *Trading Times* magazine.

"So, whoever did this," Dad said. "Tied the couple up, using a bunch of duct tape and then took everything in sight that was valuable."

"How'd they find out about Bobby?"

"Some kid in the neighborhood got caught with a gun that came from the robbery," Dad said. He paused. "The other one told Bobby not to sell it to anyone, but he didn't listen. So when the kid got caught with it, he ratted on Bobby."

"Who was it?"

"I don't know," Dad said. "But the other one's taking care of it."

I nodded.

"You goddamn kids." He shook his head. "It's always something."

If he only knew this side of it, I thought.

"Your face looks good. Prison must be agreeing with you."

"Fuck you," I said.

We both smiled. Ricky probably put him up to saying that.

"Will they be able to identify Bobby?"

"I don't know," Dad said. "But the old man was a retired cop."

"Uh-oh."

"Exactly," Dad said. Whenever something happens to a cop, somebody goes to jail.

So did this mean Bobby was on his way to prison? And Rick was behind it, no doubt. He wasted no time in finding another fall guy. I thought about how I'd been following Rick my whole life. And now he was working with Bobby, who might be headed to jail. I wondered what it'd be like for Bobby if he came here. He was tougher than me, but he was also smaller. Though by penitentiary standards, he wasn't that pretty—it wouldn't make much difference if they decided to rape him. I wished I could talk to him, and help him avoid what happened to me.

"Sharon's pretty upset about it," Dad said.

"I'm sure she is. It must've come as quite a shock that her precious little angel would be involved in something like this."

Dad didn't say anything. He knew she thought her kids were special, and that Ricky and I were the bad ones. "She blames Rick for a lot of things," Dad said.

"It's not like I needed his help in getting here, I did that on my own." There were other things we'd done together that could've sent me there a lot sooner.

I thought about those times, when as a kid, I sat in the visiting rooms of juvenile detention centers and listened to Ricky's stories about what went on there. And how Dad jumped in, to tell us what it was like back when he and Uncle Ronnie were there. It seemed like those were the only times he and Rick ever really talked.

I looked up and saw that Dad had zoned out again. Physically, he was still there, on the other side of the glass, but his sad blue eyes told the real story. Through the small steel frame in the concrete wall, I saw my dad's sorrow— his own lost childhood; his longing and abandonment by his mother; his father's absence; and a stepmother who cared more about her own children— and looked upon him and his brothers and sisters as nothing more than a nuisance. I could see the heartbreak of my mom's betrayal and now the slow, steady downfall of each of his children. He checked out, because his life was too painful, and each time he tried to check back in again—he wasn't strong enough to bear it. I connected with his pain and longing for something better.

"Time's up," the deputy said.

Dad nodded and reached in his shirt pocket, where he kept his cigarettes and lighter. "I need a smoke," he said.

"OK, Pop. Thanks for coming."

"I'll try to get up to see you as soon as I can."

"OK, Pop. Thanks again, for coming."

"All right, then." He said. He backed away from the window, but kept looking at me. The sadness disappeared behind his smile. "I'll see you, then."

Later that night, not long after I'd fallen asleep; I awoke suddenly from a nightmare. I was sweating heavily, and it took a few minutes for my breathing to settle. It was another flashback of my rape at Riverside.

In the dream, I was on the bottom bunk in Chet's dorm, with the blankets draped on each side of the bed. But this time, when Chet finished raping me, it wasn't Red who pulled the blanket back to go next—it was my brother, Rick.

The dream rattled me for several hours, not knowing what it meant. Rick had never molested me, nor had we ever had sex, so why would I picture him in that dream?

I lay awake for a long time, thinking about how I had always worshipped him. The wool blanket I rested my head on was damp with perspiration. I remembered how he looked at me, that last night before I'd gone to prison, as we made the trip downtown in his van to buy me a hooker. He knew what I was facing; yet he didn't want to scare me.

I thought about the trouble he and Bobby had gotten into together and how Dad said he wouldn't get caught unless Bobby told on him, which we knew he wouldn't do—so that meant Rick was probably safe. Everyone seemed to be going to jail but Rick. It was a trick he must've learned after going there so many times himself.

When Rick had come to visit a few weeks earlier, he lied to me twice. He said he didn't have any money, and then told me about his new truck. Then he said his phone got disconnected, but he didn't mention the new number that was turned on under his wife's name. And now he was taking Bobby down.

It's not as if Rick was responsible for my going to prison. Between the hotel thing and the robbery of the Photo Mat, I blame myself. But there were other crimes we'd pulled that he could have left me out of. When someone had stolen something they wanted to sell, Rick was the guy who could fence it. But he often lied about how much he got for these goods and would later brag about how he ripped people off. He could never just keep it to himself. He thought it was funny—and he had to brag about it. Like that time he went through the jewelry we'd stolen from a house, and he threw a diamond ring in the garbage—said it was worthless cubic zirconium. Only after I'd left, did he picked it out of the trash and hock it for nearly $1,500.

That was a lot of money, especially if I'd thought about it in terms of Zoo Zoos and Wham Whams and cigarettes and shampoo and whatever else I could get from the inmate commissary. I could have lived on that money for a couple of years. But now he couldn't even send me ten bucks or allow me to call him collect.

Truth be told, my fantasies had as much to do with my being incarcerated as anything else. Ever since I was a boy, sitting in visiting rooms of juvenile youth homes and later on in the prison waiting room, listening to his stories about what went on inside—I wondered what it was like. Would I live the same adventures that Rick seemed to lead? Could I make everyone laugh about it the same way? And later on, when he talked about the punks and the sissies, it was the first place where I knew they existed. Now that I was inside, it was nothing like I'd imagined. I was stuck here for another three years.

I grabbed the scratchy blanket I'd been using as a pillow and curled up with it, sideways, on my bed. A cockroach scampered across the floor—pausing at the base of the metal toilet. A silhouette of bars crisscrossed the walls. So who was it that had really fucked me—Chet, Red, or my brother Rick?

25

When All Else Fails . . .

Mom had promised me that I was not getting a shot. She knew how much I hated them, because last time, it took several nurses to hold me down. So when the receptionist pointed us to He-ma-tology, I was hoping to meet Batman and Robin or maybe Superman, yet all I saw when we arrived there was a row of vampires.

In 1965, the nurses drew blood by way of a tube that was attached to a mouthpiece. The air pressure from their tongue provided the suction.

"Don't even look at them," Mom said, handing the paperwork to the nurse. But I grew suspicious when they called my name.

"What for?" I said. "You're not going to give me a shot."

"You'll just feel a tiny pinch," she said. And with that, I bolted down the hall.

Mom screamed after me as I ran through a set of double doors and out into the parking lot where the rain coming down in pelts. I was nearly soaked by the time I reached our car. And so was Mom, by the time she caught up to me.

"Timothy James Parsell! You unlock this door right now." Mom had her hands on her hips, which I knew meant she was serious.

"No," I shouted. "You promised." When she tried her key in the door, I started to cry, putting all my weight on the lock. No matter what—I was not getting a shot.

The next morning, I was taken down to the bullpens for transfer to Jackson Prison. Now that I had been sentenced, I'd have to go through Quarantine and Classification again, though I hoped it wouldn't take as long as the first time. I couldn't wait to get out the county jail. I'd felt liked I'd been fucked multiple times since I got there, and they couldn't move me out soon enough. The first time was when Nate and Loud Mouth raped me. And the second time was with that fat fuck of a probation officer. But the final blow came from the judge, when he vacated my plea agreement and gave me almost twice as much time than I thought I was getting.

The deputy who'd escorted us down, walked with a swagger that seemed to express his boredom. His hair was sticking up in the back, like he'd been sleeping with his head resting against the wall.

I was taken to the same bullpen as when I first arrived. It was beginning to feel all too familiar. The four identical cells, on the opposite wall, were dark and empty. At 5:00 in the morning, the reception area wasn't completely quiet, but it was probably as close to peaceful as it ever got. I sat on the bench and stared at the floor. My state shoes looked dull and needed a shine. No matter what these fuckheads did to me, I was not going to lose my sense of good appearance and pride.

The inmates to my side had been talking a few minutes before I realized what they were saying. "You can just have him come over here," one of them said.

I looked up, and he was squeezing his crotch and nodding toward the toilet. The guy next to him was Loud Mouth—the con from upstairs who had raped me.

"Square Business," he said. "He sucked my dick while Nate fucked him in the ass."

Two more approached so that four of them were now standing in front of me.

"Hey white boy," one of them said. "Why don't you come with us."

"Yeah," another said, who was standing by the toilet. "Come give us some face."

A variety of things passed through my mind, but terror and rage were the dominant factors. "I ain't laying like that," I said.

Just then, Loud Mouth walked up and slapped me, and the others laughed.

"Hey!" I blurted out, and I bolted toward the front of the cell. I was not going to let it happen to me again! One of them grabbed my arm, and I screamed, "Deputy!"

He let go and the other inmates scattered.

They waited a moment for the deputy to appear, and when he didn't, they came at me again. "Come here, you little bitch. You know you want it."

I called out to a deputy who was standing in front of the cell next to ours, but he walked away.

A moment passed, and one of the inmates came toward me again.

"Deputy!" I screamed. The inmate backed off.

"We'll get your ass, you little faggot."

A couple of them laughed.

I stayed by the door, calling out to a deputy whenever one passed by the cell. But none of the deputies would stop or listen. The inmates hesitated for a minute or two longer and then moved in on me again. The electric motor to the door suddenly kicked in, and the bars lurched open. I sprang from the cell.

"Where are you going?" a deputy yelled.

"I ain't going back in there," I said.

"Oh you're not, huh?" He reached for me, and I skirted around him, breaking for the other side. He chased after me, while two others cut me off and tried to tackle me.

"Those fuckers are trying to rape me," I screamed. I broke loose and ran to the other side of the control booth. One of them grabbed my shirt and ripped it. Two more rushed me, and I was pinned to the floor.

"You're going back in that cell," the first deputy said.

"No I'm not," I shouted.

They picked me up and carried me to the bullpen, but I grabbed the bars to one of the empty cells. "I'll sue you motherfuckers! I'm not going back there!" With both hands I clenched hold of the bars. They lifted my legs off the floor while the others tried to wrench my hands free.

The inmates laughed from the other side.

One of the deputies elbowed me in the face, and my nose started to bleed. They dropped my feet, and one of them pushed me back against the bars.

"Just stop it," he yelled at me. The other deputies let go.

"I'm not going back there," I screamed. "I don't care. You can fuckin' shoot me."

"Yes you are," the first deputy said, and I bolted from them again.

I felt a sting on my chest, from where someone had scratched me. The deputies put me in a headlock and pulled me into an empty tank, where they knocked me to floor and started to pounce on me. They were trying to force handcuffs on me when the sergeant appeared in the doorway and ordered them to let go of me.

"OK," he said to others, "I'll take it from here."

My back felt bruised, and my side was numb. I struggled to stand up, but the best I could do was sit up. It was dark in the cell, and all I could see was his outline.

"What's your name, son?"

"I'm not going back there," I said.

"I said, what's your name?"

"Those fuckin' niggers were trying to rape me."

"Oh, now we're niggers," a inmate shouted from across the hall.

It was the quietest I'd ever heard it get in there.

"Just calm down," the sergeant said.

"Bring him over here, Sarge," an inmate yelled. "We'll take care of it."

"Yeah, Baby," another shouted. "You snitch ass bitch."

I didn't care what they called me. Or what the deputies would do. They could bring in the goon squad and kill me for all I cared. I wasn't going back inside that cell. What those motherfuckers had already taken from me was all they were going to get.

The deputies who had grappled with me were standing outside the bullpen, laughing, just like the inmates.

"Relax," the sergeant said. He helped me off the floor and handed me his handkerchief, lifting my hand to hold it to my nose. "No one's going to do anything to you."

He stepped back from the dark holding cell, and out into the light, where I noticed for the first time that he was black.

The electric gate jolted closed with a loud bang.

"*Those fucking niggers tried to rape me,*" a con mocked from across the hall.

The inmates laughed.

26

Black Panther . . .

It was a regular cellblock, like all of the others, except I wasn't allowed out into the common area in front of the cells. They said it was for my own protection, but it felt more like punitive segregation.

After the incident in the bullpens, the sergeant had me moved upstairs to the Lavender Wing. I hadn't told them I was gay, but it didn't matter. "You'll be safe here," a deputy said. Making my way down the row, I sensed eyes staring at me as I hurried past each cell. When the deputy pulled the release brake and closed the sliding bars, I felt relieved. No one could get at me, in here.

I overhead the sergeant say he wasn't going to move me in the same transport vans that carried the inmates I had called niggers, so he postponed my transfer to Jackson. I knew, as soon as I had made that remark, that it would inflame the situation further, but I had hoped it would force the deputies into taking the action they did. Being a crazy racist, or even a snitch, was preferable to being gang raped and turned into the group bitch.

I'd also heard later, that when Nate and Loud Mouth appeared for their sentencing before Detroit Recorder's Court Judge, The Honorable Geraldine Bledsoe Ford, they both nearly fainted when she told them to look out the window and count the almost one hundred pigeons that were clustered outside. But even the ninety-nine years to life she'd given them, for the armed robbery and murder they'd committed while on parole, wasn't long enough to erase the pain of what they'd done to me. Not even a death sentence could've lessened my rage. They should have been charged with raping me, because that might have served as a deterrent to others who were doing the same. But that would've required my coming forward, which I was still too afraid to do.

"You've gotta let that kind of thinking go," Black Diamond said from the cell next to mine. "Cause that shit will just fuck with your mind."

I hadn't noticed her when I first came in, because I'd mostly kept my head down until I reached my cell. I was both upset about what happened in the bullpen, but also a tinge embarrassed for being placed on the wing with all the queens.

"Birds of a feather, honey," Black Diamond said to me.

I first heard about her in Quarantine and then again down in the bullpens. Some queens achieved almost celebrity status, and Black Diamond was among them. She wanted to be called Cat Woman, because she was dark like a panther and because of how she slinked down a prison catwalk. But the name had already been taken. Black Diamond came about because she was exceptionally ugly. "A diamond in the rough," as she'd tell it. Others said, "That bitch is so ugly that she has to sneak up on her food tray."

She was friendly from the moment I arrived, so we talked from the front of our cells. She gave me a book to read and even leant me a few cigarettes, even though she knew I couldn't repay her. The book was *Meridian* a novel by Alice Walker.

"I'd lend you this other one," she said, "but I'm still reading it."

"What it is?"

"*Black Widow Mama.*"

"That's OK," I said. "I probably wouldn't want to read it, anyhow."

"It's my life story," she said. "It's about a Chicago Drag Queen."

"Oh. Are you from Chicago?"

"No, but I'm a Black Widow, don't you know."

The queen in the cell next to her yelled, "She done killed nine of her husbands. The bitch is like a praying mantic."

"Do you mean praying mantis?" I asked.

"Whatever," the queen shouted. "The bitch is a cold-hearted killer. Got arsenic and shit runnin' through them veins."

"All right Miss Ginger. Don't get me started on your nasty self." I could picture Black Diamond's eyes pivoting back and forth. "Just put Miss Ginger on your pay-no-mind list," she said. "She got a birthday comin' up and is about to turn twenty-five, which for a prison bitch, is like turning eighty." Black Diamond stuck her arm out of her cell and snapped. "Better take your Geritol, Girl!"

"We used to have a Mary Ann in here too," she said. "But her man posted bail this morning. The lucky ho. She's probably back out on the track, clickin' those ruby heels on Woodward Avenue. Anyway, Ginger here has offered me a pack of cigarettes if I read to her, so if you want, you can listen for free. But we have to wait till shift change 'cause the book is contraband and that's when Smitty's on." The jail prohibited books or magazines about queers. "Smitty's one of us," she whispered, "but we still have to do it on the Q.T."

"On the Q.T.?"

"On the Quiet Tip, girl! How long have you been down?"

I didn't respond.

"I'm just sayin', cause you need to toughen up if you want to make it in here, girl."

"I'm not a girl," I said.

"Well, you're a girl in here, honey."

"You tell her, Miss Thing," another queen shouted.

"You might as well have a vagina honey, 'cause once you're up here with all these scandalous queens, your ho' card is thoroughly punched."

"Speak for yourself," Ginger yelled. "Some of us ladies know how to be discreet."

"Uh-huh," Black Diamond said. "You forget, bitch, I knew your ass in juvenile hall. Back when you were doin' boys for Hostess Ding-Dongs."

"Hello!" someone chirped from the end of the hall, as if keeping score.

Thanks to the meal cart express, they all knew what happened down in the bullpen, as well as what had happened upstairs with Nate. "And even if they didn't," she said. "They know about you now, 'cause you're up here on Queens Row with us."

"That's right," Ginger added. "Ain't no secrets in here. Everyone knows what happened to you."

"Even at Riverside," Black Diamond said.

It took a moment for that to sink in, and I felt my heart sink with it. I sat back on my bunk without saying anything. So everyone knew. I felt humiliated and ashamed.

"Girrlll. You had it going on. If Miss Thing here could've passed herself off as straight and got up on one of those regular floors! I'd a been right up there on it."

I didn't respond.

"But I know what you mean, though. That shit is fucked up when you don't want it, and they decide they're going to just up and take it from you."

"That's right," Ginger said. "But there ain't a whole lot you can do about it."

"Yes there is," Black Diamond said. "You can hurry up and get yourself a man. These motherfuckers think that just 'cause we like dick, it means they can fuck us whenever they want, even if we don't want it."

"And the guards ain't gonna help you none, either," Ginger said.

"*I thought you liked dick?* is what one of them guards told me," Black Diamond said. "That was after a bunch of motherfuckers had Miss Thing spread out over a card table. Shit, I was in the infirmary for almost a month after that. But I don't like to think about that. Shit gets too damn depressing."

I just listened as Black Diamond went on. Perhaps it should have felt validating to hear someone else share an experience that was somewhat similar to my own. I knew I wasn't alone—but Black Diamond was right—it gets too damn depressing to even think about it. So I don't—I changed the subject in my mind.

"'Well a dick's a dick,' is what one of these men told me—and he was serious, too. Uh-uh, I told him—it don't work like that. Is a pussy a pussy? And he said, 'Hell no'—so what makes you think it's the same for me? So that's why you need to be real careful with yourself, white boy. 'Cause these motherfuckers all know you're on Queens Row, and they all know your business, so when you go back down to them bullpens—you need to be extra careful with yourself."

"Thanks," I said. It was good advice about being careful, but I rejected the notion of being branded by being placed on Queens Row. And I started being careful right then, by placing the book and cigarettes she had given me back on the cross section of her bars. "Thanks anyway," I said.

When Black Diamond first gave me the book and cigarettes—I told her that I couldn't repay her. She said, "That's OK, you can hook me up later. I'm sure there's something we can swap." I was pretty distrustful of everyone by then, but I thought I was safe, being locked up in a single-man cell, but then I learned they showered us two at a time, and that her cell and mine were numbers 9 and 10.

"Well, you know, I've got quite the reputation . . ."

I knew about her reputation. "She sucks a mean dick," was the other thing I'd heard about her, which I suspect was her primary (if not only) attraction.

I had never received a blowjob before, so I wouldn't know what I was missing, but I was pretty sure I wouldn't be able to get it up for her. "Thanks, but no thanks," I said.

"Well, suit yourself, but you can't blame a girl for trying."

It may have seemed like a trivial thing, a simple book and a few cigarettes, but as I was quickly realizing, nothing came for free in prison.

Black Diamond placed them back on my bars. "Don't worry about it," she said. "My man puts plenty of coin in my commissary."

"Thanks," I said, but I felt uncomfortable taking it.

"You know, Tim. If you don't want what's been happening, to keep happening, you gonna have to learn how to work it."

"That's right," Ginger shouted. "Your pretty white ass is too fine to be up in here suffering. But don't just survive girl, you gots to learn how to thrive!"

"Never mind her," Black Diamond said. "She's just a nasty old cell hop."

"Don't be getting' shady with me, Miss Diamond. I'm just trying to help the boy. He's sitting on a gold mine, and he don't even know it."

"Ain't nobody gettin' shady with you, but you need to stay out my business. If that boy listened to you, Miss Gingivitis, he'd be turning tricks till he needed dentures."

"Oh yes you are, you ugly bitch, you're over there livin' on Shady Lane with all that smack you're jackin'."

"Say what?" Black Diamond said. "Do you talk to your momma with those lips, or do you just use 'em to suck the Milk Duds out your daddy's ass?"

"Hello!" the scorekeeper yelled.

"Look," Black Diamond said, "If you don't shut your twat, I ain't gonna read to you no more."

Ginger didn't say anything.

"OK then. Now stay out my affairs." She turned her attention back to me. "I'm just sayin', as long as you keep hanging to the outside world, and walking around here like your some kind of lost sheep, then these motherfuckers are just gonna keep doggin' you. So you need to put that shit right out your head and start playing this game for real."

"Oh, shut up, you ghastly ho'," Ginger said. "*I ain't gonna read to you no more!*"

"Look, bitch! I'm not kidding," Black Diamond said. "You better shut up."

"She's right," Ginger said. "You gotta stay strong, girl. Throw some shade and make these motherfucker pay! You've gotta go from *What can I do?* to *What can I do you out of, baby?* You know what I'm saying to you, girl?"

I wasn't sure I knew exactly, but Black Diamond was right about one thing—it was time I let go of the outside world. I was spending too much time thinking about it. Retreating from whatever was happening inside prison—to my memories of childhood and home—like my brother Rick had told me to do. "It would be my memories that helped keep me together," he said. But Rick had been wrong about a lot of things, and so maybe he was wrong about that too. So I was now ready to let go of the past, and to concentrate on being present, so I could learn what I needed to learn to survive in here. I don't know that I was ready to learn how "to work it," like Ginger was saying, but I was definitely tired of being a sheep that kept getting "dawged" by other inmates.

The next morning, I was transferred to Jackson Prison.

When I arrived at Quarantine, the deputies who had transported me to the state prison must have told them what happened to me earlier at the county jail, because I was processed immediately and placed back on Two-Special—the set of cells next to the guards station on the second tier. Ironically, I was put in Grasshopper's old cell, which had been next to mine the first time through.

I wondered how Grasshopper was doing, and if he had learned how to adapt by now. Perhaps he got a man to protect him. And if so, maybe he got as lucky as I had, by having someone who cared about him like Slide Step seemed to care for me. So much seemed to fall to chance, if you weren't proactive in some kind of way. "You can hurry up and get you a man," Black Diamond had said to me. "You choose one of them, before they choose you."

Since I had already gone through medical and educational testing last March, I didn't have to wait the full six weeks to meet with the Classification Committee. It only took three. Yet it seemed much longer. By now, I was eager to get back to Riverside. It wasn't the prison I missed so much, as it was Slide Step. With him there, I didn't have to worry about what was going to happen to me. And even the sex wasn't so bad. At least he didn't try to hurt me. And anything else an inmate could have in there—Slide Step made sure I had it. Including Brett! Yet oddly enough, I'd hardly thought about Brett at all since I'd been gone. It was Slide Step who I kept thinking about.

"Why do you want to go back to Riverside?" the head of the Classification Committee asked. He was a man in his fifties with short dark hair and glasses. He didn't look the type who would understand.

"I like it there," I said. "Can I please go back?"

"But it's a higher security and you now qualify for medium security placement."

He looked at the other two members, who were looking back and shaking their heads. "We don't understand why you'd want to go there, when you can go to a lower security facility with inmates who are closer to your own age."

"I feel safe there," I said.

I couldn't think of what else to say, and for the first time, I realized how deeply I had cared for Slide Step—because the pain I was feeling, deep down in my gut, had nothing to do with concerns for my safety.

"Please," I begged. "Can I please, just go back there?" But this sudden realization of how I felt for Slide Step, was too late.

"No. I'm afraid not."

My heart sank.

"We're sending you to the Michigan Training Unit, where you can finish high school and acquire a trade, so you can be productive when you get back out."

I didn't want to get back out. I wanted to go to Riverside. I didn't care anymore, about guys my own age. I just wanted to go home, to Riverside.

27

Greener Grass

We had gone out to eat at a family restaurant. Everyone was there except for Ricky. He was down in Florida serving time for forgery. Dad was hungover and was making up to Sharon for a disappearance.

I looked over at the family sitting at the table next to ours. The son, who was about my age of fourteen, was talking and everyone at his table was listening to him. His dad smiled as he placed his hand on the back of his son's neck. Everyone laughed.

The boy's clothes looked different than mine—they were cleaner and new—and he sat up taller in his chair, even though he seemed shorter than me.

I wondered how different my life would have been, if I had lived with them.

According to the orange-covered rulebook, The Michigan Training Unit was a medium-security prison for the more *educable* inmates under twenty-one years old. The focus was on rehabilitation, and everyone there was required to work and go to school.

For all the structure that had been missing at Riverside, the Michigan Training Unit had made up for in programming. They offered high school and college, GED preparation, and training in vocational trades. The place was so strict that if you stepped on the grass between the walkways, you were issued a misconduct report.

The warden, Mr. Richard A. Handlon, prided himself on running a model facility. He was a man in his fifties, who was fat and bald and wore his pants so high above his waist that he looked like Humpty Dumpty. But Warden Handlon was not the kind of man you could fuck with, because he didn't play. The rules were strict, and if an inmate received too many tickets or filed one too many grievances, he'd have them "rode out" or transferred to another prison.

For the most part, the inmates in medium-security were all within a few years of parole, so it wasn't as dangerous as a close-custody or maximum-security prison. But just because there was less violence, didn't mean there was none at all.

When I first arrived, I was assigned to G-unit, which was a converted shop class that resembled an army barracks. It had a high ceiling with long double rows of bunk beds and lockers. Fish had to wait up to three or four weeks until a room opened up in one of the six main housing units.

From the outside, the main housing units looked like student housing. Two-story tan brick buildings with faded turquoise trim. But inside, there were open-tiered cellblocks, with single-man rooms in place of the cells. In the newer buildings, the windows opened onto lawns and were large enough to crawl in and out of. Inmates also had the privacy of rooms with doors that locked, and each of us was given a key to his room. The central chow hall once a week served cheeseburgers and pizza. Were it not for the double barbed-wire fences and gun towers that surrounded the compound, it could have passed for a college campus.

But it wasn't just my surroundings that were different: the inmates' behavior and attitudes were different, especially when it came to queers. Perhaps it was because many of them had just come from the outside world and they didn't have long to go before they got out. Or maybe it was because everyone was so young. I heard a guard say that younger inmates were more difficult to control because they were quick tempered and got into fights easily. I had hoped to keep secret all that happened to me earlier, but the inmates had already heard about me.

"He's laying that way," I heard a guy whisper. "He was *fucking* at Riverside."

I was up on my bunk reading, when someone said, "Uh-oh, Don't squeeze the Charmin." That's when one of them grabbed my ass. I spun and swung at whoever it was, jumping down from my bunk all in the same motion. It electrified the barracks, where hostilities were already tense. The inmates started yelling and cheering.

He was a black man, about my size, and we exchanged a few slugs before wrestling to the floor. "Kill that peckerwood," a black inmate shouted. "Don't take that shit from a nigger," a white hollered, and another fight broke out on the sidelines.

The racial make up was almost evenly split, so tensions were higher than I'd seen earlier at the other prisons. The guards handcuffed us quickly and took us to A-unit, where we were placed in isolation. Three days later I would go to "court."

Since major misconducts could result in the forfeiture of good time (time off your sentence for good behavior), inmates were granted due process and given a hearing. The Hearing Officer was a thin, dark-skinned black man who wore a navy blue suit and tie. The inmate advocate was also present. She was a young white woman who dressed plainly.

The Hearing Officer read from the incident report. "At approximately 1600 hours, C.O. Miller observed an altercation between inmate Parsell #153052 and inmate Williams. . ." There was more to the report, but he stopped reading and looked directly at me. "So what happened?"

"The guy squeezed my ass." I shrugged. "So I hit him."

The Hearing Officer nodded then glanced at the advocate. She said nothing, tucking her long brown hair behind her ear.

He placed the report on the table and checked the box marked, *Not Guilty*.

"OK, then," he said, without looking up.

We were sitting at a small conference table, and I watched as he wrote something in the *Findings* section of the report. His handwriting, like his hair and suit, was neat and orderly and his gold wedding band looked new.

"You'll get out of segregation this afternoon," the advocate said with a quick smile.

"I'll call Housing," the Hearing Officer said, "and get you moved to a regular unit."

"Today?" I asked, sounding surprised. I was told it took up to six weeks.

"Well, every now and then, when we see someone who's being pressured, we try to move 'em out of the barracks sooner. You did the right thing, by fighting back. It's the quiet ones that get themselves into trouble over there."

"Thanks." I smiled.

He didn't smile back. "Now, don't let me see you over here again."

"No sir, you won't."

As I bounced out of the Hearing Room, Inmate Williams was waiting in one of the chairs in the hall. A guard stood next to him. "Don't think this shit is over," he said. "You're still gonna need a man, bitch."

"I got your bitch," I said, walking up the hall.

Neither of us had actually won the fight, though it might have been enough to have defended my manhood. Surely they had heard that I'd been turned out at another prison.

I wondered how different my incarceration might have been, had I been sent to MTU originally. Or how differently my situation might have turned out, had I fought Chet in the showers at Riverside; but what chance did I have against the Thorazine? What chance did a seventeen-year-old boy have against any of them?

When I got back to A-unit, the guard was yelling "chow," and so I started toward the door. Suddenly a white inmate grabbed my arm.

"Let the crows go," he said.

The blacks filed out of the building first, followed a few minutes later by the whites. When I turned back to the inmate who had stopped me, he was gone.

Like everything else inside, the racial balance was controlled by Warden Handlon. The staff denied it, saying the mix had more to do with the youthful population than it did anything else. At any rate, it seemed to make matters worse, since at most other prisons the tensions didn't seem as high when one side grossly outnumbered the other. And though large-scale violence never broke out, there was frequent grumbling between the groups about rioting.

The oldest inmate there was Little John. He was forty-five and worked as a waiter in the Officer's Dining Room. He had worked for Warden Handlon for years while he was over at the Michigan Reformatory. Little John still wore his pant legs rolled-up like knickers, the way he did when he had first come to prison in the 1950s.

I heard someone call him the warden's house nigger, but no one had the nerve to say that to his face—not even the blacks. Everyone knew not to fuck with an older inmate.

I remembered Manley telling me that older convicts didn't like games. "Most of them have been down too long, so they don't have the patience for a lot of bullshit. They ain't gonna get up in your face like these young silly jitterbugs and talk a lot of smack. They'll just sneak up behind you, and quietly kill you."

Manley had also said that older convicts are more levelheaded. You're always better off with an older inmate than with someone younger. "These youngsters got no sense," he said. "They're too young, dumb, and full of cum, so they'd just as soon cut your head off and fuck you—and *then* ask if that pussy is any good; whereas the older cons are a lot smoother. They're just as dangerous, mind you—but they'd rather coax or trick that pussy out of your ass than just up and take it from you."

Perhaps I was being naïve to think that since I was at a new prison, that I might be able to leave my past behind. I thought about the advice Black Diamond had given me: as long as I kept walking around like a lost sheep, people were going to keep dogging me. I was hoping to put an end to the question of whether I was gay or not, but as I turned the corner on the yard, I ran into Josh from Riverside. Josh was the chubby white guy that Slide Step had set me up with in the shower. It made sense to me now—how the guys in the Barracks knew my story.

"Hey, Tim. How you doing?"

I kept walking. "All right," I said.

"Wait up! I hear you're moving to C-unit."

How did he know that?

"One of my homeboys is a clerk in Housing." He said it like it gave him some kind of clout. "Anyway, it's a rough unit, so you're going to need protection."

I didn't say anything.

"It's one of the worst units in here," he said, sounding sincere. "So I'd like to introduce you to a friend of mine."

"I'm not interested," I said, but just then his friend, Rock, walked up to us.

Josh said, "I know you'd rather be with a white guy."

Rock was so big he dwarfed me. He was a twenty-year-old bodybuilder, who was serving the last of a three-year sentence for selling drugs. His short wavy hair was a reddish blond, which matched his mustache and small goatee. He stood about six foot five, and his chest was so large I would have practically had to climb up on it, just to touch his chin. Rock was very sexy. In spite of myself, I started to grin.

"OK," I said. "But only if I have to."

When I moved to C-unit, it didn't seem like a rough unit, but I wouldn't really know for sure because by the time I got there, everyone knew that I belonged to Rock.

If MTU had a football team, Rock would have been captain, although he lacked the discipline to follow orders, and he took pride in the way he skirted authority. Since he was about to be discharged on the maximum of his sentence, he didn't have to worry about pleasing the parole board. He had a way of carrying himself that, combined with his size, allowed him to hold court on the section of the yard where the bodybuilders hung out.

Rock's friends, all of whom were white, seemed to know each other from the streets or time served together in juvenile hall. Rock wasn't the best looking among his friends, though he was the largest—and he carried himself like he knew it. He was the kind of guy the girls back home would have been crazy about—except that he liked to brag about mistreating them. "I used to dog them bitches," he once said, sitting back on the grass with a pint of ice cream.

"Man," Josh looked on admiringly, "he used to *buke* those bitches. He'd say to them, 'Shut up bitch, and get your ass in there and clean them dishes.' And they would too!" Josh laughed. "They were only too happy to do it."

Rock leaned back and smiled.

Buke was a word I remembered Slide Step using, when his team had beaten another team badly. Perhaps it was a bastardization of the word *rebuke*, yet I doubt anyone even knew. Rock's bragging about his abuse of women should have been a sign of things to come. But I was lost in staring at the curves of his shoulders, chest, and arms. I hardly noticed when he handed me the rest of his ice cream.

If Slide Step had two sides to him—a public and private side—Rock had only one: asshole. He never spent any time with me, and whenever I was forced to have sex with him—I would pretend he was somebody else. Anyone, it didn't matter who. I'd come to despise him that much. Afterward, he would talk about girls and pussy and anything else he could think of to emphasize his masculinity. And then he'd say something stupid like, "Why don't you go off and swing on a dick somewhere."

The only time Rock ever looked me in the eyes was when he was probing for something he could fuck with me about later. Once he found something, he'd get a smirk on his face like he couldn't wait to go back and tell his friends. I tried not to give him the satisfaction, so I'd laugh it off, like I thought it was funny, but he always seemed to see right through me. Right before he was released, he traded me to a black guy for a carton of cigarettes.

The school and the library became my sanctuaries. The Department of Corrections announced that at the end of the year, they were phasing out regular high school, so starting in January; inmates could take only a GED (General Equivalency Diploma). I kicked into gear and completed all the modules I needed to graduate and finished my senior year with As in all subjects. I graduated first in my class (of one).

I'm sure the program was watered down for inmates, but I took advantage of classes and finished high school the same year I would have back home. Hill Top High School, Class of '78. It was named for the school at the Michigan Reformatory, which sat on top of a hill.

I gave up thinking about family and home and memories of happier times. It wasn't working any more, so instead I thought more and more about what it would be like when I got out. In the library, I read magazines and dreamed about my future. *Time* magazine ran an article about the discothèques in New York City, where I'd never been. There was a picture of a gay bar that had hundreds of men, and I got excited. It seems hard to believe now, but that was the first glimpse I had of the possibilities for gay men outside of a prison.

By and large, the men at MTU were young and sexy. All the good-looking bad boys in the state of Michigan had ended up there it seemed. But however sexy they may have been, I wasn't enjoying any of it. Sex was an unpleasant task, and I would have to slip outside of myself whenever I was forced to have it. After a while, it was a constant struggle to stay present at all. Yet I needed to stay alert to the constant threats. In my mind, I was always racing ahead—calculating the possibility for danger—looking for an out or an exit. Or I was going backward—replaying conversations and scenarios, scanning for something I might have missed that could come back and hurt me.

It was ironic that while I was at Riverside, I wished I could be among younger men. Now that I was, I wanted to get back to the other side. I didn't have many friends to begin with, so when Rock traded me to a black guy, it made matters worse. Now none of the white guys would have anything to do with me. But I got good at pretending I didn't notice their hostility toward me. Though there were one or two guys with whom I'd occasionally share a prolonged stare—and then we'd slip off and meet in an empty bathroom. The sex helped bring me into the present, but it was never a mutual transaction, and it rarely lasted long. Then I'd retreat back inside myself to hide in that place where no one in there would ever see my true feelings—all the fear and insecurities that I always carried with me.

The black guy that Rock had sold me to was named Moseley. He was the inmate from the bullpen at the county jail, who had been annoyed that I'd never seen a cockroach before. The first time I saw him at MTU, I was horrified. He was standing back from the urinal, with his hand on his hip, staring at me coldly, as he took a piss. His dick, which was soft at that moment, was larger than any I had ever seen. It looked like a small elephant trunk—and he wasn't shy about showing it off. I walked out of the bathroom thinking, he'll never get that barrel near me.

Moseley met Rock in the weight pit, where he and others spent their time bulking up. When Moseley had first appeared at my room, to tell me that he was now my man, he nearly filled the frame of the doorway. He had broad shoulders and a thick neck, but his legs and waist were smaller, and out of proportion with the rest of his body. He once showed me his ID, which included a photo taken when he first came to prison; he looked almost as thin as me. "No one is as skinny as your bony ass," he said. And he was probably right. Far from bulking up, I'd lost weight since coming there. When my street clothes arrived, they hung loosely on me.

Sharon had finally sent my clothes—at least the ones that were left after her sons raided my closets. I felt self-conscious when an inmate commented on how "cocky" I was acting now that I was wearing street clothes. There was something depressing about wearing state blues—and I wasn't the only one whose spirits lifted a little after putting on his street clothes.

Moseley was heartless when it came to sex. He didn't care the slightest that his dick was agony for me. And the only saving grace I had was that he was leaving in a few weeks to go to the Corrections Center.

In a strange twist of irony, the way Moseley had ripped open my rectum, may have saved my life from contracting AIDS a few years later when HIV infection became so prevalent in the early 1980s—especially considering the self-destructive ways I was acting out then with drugs and booze.

Had it not been for those times I shared with Slide Step at Riverside, I don't think I could have survived those first few months at MTU. I searched for what it was that I got from him, but I couldn't put it into words. Yet I knew it was a lot more than what I was getting from Moseley. I couldn't show Moseley what I was feeling inside. To show that, would have invited more attacks—if for nothing more than his passing entertainment. So I pretended nothing bothered me, and in time I got so good at it, I could fool even myself.

Each time I went to the bathroom following sex, I would start bleeding. The doctor at MTU sent me over to the infirmary at Riverside, to see the visiting proctologist. When they brought me over in the van, and we made our way up the winding landscaped drive, past the small watermill and a sunken garden—I thought about asking the hospital staff if they could keep me there. I had filed several grievances, requesting a transfer back to Riverside, but the response was always the same: Without a disciplinary reason or compelling need for protection, your request is denied. If I were to complain of being raped, I would have to tell them who it was that were raping me.

"I'd kill a fucking snitch," I'd heard said many times. It was one of the few sentiments that crossed all racial lines.

When I got there, someone quickly sent word to Slide Step, who ran right over.

"Are you all right?" He yelled up from the courtyard, to me at the window. I could see his breath in the winter air.

"Uh-huh," I nodded. Seeing him made me miss the place more. "MTU sucks," I shouted to him, "They won't let me come back."

"That's what I hear, Squeeze."

"I miss it here," I said. And I missed hearing him call me Squeeze, but I couldn't say that out loud. It would have taken too much for me to go there, and I think Slide Step knew this. He felt the same way. And though we were now each in separate prisons, we both still lived in a world that prohibited the expression of feelings.

He looked up and nodded at me. "You just don't know, Squeeze."

We stood there another moment, until the nurse came out and called me into the office. A guard walked up to Slide Step threatening him with a ticket for being out of place. He waved at me and backed away.

Loneliness, which had long been my boyhood friend, was starting to suffocate me.

The proctologist placed a long, metal tube-like instrument on the tray next to the examining table. I asked what he intended to do with it. It looked like a telescope, with an eyepiece on one end and a small light built-in to the tip at the other end.

"It's not any worse than what's been going up there," he half-joked, but when he saw I wasn't smiling, he looked as though he regretted saying it. He cranked a knob at the side of the table and one end folded down and receded into a place to kneel on. "Get up here and bend forward over the table," he said. "This shouldn't hurt much. The position will make it easier for you." He squeezed some K-Y jelly onto his gloved finger and then massaged the opening of my ass. I could feel my body tense up, because I wasn't sure I could trust him, but like everything else, there wasn't a whole lot I could do about it. It felt humiliating, but he was right—it wasn't anything worse than what I had already been through.

"Listen, I understand," he said, when he was finished examining me. "You guys are young and all full of hormones."

I looked down at the floor. My hopes of his helping me were quickly dashed. He was wrong—he didn't understand. How could this man not see what had happened to me?

I had a fissure, a tear on the rectum wall, but it wasn't so serious that I would need stitching or surgery. "I want you to take a sitz bath with Epsom salts, and use this medicine I give you. And try not to irritate any more for the next couple of weeks."

Did he think I had any control over the situation? I just nodded and looked away.

When I got back from Riverside, Moseley wasn't happy with the doctor's orders, but since they were moving me to A-unit to be next to the infirmary, there was nothing he could do about it. Inmates weren't allowed inside the other units and so now maybe, he wouldn't be able to run my life. I avoided the yard as much as possible. On a good day, Moseley was as thorny as the barbed wire fence that surrounded the prison, but now that he couldn't fuck me, he had become enraged. I was counting the days until he left for the corrections center—a halfway house out in the world. There were twenty-three to go.

"What are you going to do when you get there?" someone asked.

"I'm gonna hang with this boy I used to own," Moseley said.

"A fag?" his friend asked.

"Fags got money too," he said. He didn't care I was standing right there.

When Moseley made me meet him in one of the bathrooms at the school, I received another misconduct for being out of place. So when I went to my hearing for the ticket, the hearing officer asked if I was having problems with Moseley.

"He has a reputation for harassing younger inmates," the hearing officer said. "Do you want to tell me about it?"

I shook my head. This time, I couldn't bear to look at the Inmate Advocate. He frowned and I knew suddenly that he was on to me. "OK then, five days top lock. And if you're caught again, we're gonna take a look at your good time."

At least it would be five days I wouldn't have to meet Moseley at chow.

After serving my five-day sentence, I was standing at the bulletin board looking at the menu, when someone appeared beside me. I'd become accustomed to ignoring people unless they put their hands on me, so I paid no attention to him. I finished reading the dinner menu and finally looked over. It was young Paul, from Riverside. Taylor's boy.

"Hey, Squeeze!"

"Hey, Paul! What are you doing here?"

"Freedom, man." His green eyes were sparkling. "Freedom," he repeated.

"When did you get here?"

"Just now. I heard you were here, so I cracked on the housing officer to get me over here."

"No kidding?" I was surprised, given how indifferent he was to me at Riverside.

"Square business," he said. He was almost beaming.

I wondered if he was just relieved to see someone here that he knew.

Paul King was nineteen years old, serving a ten-to-twenty for armed robbery. He'd been down since 1976, so he was now into his third year. Since he'd reached five years from his first out date, they lowered him to medium-security.

"How do you feel about it?" I asked.

"It feels fuckin' great. Are you kidding?"

"We'll see if you still feel that way after a few weeks in this motherfucker," I said.

"Count time," the guard yelled, from the desk at the axis of the two open-tiers.

Count times at MTU were identical to Riverside's. We had to go to our rooms while the guards came around counting heads. It took about thirty minutes to clear us.

"You can tell me all about it at chow," he said. "Let's meet up and we'll walk over together."

"OK," I said.

I met Paul right after count, and we walked together to chow. I was suppose to hang back and wait for Moseley, who was in C-unit, but every now and then the guards would catch me loitering and order me to move along. So I went in with Paul and decided to tell Moseley that guards had ordered me inside.

Paul talked the whole way to chow, as if he'd just been in solitary and hadn't seen anyone for days. Paul was such a chatterbox that it was hard to slip a word in. But I enjoyed his company and was happy to listen to him. He seemed just as eager to have someone to talk to, but later on when he settled in, he confessed that he was nervous. He said he had wanted to get next to me from the moment he first saw me.

"I thought you didn't like me," I said.

"Slide Step wouldn't let me anywhere near you."

"That's not true," I said. "He'd let me mess with other boys."

"Not me," he said. "He knew I'd try to snatch you away from him."

I smiled. He was acting like I didn't know that he was a boy, too. "How's Taylor doing?" I asked.

"He's all right," he said. Shaking it off, like Taylor didn't mean anything to him. "Taylor and Chet got locked up for some stupid shit they pulled with a guard. They had him moving drugs for 'em, and then they snitched him out—hoping to get time taken off their sentence."

"I was there when it happened," I said. "Are they still in the hole?"

"Yep. They were out for a little while, but Slide Step made the bitches lock up." After they had tried to doublecross Slide Step, he wasn't going to let them walk the yard anymore. So they were forced into protective custody.

I smiled again, but I was smiling not so much because Chet was locked up but because of the way Paul was talking so tough. Not that he was ever feminine, but he was talking a lot of shit for someone who had had a man at least once.

"You know a lot of people thought Taylor was my man. And he was," he said, "but I ran that. These motherfuckers just don't know."

"Don't know what?"

"I'll explain it later," he said.

Moseley stopped at our table. "What happened to you?"

I looked up and felt my face burn with embarrassment. Paul was the closest thing I'd had to a friend since I got here, and now Moseley was taking charge.

"The guards made me go inside," I said.

He just stood there and watched me.

"Moseley!" one of the guards next to the window yelled. "Let's go!"

I looked at Paul and back to Moseley again. Paul stared down at his tray and then looked away. Moseley was now eyeing Paul, too.

"Let's go Moseley," the guard repeated.

"Wait for me outside," Moseley said to me. "I want to talk to you."

Paul glared at him as he walked away. "Don't take that shit from nobody," he said, finally. "You are way better than these motherfuckers."

I looked down at my tray. My half-roasted chicken looked raw and picked-at.

When I first sat down with Paul, I hadn't anticipated the reaction I got from Moseley. And yet, at the same time, there was something in the way that Paul spoke to me, that sparked hope. I was so close to being at the end of a rope. It was probably the closest I'd ever been to considering suicide.

When the guard released our section, we dumped our trays and walked out together. Moseley stared at us as we walked past.

I stopped outside the chow hall door and lit a cigarette.

"You got another one of those," Paul asked. I handed him one and lit it for him.

"Let's go," he said.

"I can't. I have to wait for Moseley."

"No you don't." Paul sounded incensed. "Fuck that!" He grabbed my arm.

I hesitated. "C'mon," he said. "I'll show you how this game is played."

I looked back at the door for a second, and then went along with him, my heart pounding. "He's going to the Correction Center in a couple of weeks," I said.

"Even better," he said. "You can't let these bitches run you like that, Tim. Believe me, I know. Stick with me, and I'll teach you. You'll be having these motherfuckers eatin' out of your hand."

I'm not sure why I went off with him. I looked at him and hoped he wasn't bullshitting me, but Paul's face was proud, unflinching, and his eyes were bright and full of fire.

"So," he said. "I hear you like to suck dick."

I stopped suddenly, and my smile disappeared.

"Relax!" He grinned. "So do I!" He shook his head and frowned. "C'mon, silly rabbit. I'll show you."

He hooked his arm inside of mine and led me into A-unit.

28

Consider Yourself Part of the Family

The first time I saw a live musical was at Adams Junior High School. It was Oliver Twist, *starring Tim Blankenship—a fellow seventh grader. They gave two recitals during the day for faculty and students, with two more at night for family and friends. I was neither in the cast nor crew; so after sitting through three of the first four performances, it should have been an early clue that something was amiss.*

I had arrived early for each show and sat up front on the carpeting of the school's multipurpose room, eagerly awaiting that moment right after a cast member would sing, "Boy For Sale," and as Tim Blankenship climbed up on the coffin (loaned to the Drama Department by a local funeral home) and started singing, "Where is Love?" The tears welled up—in both of our eyes—as parents and teachers whispered all around us, "What a good looking and talented actor Tim was and how he looked like he was almost crying!"

It was the first time I was called a fag at school.

I lay there staring up at the bottom of Paul's mattress. Like at Riverside, we had sex under our beds with the sheets and blankets pulled down on the sides to hide from view. Paul was small, and I was skinny so we fit there comfortably. "How did you get the extra pillows?" I asked. My head was resting on two and there was another on top of his bed. "I know the quartermaster from M-R," Paul bragged.

His short whiskers tickled my skin. He was lying on his side, with his arm draped across my chest, and his right leg bent over mine. My arm felt natural resting on his shoulders and back. I wanted to cuddle up to sleep like that, and then maybe I could finally escape the nightmares that had been haunting me since the county jail.

It was the first time someone had satisfied me, the way I had been forced to satisfy others. And it was completely consensual. I just wish it could have lasted longer. Paul was a magician the way he worked his tongue and lips. And there was something very generous in the way he touched me. I offered to return the favor but he gently pushed me back down on the blanket, saying that it was OK—maybe next time.

"You're funny," he said, "the way you wiggle and shake."

"It gets real sensitive," I said. "I can't help it."

"I know, but I've never seen anyone shiver like that."

I smiled. Paul was amazing, and I didn't know it was possible for someone to make you feel that good. This seemed to go beyond the physical—because my whole being felt tasted and satisfied. For a moment, I felt like pouring my guts out to him, because I finally felt like I'd found a friend that understood me, but I was still feeling cautious.

"Haven't you ever had sex with someone you enjoyed?" Paul asked.

"Once," I said, thinking about Brett. "Well, maybe twice, but that one's a secret."

"Who?"

"Uh-uh. My Dad always said a guy who'll tell on himself would tell on anybody."

"C'mon. Who?" Paul leaned up on his elbow and looked at me.

"Scatter," I said.

"How was he?"

I smiled.

"Cut or uncut?"

"Huh?"

"Was he circumcised?" he asked.

I didn't know what he was talking about.

"This," Paul said, pulling on his foreskin.

"Oh, that's what you call that."

Everyone in my high school must have been circumcised. Before coming to prison, I'd never seen that extra skin there and it never really came up in conversations back home.

We heard heavy footsteps approaching and the sound of jangling keys. Paul tensed up and the pounding of my heart increased under his weight. The sound grew louder as it neared and we lifted our heads toward the door. We almost jumped when he heard the squelch of the guard's walkie-talkie. The noise continued past our door then faded down the hall.

Paul put his head back down on my chest. We were good until the 9:30 count. The other inmates were down in the day room watching TV, or in the card room playing pinochle or spades. I still wasn't out of Moseley's clutches, but he was in another unit, and I wouldn't have to contend with him until the next day.

"Don't you wish we could double-bunk?" I whispered.

"With my luck," Paul said, "I'd get an inmate with funky feet."

"Who snores all night," I added. "And farts in his sleep."

We both laughed.

"Shhh," Paul said. The guard was coming back up the hall.

After he passed, Paul said we'd better slip back out again. If the guard were counting heads, he'd notice us missing.

The guards changed shifts during the 9:30 count, and we were let back out again until 11:15. Lights out was at 11:30.

Inmates started their job assignments or school by 8:30 in the morning, and we weren't allowed back inside our housing units until 3:30 or 4:00. The afternoon count was at 4:30, and dinner was between 5:30 and 6:00 P.M.

When the weather was good, we were allowed a couple hours of yard in the evenings, but we had to be back by 8:30. The yard was in the back of the prison, which you accessed through a gate next to the gym. In the winter, the yard was closed, and inmates used the inner walkways to go to and from the gym, which also housed the store.

The next day, I was sent to Classification to receive my next job assignment. Since I had finished high school, I now needed a job. I had signed up for college, but that was considered extra, which I would have to attend in the evenings, in lieu of open recreation. One of the classes I signed up for was Corrections 101 where I learned that if I attended college courses while in prison, statistically speaking, my odds of coming back there was less than a third of that of other inmates. Some guards seemed resentful toward us going to college, as if we were undeserving of school or were taking something away from them. But only a few seemed to feel this way—and anyway, it didn't matter—since I was determined to never come back here again.

Miss Bain, the Classification Director, had her office in the school. She was a young black woman, and the inmates were crazy about her. Not that she did anything to garner their attention, other than being a beautiful woman who worked inside a prison that was filled with horny men.

"Gee, Miss Bain," an inmate said to her, once. "You sure look pretty."

"That's very nice," she said. "But I don't really need to hear that now. Do I?"

As rumor had it, the inmate was assigned to the kitchen for the rest of his stay, washing enormous pots and pans. With over eight hundred inmates to feed every day, he was kept busy.

As I made my way to Miss Bain's office one day, Moseley saw me coming and headed over to me. He had sent word to me that morning, via an inmate who told me Moseley was angry with me for not waiting for him after chow the night before.

"Don't let him try to blame it on the guards," Moseley told the inmate. "'Cause I saw him run off with that redheaded hood rat from Hamtramack."

When I saw Moseley on the walkway, I picked up my pace and tried to get to the school without making it seem obvious I was trying to avoid him.

Moseley cut me off before I reached the building. "Don't even try it, bitch."

"Moseley!" a guard yelled from around the corner. We both looked up. It was C.O. Miller. "Get your ass over here!"

He ordered Moseley around like a dog, which he knew he could get away with since he knew Moseley was about to go home. Even one ticket could delay his release.

When it came to the enforcement of rules, each guard was slightly different. Some would issue a warning or two before they wrote you up, while others, like the newer guards—would give you a ticket right away. But it also depended on who the inmates was, as well. If he were a known trouble maker, even the more lenient guards would write him up for a minor infraction, while a stricter guard might let something slide for inmates who kept to themselves and didn't cause problems.

It was a game everyone learned how to play, and the longer either side was there, the better they got at playing it. The guards were understaffed anyway, so they couldn't possibly enforce all the rules. If they did, the inmates would probably revolt—so it was a constant balance. Yet as an inmate got closer to parole, the guards had maximum leverage, which is why C.O. Miller was able to talk to Moseley like that.

Moseley pointed his finger at me. "I'll deal with you later."

I tried to pretend like I didn't know what he was talking about, but it was obvious to both of us. I dashed into the building. I should have waited for him the night before. I knew there would be a penalty, but I left anyway. Now what was I going to do?

Miss Bain's skin was a light brown color and her eyes were bright and expressive. She reminded me of Diahann Carroll, the actress that played Julia on TV.

Like the other professionals and administrative staff, she wore no uniform. Instead, she had on a dark brown suit, with a gold and turquoise blouse. She smiled at me, and told me to have a seat. As I'd find out later, she had majored in social work but when she graduated from college, jobs were scarce—so she went to work in corrections. She brought her passion for making a difference to the position, and so she stood out among the others. Meeting her for the first time, I doubted right away the rumor about her sending that guy to the kitchen.

"How are you?" She smiled.

"Fine," I said. "And you?" I was surprised to meet anyone this gracious.

"Very well, thank you." She read through my folder. "A Photo Mat, huh?"

I nodded and looked down at the floor. "It was pretty stupid, I know."

"Congratulations on your high school diploma, Tim."

She called me, Tim, and I almost beamed inside. It was a simple thing, but it felt so nice to be called by my first name.

"Have you given any thoughts about what you'd like to do next?"

"Not really," I said. "But I don't want to be in the kitchen."

She grinned. "Nobody ever wants to work the kitchen. Do you have any skills?"

Prison jobs varied anywhere from 41 cents to a dollar a day. So if your haircut came out lousy, or your eggs were burned and green—it was probably because some asshole had overstated his qualifications in order to get one of the better-paying jobs.

"I can type."

"Really?" She looked up at me.

"Uh-huh. I took it up in seventh grade."

"How well do you type?"

"About sixty words a minutes, without errors. Faster if I'm allowed a few." I was exaggerating a little, but I really could type.

"Can you write? I'm starting a prison newspaper, and I need writers."

"I keep a journal," I said.

"OK, I'd like to see a sample from you."

"On what?"

"Well, I don't know. What do you like to write about?"

I didn't know what to say. I blushed at the thought of what I'd like to write about.

"What?" she said.

"Oh, nothing," I said. I hated that I blushed so easily. "Can I think about it?"

"Sure. Can you get something to me by this Friday?" And with that, I bounced from her office. The prison newspaper! But what would I write about? I wanted to write about her—how she talked to me like a real person and how that made me feel. How nice it was to be called by my first name and how it was to believe that I was human again, in that little interchange. And that's exactly what I wrote about. I wrote about what a difference it made to be treated with dignity in a place that didn't seem to value it much. I wrote about how it elevated the spirit and how much that meant to me. I'm sure it wasn't well written, but she hired me anyway.

"Hood rat!" Paul said. "What the fuck is a hood rat?" He was incensed. "And I ain't from Hamtramack either. I grew up in Wayne."

Wayne was the town next to mine. Paul and I would have gone to the same high school, had he not dropped out and gone to prison. "How dare that motherfucker!"

"I don't know what I'm going to do, Paul. He looked like he was about to hit me."

"Listen, I'll take care of it," he said. "Don't you worry about nothing."

"Yeah right," I said. "What are you going to do? Blow him?"

"He's not my type," Paul said, "but don't worry, he's not gonna bother you again."

"You talk a lot of shit for someone who weighs about 120 pounds— *soaking wet.*"

"I'll kick your bony ass," he said.

"Oh now you're a big fuckin' man. If you're so fuckin' tough, why were you Taylor's boy?"

"Because I was raped," he said to me.

I didn't know how to respond.

"And because I'm gay," he said, finally. "That's why."

I stood there foolishly, wishing I hadn't said what I had.

"And like I said, pretty boy. You're not gonna have to worry about Moseley. Trust me. I'll take care of it at lunch."

As we walked to lunch, Moseley was waiting for me in front of the chow hall. They alternated the order the units were called to the chow.

"Wait here," Paul said and he walked up to Moseley. "Can I talk to you?" he said.

Moseley looked down at him without responding.

"Seriously," Paul said. "It'll only take a minute."

The two of them walked off, and I could see Paul talking to him in an animated way, with his hands making all kinds of gestures, but since they were going in the other direction, I couldn't hear what they were saying. As usual, Paul was doing all the talking. A moment later, they turned around and started to walk back. Frightened, I quickly went inside the chow hall.

The line split into two sides as it approached the metal serving trays. I inched my way to the left, and Paul came up beside me. Moseley went to the other side.

"It's taken care of," Paul said.

"What?"

Moseley was now getting his food directly across from me, and though he knew I was standing there—he wouldn't look at me.

After we sat down, I asked, "What did you say to him?"

"Don't worry about it."

"No! What did you say?"

Paul refused to tell me until we got back to our unit. I could tell by looking at him, that he wasn't going to budge. Not knowing was driving me crazy.

"Ever been to New York?" I asked, changing the subject.

"I went to Chicago once."

I was still thinking about the article I read in the prison library about the gay discos. I remembered how the guys in picture didn't seem like queens at all—they looked like Paul and me—though they were older.

"Ever go to a gay bar?" I asked.

"Nah. I wasn't old enough. Shit, I turned eighteen in here. But I'd like to, though. Gays are the only people in the world that have to go out and find their own tribe."

I remembered how I responded to disco music the first time I heard it. And now, how surprised I was to learn that it had originated in gay clubs. I wondered if it was some kind of weird subliminal mating call that drew gay men to New York.

The other two inmates at our table got up and left.

As soon as they were out of earshot, Paul leaned over and said, "I told Moseley you were about to go to The Man."

"You told him I'd snitch!" I nearly shouted, outraged that Paul had put me in jeopardy.

Several inmates looked up from the other tables.

"Why did you do that?" I demanded.

"Because he ain't gonna do nothin', that's why. He's leaving in a few weeks, and he's not about to do anything that will get his Correction Center pulled."

"So you made me out to be a snitch?"

"No, I didn't make you out to be a snitch. You didn't snitch on anybody. I just told him that you were about to."

"Isn't that the same thing?"

"Nope. Listen Tim, around here. It's not what you do. It's what these motherfucker's think you're going to do. Perception is 99 percent of the law.

It's not how you act, it's how they think you're going to act. How you carry yourself is **99** percent of reality."

I stared at him, not knowing what to think. "What about his friends?"

"Well, I'm gonna teach you how to play on these motherfuckers," he said.

"Play them?"

"Play on them," he corrected.

"Play on them for what?"

"You have to learn how to work these motherfuckers. Turn the shit around on their ass. It's the only way to survive in here. Especially if you're a young, pretty motherfucker like you or me."

Paul paused for a second and stared at me.

It was a lot to take in at once, and it was pretty shocking for me to see someone my own age who was as wise as Paul was. I also felt encouraged. He not only knew how to work the system, but he knew he was gay and was open about it.

"Listen, I didn't make up this game. These motherfucker's did, and so I'm just a player in it and I don't have a choice. Not if I don't want to keep getting pounded like a piece of meat. It's play or be played, so fuck 'em baby boy, you play on these motherfuckers to get some control."

He took a bite of his macaroni and cheese and smiled at me.

"Listen, I can sit around all day long feeling sorry for myself. Pissin' and moaning about how unfair it all is—but it ain't gonna change a fuckin' thing. After chow, I'm still sitting up in this motherfucker and in this situation. But hey! We're not talking about a bunch of PhDs around here either. Fuck, half these guys can't even read. I know I'm smarter than they are—so how do I turn it around on their silly ass?"

I knew he was right, but I still didn't know how to play them. For Paul, it seemed deeper than just defending himself—it was as if his whole identity was at stake. Or perhaps it was his dignity. If Paul had nothing else, he had his self-respect. He was proud of who he was, and that was worth learning how to play the game.

It was consistent with what Black Diamond had said, about having to learn how to work it if I didn't want have keep happening what's been happening.

Paul was right. I hated being the one getting fucked all the time. Plus, I wanted to know how he learned to accept himself.

Paul's hair was straight and long, and he kept it pulled back into a ponytail. His cheekbones were high, and his chin dimpled. He had both a feminine and masculine edge.

I was different from him. I wasn't proud of who I was, and I still felt responsible for all that happened to me. My secret fantasies had drawn me to prison in the first place—but I was too young and dumb to see the reality that laid ahead. Shame and guilt continued to haunt me.

Up until then, sex had remained an unpleasant obligation. I did it because I had to in order to survive. Yet some parts of me, liked it, which only added to my seventeen-year-old confusion. I could never say out loud that I enjoyed any of it. Some parts of it I liked, but I never thought I would be able to admit it to anyone. Paul on the other hand seemed to adapt easily to prison life. Confident. Self-assured. He knew who he was and what he was doing. He was in control.

When it came to being fucked, I still hated it, even with Paul, though I only did it once with Paul—to please him. With Slide Step, I rolled my hips, because it eased the pain, and gave me something else to think about other than his battering-ram dick. It was always painful, especially when he first entered me, but Slide Step went slowly and the pain eventually eased. He enjoyed it, and I wanted to please him because of the attention he showed me afterward. Paul didn't like it when I rolled my hips. He preferred it if I just lay there. It was more difficult for me without the rolling motion, and it forced me to be present with the uncomfortable pressure.

"Relax," Paul kept saying.

"I am," I said, with hardly enough air inside of me to speak.

Paul stopped, and for a brief second could sense his frustration. He kissed me on the neck and ran his nose through the curls of my hair. It mixed with my sweat and tickled my ear. But it was no use. I was still too tense and shifted under his weight. I had no meat on my bones so my hip cut through the blanket and felt pinched on the concrete floor. It also gave me flashbacks of Moseley and Nate, Loud Mouth, and Red.

"Shh," Paul whispered, "and just relax." I felt him twitch inside me. "Shh," he repeated, and for a moment the ache almost went away.

I didn't want to get fucked, but I felt I had to please Paul. And besides, I looked forward to his blowjobs. Paul delighted in giving them to me, and

I enjoyed receiving them. All in all, it was a fair trade. Or at least the fairest of those I had received to date.

To get through sex with Rock, I would pretend he was someone else, but that only worked a few times. I'd slip free of my body, allowing my consciousness to drift someplace else. Anyplace but in the present moment. But Paul made me want to stay present. Unlike all the others, he doted on me, which made me want to be with him. He was interested in me, and he worked hard to please me. For the first time, someone was pleasing me, and I wanted to feel it.

Paul said I was the only person he had ever been able to cum with—I don't know why that was, but he said coming had never before been that important. He never asked to fuck me again, and when I offered, he said that was OK. It made me feel guilty, knowing how much he liked it, but it never stopped me from accepting his continued blowjobs.

My favorite time with Paul was usually after sex—when we cuddled on the floor, under his bed and talked.

Paul's parents were abusive. We compared notes, and the stories of his childhood made me feel grateful I grew up in the house I did.

"I started running away from home when I was seven years old," he said. His eyes stared off into nowhere as he spoke. It took him some time to confide in me, but he eventually shared that his older brother had been abusing him—sexually.

"I was sent to Star Commonwealth for Boys at ten years old, and BTS— Boys Training School when I was twelve." He said it like he was proud of it, almost sitting up taller with each graduation to the next level of incarceration. "I came to the joint at seventeen." But then he started to shrink again. "My mom was violent and beat me, and my dad was hardly ever home. Out drinkin' somewhere or getting laid by some whore. When he did come home, he was always drunk, and then he'd get verbally abusive."

"Like how?"

He shrugged.

"How?" I repeated, wondering how his father compared to mine.

"I could take his punches," he said, softly. "But when he called me a queer, his little cocksucker—it was like he'd punched my lights out without having to lift a finger."

I wanted to ask him how he knew Paul was gay, since he didn't act like it. But I could tell it would have been useless to probe. Paul kept that part of himself at arm's length.

Instead, Paul shook it off and slid his face down my stomach—the sharp bristles of his stubble scrapping my skin.

"It's why we have to go out and create our own families," Paul said.

He was lying on my chest again, and I stroked his back and caressed his long wet hair. The smell of spent sex hung heavy in the air, trapped under the bed by the blankets used to conceal us.

The springs of his bed above were familiar to me now. The squiggly curves reminded me of the lines my mother used to make on the side of the cakes she baked. When I was a young boy, I remembered she'd let me lick the spoons and the mixers, until my belly ached from too much sugar. She was so good in the kitchen that my aunts used to tell her she should open a bakery. Mom made the cakes, and my Aunt Patsy was known for her pies.

"Do you think you'd ever like to have kids," I asked.

"No way," he said.

"Why not?"

"I'm not into pussy for one," he said.

"Ever have it?"

"Yeah, but the girl I had it with wasn't the best example," Paul said. "And besides, I wouldn't want to bring a kid into this world, no-how."

"Why not?"

"Who'd want to bring a kid into this rotten world?" He kissed my belly. "Anyway, I've already got my baby."

I smiled, and stared back up at the springs.

"I'd like to have a kid," I said, "and I think I'd like to learn how to bake."

29

The Oracle

I was amazed that one word could be worth so many points.

"Mongrels?" Sharon said. "What the hell are mongrels?"

"I don't know. I read it in the newspaper." Mayor Hubbard told some New York paper he didn't think whites should have to live with blacks because it would lead to mongrels. "Whatever they are, it's worth 117 points."

"It is not," Sharon said. But it was, because the word spanned two red premium squares, which meant you tripled the score, and then tripled it again, plus I had a double letter count on "G". (13 x 3 x 3 = 117).

"And," I said, now nearly gloating, "I get 50 bonus points for using seven letters in a single play!"

I loved Scrabble!

"Go to bed," Sharon said. "It's past your bedtime, anyway." But that was only after she challenged my word and forfeited a turn.

"It doesn't say I have know what it means. It just has to be a word."

"Well, just get your ass in bed," she said.

It took a long time to fall asleep that night because I couldn't stop smiling. I learned a valuable lesson—that even if I didn't know what something meant—it paid to study the rules of the game.

Sharon was pissed, and for once I had finally beaten her!

We decided to name the prison newspaper *The Oracle*. Spaulding, our editor, had found the word in Webster's Dictionary. He read us the definition and everyone agreed it was perfect because it reminded us of Miss Bain. An oracle is a person (as a priestess of ancient Greece) through whom a deity is believed to speak—a person giving wise or authoritative opinions.

Spaulding had worked closely with Miss Bain to pick the team of five reporters, an assistant editor, and me. I was hired as the administrative assistant. I'd never held a real job, much less one with a title, so I was especially excited to take part in the project. Four of us were white, and four were black.

When Miss Bain first assembled us, she handed everyone brand new journals and said that we each brought something unique to the paper. She wanted us to share our unique experiences, something no one before had ever asked me to do. She told us Warden Handlon wanted the paper to win an award for prison newspapers and that he instructed her to hire the best and brightest at MTU.

Josh, the white guy I knew from Riverside, was our legal writer. He was studying to become a paralegal and worked in the law library. I hated him for setting me up with Rock when I first arrived at MTU, but I wasn't going to let that stop me from advancing myself.

Spaulding was also white, and the oldest among us, had worked on a newspaper at Jackson prison. At twenty-four, he was older than most inmates at MTU. No one knew why he was there, since MTU was for inmates who were under twenty-one. The rumor was that he had snitched while on the North Side of Jackson. Warden Handlon believed that anyone who had served time in Jackson didn't belong at MTU, since its focus was on younger inmates who still had a chance of reforming. But Spaulding was a college graduate, and his experience on the newspaper must have had something to do with him joining us. Miss Bain said that Warden Handlon was the type of man who once he set his mind to something, like winning the National Penal Press Award, he'd stop at nothing to accomplish it.

I was the youngest on the team and the only homosexual, which is why (I believe) the others hassled me about working on the newspaper.

"*She's* going to fuck it up for the rest of us," O. J. said.

O. J. was one of the reporters. He looked like the then-famous football player who appeared in rental car ads on TV, but that isn't how this O. J. got his name; he'd tell us many times. He was Otis Junior, the fifth or sixth *junior* in a row.

"My daddy was Junior, and my granddaddy they called June Bug, so they named me O. J. —long before that other nigger won the Heisman trophy."

I stared at him in confusion.

"See!" he said. "She probably doesn't even know what I'm talking about."

"I'm not a she," I said. "I've got a dick."

He and the others shot me a dirty look.

"Watch your language, bitch. Can't you see there's a lady here?"

I looked up and saw Miss Bain standing in the doorway.

"Sorry, Miss Bain. I don't like being called a girl."

She nodded at me and glanced disapprovingly at the others.

"Whatever you are," Rodney said, "None of us want you messing it up for us."

"What are you talking about?" I asked.

By being on the newspaper, we were granted free access throughout the prison, to follow up on news stories, but the other guys were worried that I would ruin that by getting caught having sex in one of the units.

"If you get caught," O. J. said, "they'll take that privilege from all of us."

"I'm not looking to do anything!" I wanted to ask, "What about you guys?" Who's to say they wouldn't be out raping a fish or forcing some gay guy to blow them?

"All right," Miss Bain said. "You can knock all that off right now."

"I'll knock it off," Lee said, his eyes trying to check out my ass.

The others laughed, and Lee winked at me.

I was angered by how they'd pick on me one minute and then the next, turn nice and ask if I'd go off and have sex. But of course that only meant my servicing them.

"Now we can let go of stereotypes while your working with me," Miss Bain said. She walked in and sat on the edge of a desk. "I've hired Tim because he can type, better than anyone in here, and because he has shown some other talent . . ."

"Yeah, we know about that," O. J. said.

"I said that's enough!" Miss Bain sounded annoyed, but she didn't raise her voice. She didn't have to. These guys wanted to stay in her good graces.

"I can't believe how you all are treating him!"

O. J. and the others shifted in their seats.

"I would expect some of you, at least, to have some sensitivity to prejudice and discrimination."

"It's not the same thing," O. J. started to say, but Miss Bain cut him off. "Yes it is. It's not black and white, or even a gay/straight thing, it's. . ."

"It's in the Bible," O. J. said.

"And we all know how closely you live your lives by that."

O. J. smiled.

"The Bible also condones slavery. Did you know that?"

"Hey Miss Bain?" Lee said. "Why are you sticking up for fags?"

She stood up and closed the door. "Open your journals, gentlemen, and write down these words: Hate and Ignorance. As reporters, you're going to need to know the precise meaning of words."

She sat on the edge of her desk. "This is not about homosexuality, Lee, its about hate and ignorance, and though you may think you know what those things mean, I want you to look them up anyway. As long as we keep focusing on where something is landing, instead of what it is that's being tossed about, we're going to keep missing the point."

A couple guys nodded.

"Whatever Tim's lifestyle is, is of no concern to me." She looked around the room. "Now this isn't just another job assignment, and if you came here because you wanted a free pass throughout the prison, tell me right now. I'm sure we can find something else for you to do—in the kitchen."

Spaulding started to say something, but Sherry Bain held up her hand.

"Now listen to me, because I only want to have this talk once. While you're working with me, I expect you to behave like gentlemen, which means I expect you to treat each other respect and with some degree of dignity." She glanced over at me.

"Words can be a powerful weapon, but as gentlemen, I'll expect you to leave some of that out there on the yard. Because I don't really need to be hearing about your bitches and ho's and fags and . . . some of those other things." She looked at O. J.

Everyone laughed, at the way she pivoted her head back and forth as she said it. She was acting very "street" all of a sudden, and it seemed out of place coming from her.

Spaulding said, "You being a woman, in the field of male corrections, you must be especially aware of these kinds of issues."

Miss Bain stifled a grin. "It probably has more to do with my upbringing, but, yes, wading through some of these back waters has been an interesting challenge. Though not as difficult and you might think."

"Since Spaulding is your editor, he is going to question your words and check your facts. We need to be as accurate as we can be, so we'll teach you how to do this," she said, "with everything."

"To validate our stories we'll look for contradictions and challenge our assumptions. When following up on something, always keep an open mind, because you never know where it where it might land you."

"What do mean by that?" Rodney asked.

"Well, let's start with a simple question," she said. "How many of you thought you were given a square deal by the system?"

No one raised their hand.

"None of you?" She looked around the room. "O. J. What was your school like?"

"It was pretty messed up," he said.

"Any sports programs?"

"We used to, until they cut them out."

Lee said, "That shit is for white folks—out in the burbs."

"Do you think it's an accident that most inmates are black?" Miss Bain asked.

"Shit. Tell us something we don't know," O. J. said.

"All right. How about the movies you're all watching in the auditorium. What was last Saturday's movie?"

"*Trick Baby*," Lee answered.

"*Trick Baby?*" she said. She dropped her head is disbelief. "*Trick Baby?*" The guys laughed because her eyes said it all.

"Hey! Now that's my boy," Lee said. "That's Iceberg Slim."

"I don't care if it's Romaine Lettuce," she laughed. "That crap is doing nothing but poisoning your young minds."

O. J. looked over at Lee with an exasperated expression.

"You can roll your eyes all you'd like, Mr. O. J., but let me just say that as long as we keep pandering to this never-ending stream of negative images— ones that show young black men as nothing more than pimps and pushers, con men and racketeers—instead of stepping up and showing off young, bright talented men such as each one of you is capable of being, then the general public is not going to care two nickels about you, me, or any other minority."

O. J. looked at her, his mouth slightly ajar.

"There will just be a neverending stream of young O. J.s and June Bugs and JuJu Beans that keep showing up in prison each year."

"I'm not telling you what you should watch, but I do think we can challenge what others think about us by questioning who it is they say we are."

We sat in a kind of stunned silence. No one had ever had that kind of analytical conversation with me, and I'm sure none of the others guys had ever had one either.

"I'll tell you what," Lee said. "That shit is DEEP."

The loudspeaker blared, "Attention All Inmates: Return from your assignments."

"Question your assumptions," Miss Bain said in closing, "and look for the contradictions. I'll see you all this afternoon."

As she got up to leave, she glanced over and smiled at me.

Miss Bain was a bad motherfucker!

When we arrived for chow, I let Paul go ahead of me in the line. It was pizza day, the highlight of the week's menu. As I inched toward the serving trays, I felt someone squeeze my ass. I spun around and saw a large black guy, Reese, pull his hand away. He stared at me like it wasn't him, and as soon as we sat down, I told Paul about it.

"Who?" He shouted.

"Shhh," I said. "He'll hear you."

"Fuck that! You can't let these ho's play you like that."

My heart sank, because I didn't want to get into a fight. And I wasn't sure it was him anyway. "It was Reese," I said, after Paul insisted I tell him.

Paul got up immediately and went over to him. A few minutes later, he returned. "It's take care of," he said. "I told him I didn't want a fight, but that you were with me."

"What'd he say?"

"He said that was cool."

Paul took a bite of his pizza.

"Do you want mine?" I said. "I'm not really hungry."

"You need to gain some weight, Squeeze. Those pants are falling off you."

It was scrawny piece of pizza, and it was nearly cold. I didn't want it.

"Listen, you can't let shit like that go," Paul said, "because it's never about what it looks like on the surface. He wasn't just copping a feel. He was testing—to see how you would react."

"I think he was also testing me," Paul said.

I bit into my thin slice of pizza.

Outside the chow hall, two inmates walked past.

"That bitch is *so* ugly," one of them said, "that when she was born—the doctor slapped her momma."

Inmates loved to snap on one another, but I didn't know who they were joking about until I turned the corner and saw Black Diamond standing with another queen.

"Well stir my pudding," she said. "If it ain't Mr. Blue Eyes. How the hell are you, girl?"

In the daylight, the poor thing was even more ugly than I had remembered. Her hairline was at the top of her head and her eyebrows were arched so high that she looked like Oopsy the Clown.

"I'm fine," I said, smiling, "but I'm still not a girl, Miss Thing."

"Well all right," she said. "You can be anything you want to be, honey, with your fine self."

It had been a few months since I left the county jail, and though I heard she had arrived in Quarantine, I didn't get a chance to see her before I left.

"When did you get here?" I asked.

"Today. I guess they don't want me startin' no scandals over in the barracks—so they're moving me into A-unit before we hit the *Eyewitness News* hour, if you know what I'm sayin'. *Girrrl!* There are some fine lookin' men up in this place, honey."

"How's Ginger doing?" I asked, remembering her cellmate from the jail.

"Girl got herself a dime," Black Diamond said, meaning she had received a ten-year sentence. "She's over in Gladiator School. But she'll be all right, already got herself a man picked out, so won't nobody fuck with her."

"And you?" I asked.

"Well, I'm just gonna have to wait and see what time it is before I pick me out a timepiece. But I'm sure enough gonna get me a Roladex or at least a Long Jean's Wittnauer, if you know what I'm sayin'."

She mispronounced both names, but I didn't have the heart to mention it. We both laughed. I remembered how judgmental I was when I first came to prison, and how horrified I was when I saw those queens on the tier—gigglin' and wigglin' their butts.

Paul tugged my jacket. "This is Paul," I said.

Paul nodded, but he seemed distant. "C'mon, Tim, we've got business."

"Well all right," Black Diamond said. "Y'all go on and make that thing happen."

As soon as we got out of earshot, Paul said I needed to be careful about who I associated with, because that had much to do with everything.

"But she's been nice to me!" I said.

"I hear what you're saying, but these fuckers will judge you by who you're hanging with, who you talk to, by as much as how you carry yourself. And don't kid yourself, Tim, they're always watching." He stopped to look at me. "Listen, we can talk about this later, but neither of us has chosen a man so we need to keep a low profile."

When inmates arrived at a new prison, if they were gay or had been turned-out before, they had limited time to choose a man before one got chosen for him.

"But I want you to be my man," I said. "Can't we keep doing what we're doing?"

"Of course," he said, "but it's only a matter of time before they start turning up the pressure on us."

Under the convict code, regardless of how we may have acted, we weren't thought of as "men" because inmates believed that gays were fundamentally lacking in what they considered *manhood*. "It's pretty fucked up," Paul said, "because I know some stone cold killers who are also gay, but that's just how these simple-minded fuck heads view things."

"Attention all inmates," the loudspeaker blared, "Report to your assignments."

"And besides," Paul said. "Neither of us has any money, so we need to get one or two of these knuckleheads to start taking care of us."

Paul's family didn't visit, nor did they write or send any money. His job paid 33 cents a day, which came to less than $10 a month. I'd been there close to a year, but I'd only had one visit. Though now that my stepbrother Bobby was going over to Gladiator School, I suspected I'd see more of my family. I received a letter from Sharon, who said the judge gave Bobby ten years.

I told Paul I didn't care about money, or anything else these guys had to offer, but he said, "Don't worry about it. I'm going to show you how to work it—so we can use them like they've used us."

He said that first, we had to sit back and study our options—to find which guys were ideal for playing on. "You watch them carefully," he said, "and see what makes them tick. Is it love or attention? Then we pretend to give it to them. Do they have an ego? Then we stroke it. Whatever it is, once you find their weakness, we use it to gain control."

Paul showed me a letter that an inmate sent him from Gladiator School. "He was in love with me," Paul said.

I nodded.

"No! He was *really* in love with me. Read the letter."

I did, and the guy had signed it, *with all my heart . . .*

"That's when you control him," he said. "Once you get 'em to care about you, they'll do whatever you want."

"Sounds like a lot of work," I said.

"This is just practice," he said, smiling. "For when we get out. Trust me on this."

I was beginning to trust him, which was hard for me to do after all that had happened beginning with Riverside. I wasn't sure I could trust anyone again, but Paul made me willing to try. He had freed me from Moseley, and he really seemed to like me. And I liked how he looked at me with that green sparkle in his eyes—first straight in the eye, down at my lips, and then back up again.

"My skin is breaking out," I said, self-consciously.

"That's OK. I hadn't noticed."

I knew he was lying, but I appreciated his kindness.

"I'm getting allergic hives," I told him.

"I don't mind, it's just more for me to look at."

"Oh brother," I said, smiling at such a tired cliché.

"I'm serious."

"No you're not."

The loudspeaker blared: "Attention all inmates: Report to your assignments." They always made announcements twice, since no one listened the first time.

I avoided Black Diamond from that point on, which turned out to be good advice. A few days later, I saw her and another queen fooling around in the bushes next to the infirmary. Black Diamond's friend called herself Ruby, and the two of them used to argue over who gave a better head. One time, I saw them swapping a couple of guys back and forth, so they could help them decide, but the two guys who were getting blown kept coming back the next day saying they weren't quite sure.

That afternoon, I was called to Miss Bain's office. Another inmate was speaking with her when I arrived, so I waited in a chair outside her door.

"I don't know where you got this, Little John, but I think you better put it away."

Little John responded in a low voice, so I couldn't hear what he had said. Then Miss Bain said, "Listen, I'm always willing to talk to inmates, but I think you and I should take a break for a while. And I think it's time for you to leave."

I stood in her door. "Hi, Miss Bain, you wanted to see me?"

"Yes, we were just finishing." She handed Little John a pass.

I caught a glimpse of a red necklace before he closed the lid of the small box. He glared at me as he walked past.

"Thank you," Miss Bain said. "I heard you when you came in, so I appreciate your timing."

There wasn't a lot I could have done to defend her if Little John had turned violent, but my presence might have prevented him from trying something.

"Listen," she said. "I want to talk to you about what went on earlier today."

"Thanks for sticking up for me," I said.

"Well, they do have a point. And they're not the only ones who are concerned about you being on the paper."

"You're worried?"

"No, I'm not, but I did get a call from Warden Handlon today."

"That's bullshit!" I fumed, afraid I was about to be pulled off the paper. She dropped her head and looked at me.

"Sorry, Miss Bain."

"Now you can't get any ticket while you're on the paper, or I'll have to reassign you."

"Does this rule apply to everyone?"

"Look, Tim, when Warden Handlon asked me to take this assignment, I told him I would—but only if I could do it without interference. You need to work with me on this. I have to pick my battles."

"I understand," I said. Though I didn't really—but I desperately wanted her to like me. She made me feel special, and I wanted to be around her as much as I could. I needed that attention from her. Of all the people to help me, I never expected a black woman. I don't think I knew any black women before.

When I had first made the mistake of telling O. J. that he did look like O. J. Simpson, he said, "I'll bet you think all niggers look alike." He and Rodney laughed when he said it, and I noticed how they stuck together like that. But mostly I felt embarrassed, because I did have trouble telling them apart at first. But how could I if I only lived in one world where everyone looked the same?

"There are a lot of things that are unfair in this world," she said, "but your job is to accept that and learn to work within it." She signed my pass and sent me back to the newsroom.

On my way out of her office, I ran into Reese and a few of his friends in the hall. He stopped talking and looked at me as I passed.

"Both them bitches are gonna need a man," he said.

When I got to the newsroom, everyone else was out following up on stories. I wasn't there when Spaulding handed out the assignments, so I didn't know what kinds of stories they were covering. But my job was mostly typing anyhow.

I picked up my journal and started writing. I struggled to keep up with my thoughts. Here was this woman, a black woman in a man's world, who was better educated than anyone I'd ever known. She stuck up for me as my mother or Sharon never had and said things like I'd never heard before. But it was more than that; it felt deeper, like I was a kid again and peeking at her from around the corner.

Warden Handlon believed that once an inmate was capable of comprehending his circumstances, he would be able to transcend them. My dad, who never completed the sixth grade, used to say that niggers were ignorant—because that's what his dad had taught him. I used to think that word meant stupid. But I looked it up, like Miss Bain said, and discovered that it meant something else. And now that I was getting an education I was starting to understand what it meant not to have one. I wondered how different I might have turned out had I paid attention to some of these lessons earlier—but how could I if I only lived in one world that didn't value learning? And would I have been ready to listen? Sadly, I had to come to prison to get an education, and maybe this woman could help lead me on a new path, because now that I knew what this world was like—I didn't want to be in it any longer. In here, I was the "nigger." And only then, was I willing to look, learn and listen to what that ugly little word really means.

30

Head Games and Power Trips

Sister Mary was quite clear. If I came to class again without my home-work, I'd be sent to Father Bruiser. That's the name given to him by the kids. The name alone speaks for itself.

"Oh, you don't want that," Jimmy Conroy said. "He's got a real leather strap, and he'll use it on you too."

I was supposed to read the catechism and discuss it with one of my parents, but Sharon's bedroom door was closed, and Dad hadn't come home. I stood there, weighing which was worse—the wrath of Father Bruiser or hearing Sharon yell at me. I nearly jumped when I heard her say, "C'mon in." I stood there motionless. "For Christ sakes! I can see your feet!" She sounded like herself this time, so I went in.

"I have to, um, have you read this to me and talk about it." I held up the second grade book.

"Which one?" Sharon asked.

"That one." I pointed to a page where Jesus was playing in a field. "Suffer the little children—come unto me."

Sharon propped herself on a pillow and began to read. Her voice was soft and gentle, and she spoke with a kindness I'd rarely heard from her before, (except when she was answering the phone or talking to a stranger for the first time). She stopped suddenly and looked over at me. "Why are you crying?"

I shrugged a shoulder. I didn't know why. Perhaps it had to do with her tenderness and the way she was reading. Or maybe she reminded me of my mother and how she used to make me feel, by just reading to me. But I could never tell Sharon this, because she hated my mom, and she wouldn't understand.

"Aw, C'mere," she said, and she held me gently against the side of the bed, stroking my hair and back.

A few moments later, I looked back at the book. "So what does it mean?"

"Well, let's see." She hesitated. "You know how you've been peeing the bed at night? Well, God will wake you up, just beforehand—to tell you that you have to go. It's kind of like that, you know?"

I'm not sure I understood what she meant, but it was the last time I ever peed the bed.

Working with Sherry Bain made me feel special, it was as if for the first time I was above prison. Simply speaking to me like an adult allowed me to pretend I wasn't one of the inmates. Her kindness had no motives, unlike the inmates who were nice only when they wanted to fuck me. Paul was different too, he was always happy to see me, even when we just sat in the back of the day room and talked.

"She studied sociology and psychology," I said to him, "but when she got out of college, there weren't any jobs, so she came to work in the prisons."

"What was she hired for?" Paul asked.

"She worked in the Control Center and then in the Tower."

"The Tower! She worked the gun tower?"

"Yep. Can you believe it?" I smiled broadly, proud to know someone as brave as she was. "I'll bet the gun weighed as much as she does, but she outscored a lot of the men at the firing range."

Paul said I was lucky to be working with Miss Bain and encouraged me to study her as much as I could. He said there was much I could learn from her example. Bringing me back to reality, he asked how I was doing with picking a man.

"I've been studying Jake," I said. "He works in the store."

"That's good," Paul said. "He'll be working when we have yard."

"He lives in D-unit, which means I won't have to spend that much time with him. Every time I come to the store, he stares at me and asks how I'm doing. And when I get up to the window, he always slips something extra in my commissary."

"He sounds like a much better choice," Paul said. He had been critical of the others I had been considering. The men knew we were "looking," and a few were eager to kick the tires. But it took me little while to notice the subtleties of those who talked a good game from those who had something going on. But at my age, what did I know about any of this?

In choosing a man, respect was the most critical factor. Whoever I chose would need the respect of others, especially if he lived in another housing unit. I studied how inmates interacted with Jake. He was quieter than most, which Paul said help him hold onto his power. I noticed that his friends seemed to look to him for approval. I paid attention to how he dressed, and the size of his commissary. His cell would be a tell-tale sign, as well, so I used my press pass to sneak over to D-unit for a peak.

Inmates personalized their cells with brightly colored towels that were sewn together to make bedspreads and matching curtains. Small rugs were purchased in the store. Inside their lockers, would be a well-stocked supply of store-bought soap, shampoo, and deodorant. Inmates who didn't have money, were forced to use the green state soap. Cosmetics were a status symbol, and those who had them made a point of bragging about it. "But a true player," Paul said, "was someone who had it all, but didn't need to show it off. For these guys, it's no big deal because they're always supplied and always will be."

Paul said the next thing to find out, was whether Jake was susceptible to being played. This was the trickier, because if he turned out to be cold-hearted, then I find myself in a situation like I was in with Moseley. Moseley didn't care about me or any other fag for that matter. To him, we were just a piece of meat.

I wondered how Paul learned all this stuff. How many times had been raped, treated horribly, terrorized before he gleaned all this knowledge? But it clearly came out of a need to survive. Like me, he had been knocked around a few times. And he started a lot earlier than me—being locked up the first time at ten years old. When he came to prison, at sixteen, he was raped immediately. And he was raped again, at Riverside, right before coming here to MTU. When Taylor was thrown in the hole, a guy named Cowboy snatched Paul off into a laundry room and raped him repeatedly over a several-hour period. So it was out of survival that Paul developed the skill he needed to minimize what was happening here.

"Get a guy to fall in love with you," he said, "and that's your key to the kingdom. That's how you'll control them—with a silk glove. You get their nose wide open."

"Nose wide open? What does that mean?"

"You figure out what turns him on, and you give it to him until he grows dependent on you—and then you pull it out from under him. You get him to drink from the well, then you shut down the well. Giving it up only when he does what you want."

Paul said it was turn on to have this kind of power over someone. You find a guy who's lonely, and you fill the void. "It's supply and demand, baby boy. And as long as you have what he wants more than you want what he's got—you've got 'em. You just have to let him think he's driving the car for a while. When it's really you who's in the driver's seat."

I still wasn't sure I wanted to play to this game, or that I was smart enough to pull it off. But Paul said, "Everyone in here has a game—some kind of hustle to get by. I'm tired of being the sucker."

Paul's way of talking turned me on. He was street smart and wise and could disarm just about anyone. Like an actor, he changed his persona on a dime; from acting tough to sweet-talking someone, depending on what the situation demanded and what he was trying to achieve—respect, money, confusion. Whatever it was didn't matter—Paul was going to succeed.

He had what I wanted.

It was chilly in the TV room so Paul went back to his cell and returned with a blanket. He draped half of it over me, and we held hands under the cover as we watched *Battlestar Galactica* on TV. His hand felt warm in mine, and I wished we lived in a world where we didn't have to hide our affection for each other under the covers.

Two black inmates in the row in front of us turned around and looked down at the blanket. "They're probably jerking each other off," one of them said.

"Fucking freaks," the other shouted.

"Pay them no mind," Paul said. "The motherfuckers are just jealous."

"Bitch, ain't nobody jealous," the first one said.

"That's not what you said the other day," Paul shot back. "When you were cracking on me for that ass."

"Well, if you'd give it up—that'd be a different story."

"Shit! You can't handle this," Paul said.

"I'll tell you what, boy. If you give a me a chance—I'll die trying."

They both smiled.

For a moment, I was afraid we would get into a fight, but Paul had a lot of heart. And inmates respected that. If you were too timid or backed down easily, they'd go in for the kill. But if you stood your ground, in just the right way, they would respect you and back away—so long as they were provided a graceful way of doing that.

"He's cute. I might get with him, later," Paul said. "He's laying *like that* anyway, just don't nobody know it."

"Really?"

"Square Biz. He's always talking smack just to keep the others off his back. Trust me," Paul leaned over. "He sucks a meaner dick than I do."

"I doubt that," I said.

"Thanks," Paul smiled.

I guess it might have occurred to me to be a little jealous, but Slide Step shown me how he was open about sex. He didn't care if I did it with someone else, so long as he knew about it. Paul felt the same way. It was just sex, Paul said, and it's not like we had a whole lot of other things to do in there.

"Pick one," Paul said.

"What are you talking about?

"Exactly what I said. You can have just about any one of them you want. Ninety percent of these guys will let you blow them."

I didn't know what to say, so I just stared at him with a goofy grin on my face.

"There's nothing to be ashamed of. You're in here so you might as well enjoy it."

"Ninety-nine percent," I said. "Really?"

"Oh yeah, but you have to be careful about who, or you'll find yourself in a pickle."

"Interesting choice of words," I said.

"Mmm, a Chilly Willy," he said. "Anyway, I'm mostly referring to the white boys. If you mess around with the blacks, you're messing with fire."

Paul leaned over and pointed to a hot looking white boy name Steve. "What do you think of that one?"

"Him?" I said.

He was young like me, about seventeen, with reddish-blond hair and a baby face. He was skinny and looked more like a target than even me. "Too sweet."

Paul nodded. "How about that one?" He pointed to a guy closer to my liking. He had olive skin and jet-black hair. He was probably Italian—very masculine looking.

"Too old," I said.

"You have to let me know what you like, if you want me to hook you up."

"What do you say to them?" I asked. I'd never talked to another guy about how to hook up. I was completely new to this and was amazed by Paul's lack of inhibition.

"I just tell them that I want to eat them up."

I felt my face blush.

Paul leaned back and smiled at me. "Your parents don't know about you, do they?"

"Hell no! What does that have to do with anything?"

"Because after I told my parents, nothing bothered me again. Shit, this is my life. They've never helped me out in here. So why should I care *what* they think? Or any of these people?" Paul raised his voice for the guys in the next row to hear.

"All I know is after I told my parents, nothing seemed to bother me again."

"I could never tell them," I said. "They'd disown me."

"Well, then they don't deserve you in the first place."

At that moment, if occurred to me that in spite of how messed up I may have thought my family was, and how they'd all but abandoned me in prison, I still looked to them as my home base. For years they were all I had. Even in prison, they were the place I'd be returning to when I got out. Suddenly, this realization depressed me. Was this really where I wanted to be? I didn't want to talk about it with Paul, so I let it go.

Before we went to bed, Paul gave me a copy of *The Front Runner*, a gay love story by Patricia Nell Warren.

"Just read it," he said. "We can talk about it later."

My first assignment for *The Oracle* was covering the inmate representative council. I was eager to do a good job—if only to impress Miss Bain—so I started by interviewing an inmate in D-unit. "It don't make no diff," he said. "The Man ain't gonna do shit about nothing no-how." Meaning the Warden's meetings with inmates was a big waste of time.

Spaulding sent me to the warden's office to read the minutes of previous meetings. Warden Handlon's secretary said it would take some time to get them together, but she would send them over as soon as she could. I had to stop by a couple times to remind her, and each time she said the she would, but I had to file a grievance to finally receive them.

"You know Warden Handlon doesn't like grievances," she warned. "You should have sent a kite." Kites were like interoffice memos—for inmates to communicate with staff; but kites didn't generate the same level of attention that a formal grievance did.

"I'm sorry, but I've been asking for the minutes for a while now."

"I'm know, but I couldn't let you read them without his approval, and then he screams at me—like it's my fault." She handed me the file.

When I got back to the newsroom, I was eager to find whatever it was Warden Handlon didn't want me to see. After several readings, I found nothing. It was the usual gripes: the inmates wanted more items in the store; the warden said space was limited and that if we wanted something new—we had to remove something else. The inmates wanted more yard time; the warden said programming was essential to reducing recidivism. The inmates wanted conjugal visits; Warden Handlon said no. From what the file told me, the inmate representative council was a waste of time.

At the first meeting, I sat with twelve other inmates—two from each housing unit—one white and one black, as we listened to Warden Handlon breeze through the agenda.

"I hold this meeting every month, so I can keep a pulse on what's important to you." he said. "It's a forum for airing complaints in a constructive manner."

Spaulding was there, since he had been elected to represent E-unit, and was the first to speak when the warden asked if there was any thing to add.

"I'd like to discuss forming a prisoner's progress association. We'd like to have permission to meet in the school," Spaulding said.

"That won't be necessary," the warden said. "We have these meetings for that." Spaulding tried to reply, but the warden cut him off. "Let's move on."

"Inmates' movies?" one of the white inmates asked. "We still have the issue of the movies being mostly about blacks." The black guys moaned in disbelief.

I was hoping Spaulding would bring Miss Bain's point about the content of the movies being a phenomenon of self-hate—but Warden Handlon said, "We'll have to table this for right now. The Reformatory and Riverside selects the movies, and we take advantage of their budgets by viewing them when they're finished."

I spoke up. "Excuse me, Warden Handlon? I noticed in the minutes that last spring you said the same thing. It we're saving money by letting them select the movies for us, why is the money still coming out of our inmate benefit fund?"

"That's enough," he shouted. "We won't have any sharp shooting in my meetings."

I was shocked, not sure that I understood why he exploded, but I could see that I better let the matter drop. The other cons looked at me like I was a fool. Here I had been proud of myself for digging up facts like Miss Bain had told us. I thought the inmates would be impressed. I should have remembered what she said about choosing your battles.

"Let's move on," Warden Handlon said.

Miss Bain later reminded me that Warden Handlon runs a tight ship. "It's not any different with staff. He's tough and demands respect. You can't question his authority, because you'll never win."

"Miss Kiley said he was mad at me for filing a grievance. Why would he care?"

"Grievances are one way his bosses measure how well he's running the facility. While he's penalized for them, they are one of many factors that indicate how he's doing. He keeps expenses low, he always looks for bargains, and if you suggest he spend money, it better be worth it."

"Well, he could just say that," I said. "He didn't have to yell at me."

"He probably yelled at you to keep you in your place," she said. "It's just his style. I wouldn't take it personally."

I knew she was telling me this for my own good. She didn't have to risk speaking out against the warden, but it reflected who she was; a brave person with a lot of integrity. I savored every minute I could hang out in her office and would have stayed the whole day if she had let me. I wondered if she hated being inside a prison as much as I did.

"I like what I'm doing," she said. "And I'm learning a lot from Warden Handlon."

"Really?"

"He's a legend in corrections," she said. "There's a lot you could learn from him, by studying him."

There was that word again—*study*. It seemed the theme of the moment. Paul was telling me to study the inmates, to see what I can learn about them—and now Sherry was saying I could learn by studying Warden Handlon.

"But I hate him," I said. "And do you really think he likes black people?"

I knew it was a cheap shot, but Sherry made me feel I could speak openly. Handlon was a member of the local country club, and he'd lived in Ionia where there weren't any blacks. Those who worked in the prison commuted from Lansing or Grand Rapids.

"Warden Handlon has the ability to see the future," Sherry said. "He knows what it takes to get by. And whatever his personal feelings might be, he's going to be part of that future."

I looked at her and nodded. "But don't you think that he's prejudiced?"

"No I don't. He's led the department in hiring minorities. He's recruited down south to bring more in, and he's the one who interviewed and hired me."

"How was that? The interview, I mean?"

"He got all up in my personal business, for one," Sherry said, laughing. "Asking all kinds of questions he shouldn't have been asking."

"Like what?"

"Like am I dating anyone? How come I'm not married? Do you have any kids?"

"You can't ask those things?"

"It's not really relevant," she said. "It was like the guys on *The Oracle* making a big deal about your lifestyle. Anyway, I get along with him pretty well. He never talks to me like he does the others, because I respect him and I have his respect."

"How does that work?"

"Well for one, when he tells me to do something I don't agree with—instead of arguing about it, I say, 'I'll do this, but I don't agree with you.' I never argue with him and I always do what he says. Some of the best lessons can be learned by doing something you don't want to do."

"Like not sharpshooting at his meeting?"

"He's been a good mentor to me," she said. "He's had more wardens come up under him than any other warden in Michigan. So I hope to keep right on learning. I have a future too, you know."

I looked at her and was amazed.

When Paul told me he couldn't be my man because he was gay, he was speaking to the misunderstandings of masculinity and power in prison. As gay men, we'd never have power over anyone, not even ourselves. Miss Bain challenged that notion. Here she was a woman, in a man's world, applying her intellect to get ahead. And she was doing this by taking on a man to help teach her what she needed to learn.

In that moment, I had no doubt she'd one day make warden, even if she was a woman, in a man's world and fighting the odds. There was a lot I could learn from her. Paul was right: I needed to pick someone and study him. Only it wasn't going to be a man. I decided right then it was Miss Bain. She was who it was that I was going to study.

"It's all about a power trips and head games," Paul said. We were in the day room a few minutes before lockdown, watching the eleven o'clock news. "It's the same shit that pimps use to season their ho's."

"How do you know these things?" I asked.

"Taylor taught me," he said. "They use fear and intimidation, or they pretend to be your savior. They trick you into believing they're the only ones who can protect you—care about you. I'm sure if you were still with Moseley—he wouldn't let you come near me, because he was afraid I'd wise you up. Keeping you isolated was how he kept you in his control."

I nodded, remembering how Rock once threatened he would kill my entire family if I ever went to the guards and snitched on him. And judging by how he looked at me at the time—I believed him.

"That's just part of the game," Paul said. "They break you down first—like brainwashing. It's what they did to Patty Hearst." He nodded to the TV.

A major event dominating the news was the Jonestown massacre. Jim Jones, a cult leader, had convinced 912 of his followers to commit suicide by drinking Kool-Aid laced with cyanide. The commentators were making a connection to Patty Hearst, the newspaper heiress who had been kidnapped by terrorists and brainwashed into robbing a bank. They called it the Stockholm syndrome in which captives became sympathetic with their captors.

"You know," Paul said. "It didn't happen exactly the way you think it did."

"What?"

"Slide Step. When you first arrived at Riverside."

"What are you talking about?"

"It's the oldest game in the penitentiary. It's called the Underplay for the Overlay. Slide Step set the whole thing up."

I felt my heart drop. As much as I loved Paul, he had to be making that up. He was jealous of Slide Step, that's all. "Get the fuck out of here," I said.

"Oh he did," Paul nodded. "He had his eyes on you the moment you hit the yard. Taylor and I were standing next to him when you came in with the other fish."

"You're a fuckin' liar," I challenged.

The guard flashed the lights and shut off the TV. It was time to return to our cells.

"Why would he do that? It doesn't make sense," I said, refusing to believe any of it—was this Paul's way of manipulating me? For the first time, I looked at Paul skeptically.

"He wanted you to come willingly into his fold, grateful to him for rescuing you. Who wants a wife that's resentful about being there? It's easier to control you that way."

"But Slide Step didn't control me!"

"Look Tim, Slide Step has been doing time longer than you've been alive."

"He's not that old!" I said. "He's *only* thirty!"

"If you count his time in juvenile hall."

I was angry with Paul, because I didn't want to hear this even if it were true, which I refused to believe.

I went to my cell and kicked the locker door. It made a loud crash against the wall and resonated out into the hall. The noise reminded me of the first time Slide Step kissed me, and how relieved I was that he wasn't going to hurt me. At least not how I thought he was going to hurt me. But now I wished he would have beaten me. If Paul's story were true, a beating would have been easier to take.

The snow outside my window came down heavily. I could barely see the chow hall through the small windowpanes as they frosted over. I'd wedged pieces of toilet paper inside the cracks to keep the wind from blowing inside.

Sitting alone in the dark, I thought about something else Paul had said. "Inmates are always looking to destroy whatever good you had left. They're jealous that you've been able to keep something hidden away. Or maybe it makes them feel better—knowing they can take from you what's been stolen from them. But fuck 'em, you just don't let it happen. And the best way to do that is to walk around like you're immune to whatever goes on here. So if someone else is getting hurt, you look away, or better yet—you laugh about it to keep others from turning on you. It's play or be played—It's just the way it is."

In A-unit, because there were bathrooms inside the cells, they locked us in at night. It was comforting to know that at least for the next ten hours, no one could get into my cell. I chose not to believe it. Slide Step cared for me, and that was real. It was as if by telling me that story, Paul was taking from me that one thing I had hidden away. I hugged my pillow and slowly fell asleep.

31

Go for the Grab

"Can I open that one, first?" I said, pointing to the long, gift-wrapped package at the back of the tree.

Sharon reached in and handed it to me. The tape on the end hardly looked tampered with, but I quickly ripped it open before she could notice it. It was the new tripod for my camera, which I wanted to set up right away.

"Let me have that one," Bobby said, pointing to the gift nearest him.

We knew what everything was because we had been peaking at them for weeks.

"Sharon," my dad said, "have them open this one here." He nodded to a four-foot box that was brightly wrapped and next to the hall. To The Kids, it was labeled, Love Santa.

We posed for a picture in front of it, waiting for the delayed shutter of my camera before we tore into it.

"I get the blue one," Bobby shouted.

"I already called it," I said, "You can have the green."

"Well, I'm not getting stuck with yellow," Billy protested.

Connie, we already knew, would get the red one, which none of us wanted. We knew that the Ford Motor Company windbreaker jackets were all the same size. The funny thing was, we hadn't opened the package yet.

"Well, you sneaky little bastards," Sharon said.

For prison inmates, Christmas is the quietest day of the year. It's probably the one day when there weren't as many fights or violence because everyone is in the same frame of mind. Sad. Even the Muslims, who didn't celebrate Christmas, seemed to struggle not to think about being locked away from family and friends.

"Same shit, different day," an inmate said, trying to pretend he wasn't depressed. When the black phone on the wall behind the guard's desk rang, the entire cellblock went quiet. People on the outside don't realize how important a Christmas visit to an inmate truly is.

A Christmas carol, played on a radio, could be heard faintly a few cells away. The staff was kept down to a skeletal crew, so movement throughout the prison was limited. Short-staffed, they did away with lunch, so breakfast came late, and dinner was served early. Dinner included a generous portion of processed turkey roll with cranberries and stuffing and mashed potatoes. Dessert was pumpkin pie with whip cream.

The guys in the kitchen sold spud juice off the back dock. Inmates who skipped the processed turkey were cooking up in their units. The commissary ran extra items, so you could order things like canned ham and sausage and fresh fruit. They even let you spend extra money from your account, and the money allowed in from visitors was higher than usual. (Normally, visitors were allowed to give you up to $15 in tokens, but on Christmas you were permitted $20.)

Because inmates were depressed during the holidays, the administration loosened things up a bit. Shakedowns were minimized, and guards turned a blind eye to minor rule infractions. Spud juice and drugs were in high supply.

Paul and I had a drink together and smoked a joint. The joint was the width of a shoestring, so I wasn't going to get very high, but my resistance was low—considering how clean my system had become—so I experienced a pleasant buzz.

Religious groups came in on holidays, but most inmates didn't bother to meet them unless decent offerings had been brought along. The Mexicans liked to go for the plastic rosary beads. They'd wear them around their necks for a few days, like it was jewelry. Most groups brought Bibles and other religious artifacts, which couldn't have interested us less.

My parents sent money for a small TV. It was $128. A 12-inch Hitachi, which made my time go by faster. Unfortunately, they cut the power off at

11:30 on weeknights, and at midnight on weekends and holidays. You could purchase a rechargeable battery in the store, which would buy you a couple of hours, but at a cost of $45, it was out of my price range. When I got Jake to buy it for me, Paul was proud of me for working him, but he looked disappointed at the same time. I opened Paul's present, and I understood why.

It was an extra battery.

I gave Paul a rug for his cell and a Cheap Trick music cassette I had ordered from the store. "No pun intended," I said.

"I'll give you a pun," Paul said, smiling.

I hadn't taken Jake on as my man yet, though he and I were still discussing the possibility. I held off making a decision, because I wanted to be with Paul as much as I could.

Just then, the phone on the wall rang and the guard answered it.

"Parsell!" the guard yelled. "You have a visit!"

I looked at Paul, stunned.

I didn't know who it was that was out there. My family hadn't seen me in several weeks, and I was starting to think that even Christmas wouldn't bring them around.

Paul looked at me and smiled. "Go for it, Squeeze."

Prison officials, recognizing the need and importance of maintaining contact with loved ones on the outside, granted us up to four visits a month. Seeing family and friends helped maintain emotional stability and avoid disciplinary infractions. I doubted I had much emotional stability left hidden inside, but a visit was most welcome.

Visits kept inmates connected to our previous lives and the world we left behind. The visiting room held up to hundred people, but even with over eight hundred inmates, it was rarely filled. Weekends and holidays were the busiest time, and if it got crowded, we would be limited to just one hour.

The room was long and narrow with rows of chairs that faced each another. When visitors arrived, you were permitted to hug once, and then once more when they left. All other contact was prohibited. On the wall, inmates had painted a mural: a watermill with childlike butterflies and a sun with a happy face. Considering all the roughnecks who were housed there, I wondered who had thought to paint butterflies or put a smile on the sun. Maybe the mural was done with visitors in mind, to help put them at ease.

A guard sat at a podium with a stack of visitor passes spread out in front of him. When your time was up, he would politely walk over and hand you one. Visitors had their hands stamped, on their way in, with an invisible ink so that on their way back out again, the guards could check it under an infrared lamp. Inmates usually stood at the bars and watched as their guests walked back out to freedom. It was always a painful moment, for everyone, and even the toughest thugs had difficulty hiding their sadness.

Bobby had just arrived at M-R and Dad and Sharon had gone to see him first. My Dad looked great—much younger since he had stopped drinking. Sharon looked the same.

"We only have a few minutes," she said. "We have to get home because we have company coming by the house tonight."

Even though I was getting better at hiding my emotions, I must have shown disappointment, because Sharon's tone changed for a second. "What took them so long to get you out here?" she asked.

"I had to shower." It was common for inmates to shower before a visit, even if they took one earlier in the day—to wash away any prison smells.

"Well *that's* what took so long," she said. "It's your own damn fault."

"It is not," I protested. Even on Christmas she was looking for a fight.

I looked to my dad for help. He was staring off at some people on the other side of the room. "What's he in for?" Dad nodded across the way.

"I don't know," I answered, wondering why they weren't more interested in their own son.

In the row behind my parents, an inmate sat with his family. There were six of them in total, and the youngest reminded me of myself, when I first went to visit my brother. I remembered how Rick used to brag about what went on in there, much in the same way this inmate was now holding his family's attention. I wondered what that boy would take away from the visit and whether he'd romanticize his brother's experience the way I had. Would he be forced to learn the hard truth like us?

"Well, anyway," Sharon said. "How are you doing?"

"Good," I said. We sat there awkwardly for a moment.

"Well, you look good," she said.

"My face keeps breaking out."

"I can see that," Sharon said, nodding. "How's the food?"

I changed the subject. "How's Bobby doing?" I didn't want to talk about the fucking food.

"He's OK, I guess, but it's a damn shame. He didn't need to get ten years."

"He should have taken a plea," I said.

"It's not right," Sharon said. "Your brother is the one who should be over there."

"That's enough," Dad said.

"We'll it's true, damn it. If Bobby would have just told them who he was with, he never would have been sent to prison."

"Now God damn it, Sharon. We said we weren't getting into this here."

Once more I was reminded that this was the home I'd return to after prison, and again my spirit sank in despair. What kind of future was that? And what difference would it make if I told them right then that I was gay? Sharon would probably have loved it. Something else she could hate me for. Mostly, I worried about how Dad would respond. He was always concerned about what others thought of him and my being gay would be a lot for him to handle. He hadn't been around that much anyway—and even when he was—he wasn't really present. But he was all I had.

"You have to tell you parents," I remembered Paul say. *"It's the only way to accept yourself."*

"I accept myself."

"Look, all I can say is that when I told my parents, it didn't matter what they said. I was finally taking over my life. It wasn't until then that I could start to be proud of who I am."

"Proud? What's to be proud of?"

Sharon voice was starting to rise.

"I'm so sick and tired of sitting in these visiting rooms," she complained. "It's a damn shame—to have to sit over there and listen to Bobby as he tried to entertain us. Like he had to make us feel good and convince us that nothing was wrong."

Sharon's anger was nothing new to me, but her sadness was. Bobby was her oldest son, her favorite, and I could see that she was heartbroken. She reached into her pocket and pulled out a hanky. Suddenly, she wasn't as large as before. I had spent so much time hating her, directing all my anger at her—but the truth was—she was the one who had been there a lot of the time. Seeing her crying, I felt sorry for her for the first time.

Maybe it was all the violence and terror I'd seen in prison that opened my eyes, but I could see in Sharon someone as frightened and powerless as I was. She was only twenty-four when she moved in with my dad, and was suddenly saddled with five kids to take care of. Twenty-four didn't seem that old to me anymore. Yes, I still resented her. However, she now seemed as vulnerable as I was. I didn't understand all of this at that moment, but I saw enough to pity her life.

She was in a rage at Rick, because she blamed him for Bobby going to prison. But not all her anger should have been directed at Rick. Bobby was responsible, too.

If Bobby had tried to entertain them, he was only trying to help. Across the visiting room, I noticed this going on everywhere. Inmates were exaggerating prison life so that it sounded amusing and relatively harmless. They wanted their visitors to laugh and have a good time, because maybe if they enjoyed themselves and kept ignorant of what really goes on inside, they'd come back and visit again.

I remembered how fascinated I was by Rick's stories. Did the pleasures they gave me mean I was gay? And then I started to wonder if I wasn't reading too much into those fantasies. Maybe it was just a phase I was going through after all. Maybe I was just gay for the stay, as some inmates say.

Just then, the inmate sitting behind my parents said loudly, "That's one right over there." He pointed at me, while the six members of his family turned and stared. Like they where at the zoo and suddenly got a chance to see some rare animal.

My heart was beating rapidly, but my parents were oblivious, thank goodness.

The youngest boy kept looking. He was about twelve, and I almost felt I recognized that look in his eye. It seemed to go beyond just a mild fascination. "Stop staring at him," his mother whispered.

"Well, I better be getting back," I said. "I have finals I have to study for."

"Finals?" Dad asked.

"I'm taking college classes."

"College?" Dad said. "What about high school?"

"I graduated. Didn't you get my letters?"

Dad couldn't read, so he was dependent on Sharon to read them to him.

"I must have forgotten," Sharon said. "Well, anyway. We better get going."

"OK," I said, ushering them past the family that was still gawking at me.

I regretted that I couldn't bring myself to tell them I was gay, but I'd get another chance the following day, when my brother Rick came to see me.

Like Dad and Sharon, Rick stopped to visit Bobby first. The Reformatory was on the way, and he didn't want to backtrack.

"Well, I'm glad you finally made it," I said.

"I've been really busy."

"I've noticed. How's Bobby doing?"

"He's having a hard time," Rick said. "Some inmates ran a hustle on him when he first got there." An inmate stopped in front of Bobby's cell and asked him to hold a package, and before Bobby could say anything, the guy tossed it into him. Then, right after count, another con stopped by saying the first guy told him to come pick it up. Bobby gave it to him, only to have the first guy come back, a few minutes later, wanting his shit.

"I gave it to the other guy," Bobby said.

"Who?" the inmate demanded, but Bobby didn't know who he was.

Rick said, "It's one of the oldest con games they play on a fish."

"Well, maybe not the oldest," I said, knowingly.

"Whatever," Rick said. "Since Bobby couldn't identify the guy who came and got the package, they threatened to kill him if he didn't come up with the money to replace it."

"What's he going to do?"

"Sharon took care of it," Rick said. "She sent him the money."

Of course she did, she was his mother. I didn't say anything. But surprisingly, I wasn't angry with Sharon. Where was my mother?

Given how Sharon went after that lawyer for me, I'm sure that if she knew what was happening to me, there would have been hell to pay. But it would take many years before I could talk about it with anyone, so for once, I didn't blame Sharon.

"The only problem with that is they probably won't just let it go," Rick said. "Especially not after Bobby fell for it and paid the money. Since he's shown himself as a sucker, they'll think there's more where that came from."

"It's easy to sit back and call the shots, *now*, Rick." The anger was boiling up in me, because this was typical of him, and I wasn't so enamored by his wisdom anymore.

"Well, they're also giving him a hard time because of you," he said, matter of factly.

"What do you mean?" I asked, fearing the worst.

We both knew what he meant, so Rick didn't need to say another word.

"Anyway, I need to get going. Belinda has been on the rag lately, and I really need to head out."

"But you just got here," I said. I had planned to talk to him about a lot of things.

"Yeah, but I had to wait out front for over an hour before they brought you out, and the same thing happened with Bobby. I don't want to get stuck in rush hour."

It was already 2:30, and he was a good two hours from home.

"Whatever," I said, disappointed. The fifteen dollars would go a long way in the commissary. "Thanks for the tokens."

"I'm on the prison newspaper," I added, in a quick attempt to win his respect before he left.

Rick nodded. "Well, I'll see you then."

I walked him to the front of the visiting room.

"Tell Belinda I said hello."

"I will." And then, just as the first set of bars started to slide open, Rick turned and hugged me. He had never done that before, and prison was the last place I'd have expected a hug from him—especially after what he'd heard about me being gay.

"Take care of yourself, little brother."

"I'll try," I squeaked out.

As he left me alone, I retreated back inside myself, to the only place where I knew it was safe.

As I came out of the control center and turned down the walkway toward A-unit, I saw Rick was still out in the parking lot, on the other side of the fence. He was leaning against the side of his new van, smoking a cigarette and staring at the ground. He looked lost in thought. I was about to holler to him, but then saw someone get out of his van and walk around to him. Whoever she was, she put her arms around his shoulder and kissed him on the side of his head. Rick kept staring down.

I suddenly knew why his wife Belinda had been "on the rag," but what I didn't know was why he felt he couldn't tell me.

32

Wolf Tickets

I was always afraid of the ball, so when the pitcher threw a curve ball that came at me from the inside I closed my eyes and fell back into the dirt.

"Strike," the umpire yelled, as the kids, and parents in the stands laughed. For once, I was glad my parents weren't there to witness my humiliation.

One time, I got the courage to step up to the plate and face my fears head on. I leaned back on my right leg, and extended my left, like I had seen a guy do in the majors. No matter what happened, I was not going to step back or fall out of the batter's box.

"Give me your best shot," I snarled. When the pitch came over the inside corner of the plate, the umpire yelled, "Strike!"

I smiled like I had hit a homerun, because at least this time, I was still standing in the box. Sure I was scared, but on the outside, I looked strong and confident.

"Look at Timmy!" one of my teammates yelled.

"Yeah," another said. "Now if we can just get him to swing."

Until we chose our men, Paul and I spent all of our time together. We walked to chow together, we ate together, and when we returned from our job assignments, we hung out in the dayroom and waited for the next count. And whenever we could, we snuck under his bed and had sex together. We talked a great deal about surviving prison and what we would do when we both got out. We never talked about Slide Step again. I think Paul knew better than to bring it up.

"There are queers in Detroit as well," Paul said. "I think I'll stay in the area."

"I think I'd like to get away from my family for a while. I'm not sure they'd ever understand," I explained.

Paul had a ten-year sentence, to my four and half, which meant he had a lot longer to go than I did. "You'll probably go to a Correction Center by the end of next year," he said. "I'll still have another five to go."

"It'll only be four by then," I said, trying to comfort him.

"Yeah, but you'll probably forget all about me."

"I'd never forget you, Paul. Are you crazy?"

He looked up and played with the curls in my hair. We fell asleep in each other's arms and didn't wake until we heard the sound of doors slamming down the hall.

It was count time, and we scrambled to put on our clothes. When we crawled out from Paul's bed, we heard the lock engage in the door. The guard must have pulled the release break at the end of the hall.

"Uh oh," I panicked. "We're fucked."

"Fuck it," Paul said. "We're busted—it's no big deal."

When the guard came around and looked in on us, he shook his head in disgust and continued with his rounds. A few minutes later, he came back and unlocked Paul's door, manually with his key. He didn't say anything as I climbed out and headed up the hall toward my cell. He left me waiting in front my door, before he came back with a pink misconduct report in his hand. He let me inside and then top-locked the door.

"What are you doing?" I asked.

"Giving you a ticket," he said. "Administrative Segregation until you go to court."

He'd written me up for being for two-in-a-room. It carried up to five days in detention. When you were placed on AD-SEG, you were kept locked in your cell until your hearing, which they had to give you within forty-eight hours.

Two things immediately crossed my mind. One, the hearing officer said that if he saw me again, he was going to take a look at my good time. And two, Sherry said I couldn't get any tickets. Did this mean I'd lose my job?

Outside the hearing room, I waited in the same chairs that were used by inmates who waited for the infirmary. Black Diamond was sitting at the end of row.

"How you doing," I said, smiling. I felt guilty because I had been avoiding her.

"Well if it isn't Sleeping Beauty," Black Diamond said. She smiled.

"I guess you heard, huh?"

"I keep trying to tell you, girl. Ain't no secrets in here."

"What can I say," I said. "I guess I'm a slow learner."

"You'll be all right. You've already done half the max they can give you."

"I don't know about that," I said. "He threatened to look at my good time."

Black Diamond nodded, but no further reassurances came.

Just then, one of the convicts who always seemed to be making jokes about Black Diamond, walked up and sat down next to her. He leaned over and said to her a seductive voice, "How you doing, baby?"

"All right," Black Diamond answered, hesitantly.

"You know you're a fine motherfucker, right?"

Black Diamond nodded. "Uh-huh."

They looked at each other a moment, and then they both got up and crossed the hall. Black Diamond gave me a sly look as she closed the broom closet door.

I stared after them for a long time, thinking how this might be the only place in the world, where in that moment, Black Diamond was seen as a fine motherfucker. It was probably the only place where she could have such an active sex life.

I didn't know whether to be happy or sad for her.

It didn't seem right that I should be fired from my job for just one ticket, but Sherry had warned me ahead of time. I had screwed up, just like the guys on the paper said I would. I was going to miss everyone. We spent a lot of time in that newsroom talking about everything from prison gossip to urban politics. Josh and Spaulding usually had the most to say, but Sherry was active in a lot of our conversations. I was going to miss her more than anyone.

One conversation that stuck out with me most was when we talked about Judge Geraldine Bledsoe Ford of Detroit's Recorders Court.

"That sister is fierce," Lee had said. "She'd send a motherfucker, I mean, she'd send a brother away for nine hundred and ninety-nine years if she had that many pennies left in her coffee can."

"Yes," Sherry said, "but did you know that her grandfather was a slave?"

"Say what?"

"That's right. And her father was a sharecropper, but that didn't stop either one of them from getting a college education. I'll bet you didn't know that."

"Well, you'd think she'd cut the brothers some slack," O. J. said.

Sherry said, "I think she has."

"How can you say that?" I asked.

Everyone looked over at me. I usually didn't have much to add, so I normally just sat there and listened. 'Yeah," O. J. said, "How can you say that? She's the meanest judge in the state."

"Well, I don't know about all of that," Sherry said, "but she is the first African American woman to become a judge in the state and sometimes holding one accountable and demanding nothing less than full responsibility is the best you can do for them, even if it doesn't look like it at the time." Sherry didn't care if her opinion might be unpopular with us—she always spoke her mind.

As I was about to go inside the hearing room for my ticket, the outside door at the end of the hall swung open and Josh came in with the cold. He saw me sitting there and said, "Good, I'm glad I caught you before you went in." He came up and handed me a piece of paper. "Here you go, Squeeze. I think this will help."

"What is it?"

"Policy Memorandum 1977-2," he said. "It lists all of the non-bondable offenses that you can be locked up for pending a disciplinary hearing."

"Yeah?"

"Well, *two-in-a-room* is not one of them," he said. "Which means the only way they can lock you up pending a hearing is if the shift commander determined that your ongoing freedom was a threat to the security and good order of the institution."

"Well maybe he did."

"Does it say so on your ticket?"

I looked at the report. It didn't mention this.

"Your due process has been violated," he said. "They have to throw it out, pursuant to *Wolff v. McDonald*." Josh grinned. Maybe all his years in the prison law library was finally paying off.

I looked up not knowing if I should trust him. It sounded too good to be true.

"You owe me one," he said.

"I'd say you owe me already." I handed him back the citations.

"Maybe you're right," he said, "but take it anyway. It should help."

When I went inside I handed the policy directive to the hearing officer, who read it, studied it for a moment and then picked up the phone. Whoever he called didn't answer, so he hung up and started writing. He put a check in the box marked *Dismissed*.

When I came back out in the hall, Black Diamond and Josh were waiting for me.

"It worked!" I said. "I got off!"

Josh seemed even more thrilled than I was. "Information is power, Squeeze." Inmates love getting over on The Man. "Now let's hope it helps you to keep your job."

"Did Sherry say anything about my being fired?" I asked. I hadn't been officially notified that I was losing my job.

"It doesn't look good, Tim."

"But now that I beat the ticket, I should be OK. Right?"

"I'm not sure that will be enough for the warden, since it was on a technicality."

"I'll file a grievance," I said.

"I doubt it'll do you any good, but you can always try. Stop by and see me this afternoon in the law library and I'll see if I can come up with something."

"Thanks," I said.

He nodded.

I smiled at Black Diamond. "Maybe you two can hook up."

"I'm already ahead of you," Josh said.

"Well, all right," I said, imitating Black Diamond. "Go make it happen, girl."

"See!" Black Diamond said. "You're catching on."

I sat outside Sherry's office, waiting to go inside. Her door was closed, which meant she was probably in a staff meeting. It was nice of Josh to help me, but I was still suspicious of him. He was smart, but nobody does nothin' for free. Not inside anyway.

I hoped he was wrong about Sherry and the warden, but when her door opened, she told me right off that she had to fire me. I tried to object, but Sherry held up her hand. "I'm going to hire you as my clerk," she said. "If that's OK with you?"

I smiled from ear to ear.

"Good," she said, "then it's settled. I'm having a desk and a typewriter moved outside my office first thing tomorrow morning."

But little did I know what lay ahead for me later that day.

That afternoon, when I returned from school, Reese grabbed my ass. "Now go back and get your little bitch," he said, "so I can grab some of her ass, too." The two guys that were standing with him laughed.

When I told Paul about it, he just nodded coolly and stared at the opposite end of the cellblock. "OK," he said, after a minute. "It's gonna be like that is it."

He looked at me. "Listen to what I tell you, and do exactly as I say."

I sat up in my chair. I was scared, but Paul's confidence reassured me.

"Before you come down to chow tomorrow, I want to take your padlock and put it inside a sock. I'll show you how to tie it, but make sure it's the longest sock you've got."

My eyes widened. "What are you going to do?"

"I'm not going to do anything. *We're* gonna do what we have to do," Paul said. "These motherfuckers have to learn we're not playing."

The next morning, we returned from the chow hall early and ducked into the shadows of the door to the infirmary. It was still dark outside and unseasonably warm, but I was still trembling as if it were below zero.

Paul had me stand behind him, with my sock dangling in my right hand.

It was heavy from the padlock secured at the bottom by a tightly tied knot. Paul peered out from the edge, trying his best not to be seen. He had brought his lock in sock as well. Yet for all his bravado, he was shaking as much as me. For the first time, I thought maybe he was in over his head.

Reese came up the walkway alone. He didn't see us standing there. Nor did he see Paul come up behind him when he cracked him on top of his head. The sound of the lock bouncing off his crown let out a loud smack—rattling the tumblers inside the lock. Reese staggered backward, and Paul hit him with a left hook and then again with the lock in his right hand. Reese ducked and then slipped and fell, scrambling to catch his footing up the walkway that led to the control center. Stunned, but emboldened by his falling, I lunged forward and swung, just missing him. Aside from that early night in the barracks, this was the first time I was really fighting back—and it felt terrifying. I took another swing, knowing that Paul would be pissed if I didn't try. I hit him across his ear, though the lock bounced off his shoulder breaking the impact. Paul came around my left and brought his lock crashing down on top of him, hitting squarely on the head just as he tried to bolt up the walk. Reese fell to the pavement. Paul and I each hit him again and then ran into A-unit, before anyone saw us.

By mid-morning, most of the inmates had heard what had happened. Reese was taken to Riverside, where he was kept in the infirmary for several days before he was transferred to another prison in Muskegon, which was often the case when inmates were assaulted.

And for a little while, at least, Paul and I were left alone. But there were a few who let me know, that if were it not for Paul—they'd "take that" nodding toward by ass.

"These ho's ain't gonna do a motherfuckin' thing," Paul said. "They ain't gonna do nothin' but sell wolf tickets." Wolf tickets were when inmates talked about what they were going to do to somebody, but they rarely backed it up unless they were traveling in a pack, and even then—Paul said, loudly, "many of these bitches are cowards."

I smiled, proudly, because he had empowered me. I had not felt so good since I came to prison, even though I knew Paul was doing the very thing he was accusing them of doing. He was just showing off and bluffing, like we were playing poker. Paul said, "That's a big part of it, you know. It's not whether you're going to something or not, the game is—in making them believe that you will. But every now and then, you have to show a good hand. Most of these guys are too short to do anything in here." He was referring to the fact that most were within a few months of parole—so they weren't going to do that much. "But I don't give a fuck," Paul said. "I've been down too long to put up with these knuckleheads. I'm liable to haul off and take off their motherfuckin' heads."

What terrified me most, was how good it felt to attack Reese. Once I got beyond my fears, I actually enjoyed it. There was one moment in particular, when I swung at Reese that I wanted him to pay for everything awful that had ever happened to me. "This is for Chet and Red and Nate and Moseley and every other fucker who's ever messed with me," I thought, slugging away at him. And as the lock came crashing down into his skull, I felt an odd sense of relief. Paul was teaching me how to survive in there. What he showed me that day, however, was the most valuable lesson of my entire stay. And it took a boy—not a man—to teach me this.

33

Broken Promises

Next Month. Next Year. Next Season. As soon as the school year is over.

For eight years I believed what she had to say. I was sixteen before I realized I was never again going to live with my mother. Yet after a while, I was too afraid to complain to her, because she might cut me off—like she had already done to my brother and sister.

Once, when Rick and I got into trouble together, she told me I could forget her phone number.

Were it not for the 4:30 count, I would have slept all afternoon. Paul shoved me as the stampede of feet came up the catwalk. "You better hurry up," he said. "You don't want another ticket."

I couldn't afford any more, since Simon was looking for a reason to separate us. Simon was the ARUM, the Assistant Resident Unit Manager, or A-hole as Paul called him. I didn't know where he was, during the first part of my stay, when I was having all kinds of problems—but now here he was—and busting our balls.

I slipped out of Paul's room and fought the tide of bodies as I made my way up the hall then down the other wing to my cell.

"Parsell," Goodman yelled. "Where've you been, boy?"

"Nowhere," I said.

Goodman was the counselor—the Resident Unit Manager. He was Simon's superior. Simon had been on our case because of how close Paul and I had become. As if our closeness were a problem. And so now what did Goodman want?

"Come to my office when count is cleared," Goodman said. He was black, and Simon was white but they shared the same office on the second tier.

After count, I went to his office and stood in his door.

"Well, if it isn't Timothy, the disciple of Paul," Goodman joked, hanging up the phone. He pointed to a chair next to his desk. "We need to talk about you and your friend."

"What about it?" I sat down.

"Well, there's concern you two are spending too much time together."

"I really don't give a fuck," I said. I could feel my anger rising, but it felt good to talk back like that. I wouldn't dare do that with any of the inmates, and there wasn't much he could do to me—other than write me a ticket. Besides, no one ever intervened when an inmate was being taunted or abused.

"There's no need to get belligerent," he said. "I'm not the enemy."

"I didn't say you were. It's just that it's not anyone's business what Paul and me do—unless we're breaking the rules."

"Is that so?"

"That's right," I said, imagining Paul being proud of me for standing up for us.

"OK," he said. "Then we don't have anything else to discuss."

"Fine." I got up and walked out, fairly pleased with myself for putting him in his place. Though it did occur to me, that it seemed to have ended too easily.

Back in my room, Paul said, "You shouldn't have done that. He was trying to befriend you."

"Well, I didn't know that," I said, disappointed that he wasn't proud of me. Far from it. "What was I supposed to do?"

"I think we need to go back there and clean it up," Paul said. "He's is the only thing standing between us and that A-hole Simon."

Goodman listened quietly as I groveled in his doorway, Paul at my side. "I'm sorry, I didn't know what to say, and I was nervous you were going to move us. We didn't do anything wrong, and Simon has been busting our balls. And . . . I'm sorry I cursed at you."

"I tried to befriend you," he said. "And you shit all over me."

"But what about all these other motherfuckers?" Paul said. "It's a bunch of shit and you know it." Paul was incensed because they weren't questioning anyone else about how "close" they had become.

"I don't know what to say," Goodman said. "Simon's gone to the commander."

Paul jumped in, "You know what'll happen if they separate us, Mr. Goodman."

"Divide and conquer," he said, nodding, "but you two guys have been fronting yourselves off by spending too much time together—and disappearing."

I couldn't understand what was happening, "You mean because we spend a lot of time together, but don't get into trouble—that we're a problem?"

It was bullshit, and he knew it. If we had been hanging out with *a man*, they wouldn't have said a thing. But because we were two queers who stuck together they wanted to break us up. It wasn't fair. Besides, they knew that if they split us up, we'd be vulnerable to being attacked.

"I'll file a grievance!" I challenged.

"And say what?" Goodman said, looking at me. "That you can't be with your boyfriend? This is prison, boy. You got no right to be with anyone."

"And you call this befriending me?" I said.

"It's too late for that now. Simon's taken it out of my hands."

Paul and I went to chow together, but neither of us had an appetite.

"It's not your fault," Paul said. "Simon was going to have us separated no matter what Goodman said."

"I hate both those motherfuckers," I said.

The next afternoon, the guard told Paul to pack his belongings. He was being moved to D-unit. "Maybe I can get over there too," I said.

Paul shook his head. "There's no way. Our best bet is to wait a week or two and then you should asked to be moved to E- or F-unit. I'll wait a week or so and do the same. Maybe the housing officer will forget you and I aren't supposed to be in the same housing unit. In the meantime, we'll have to hook up at chow and at yard."

My stomach tightened. I didn't think I could ever eat again. I was losing not only my best friend in prison, but also the boy who had protected and taught me so much.

"Can I help King carry his stuff?" I asked the guard at the desk.

"No," Simon said from the landing above. "Get Williams or Nichols to help, but Parsell you stay here."

I tried to protest, but Paul stopped me. "Don't. It's not worth it."

"Yeah, boy!" an inmate called out from the side. "Your little Popsicle ain't gonna help you now."

Paul shot him a look, but he was unmoved. "Go on, bitch, and get yourself a man while you're at it."

"That's enough," Simon said. "King! Get moving."

I walked to my cell, not wanting to give them the satisfaction of knowing I was crumbling inside. "I'll see you at chow," I said to Paul. "Hang back if they call you first."

"I'll see you," Paul said. He looked at me, and I could tell he was feeling exactly as I was. He looked up at Simon and grabbed his bags.

Later that week, when I reported to work early, Sherry's door was closed. I sat at my desk and started typing job orders that were in my in-box. I didn't know who she was in there with, but it had to be another staff member, since she never closed the door with an inmate. I heard a man's voice rise, and I went to listen at the door to see if I could tell who it was. He sounded angry. "You'd make warden a hell of lot sooner, if you weren't such an arrogant . . ." He snatched open the door and his face dropped when he found me standing there.

He was a black man, in his late twenties. He was wearing a suit, and walked out without saying another word. He looked embarrassed.

"I'm sorry," I said to Sherry. "I was just . . ."

"It's OK," she said.

"I just wanted to make sure . . ."

"I said it's OK."

That afternoon, I tried to ask what happened, because I was dying to know who the man was. "Don't," she said. It was the first time I felt like she was closing me out, the same way Mom used to.

"What?" she asked, annoyed. "You think you're the only one who gets harassed?"

I'd never heard her take such a harsh tone with anyone.

"Don't worry about me," Sherry said. "I can handle myself. There are battles worth fighting, and there are some you can only lose. So I pick mine wisely. What about you?"

"What about me?"

"There are no victims in here," she said harshly. "Everybody feels sorry for themselves, but what about what you did to get yourselves here in the first place? What about the victims of your crime? How much pity do any of you have for them?"

"I didn't hurt anyone," I said.

"Yeah? What about the people you stole from?"

"It was a company."

"And the woman inside the Photo Mat? You don't think she was frightened? Don't you see? All you're worried about is how you feel. How you've been messed over—but I don't hear you taking responsibility for anything. Regardless of what was done to you."

"I don't know what you're talking about," I said. "I'm going to school." I almost felt like crying. I didn't understand why she was attacking me.

"Sure, you're gong to school. That's great. I'm very proud of you, but what I'm talking about is growing up. Getting rid of these baby attitudes, like how wrong the world is and how everybody is always hurting you. A lot of you guys use that stuff as an excuse for your behavior—like it's OK to act any way you want."

"I do not!"

"Yes you do. That's all I've been hearing from you—how unfair it is that Simon had Paul moved. You know you two are lovers and that sexual misconduct is against the rules, yet the only thing I hear you talking about is how wrong Simon is."

"Well he is! They didn't catch us doing anything." I hated her for turning on me like this. What did she know about "sexual misconduct"? Had she been gang raped or forced to turn to a man for protection and then had to do anything he ordered her to do? I had thought she was cool. With Paul gone, Miss Bain was the only bright spot in my life. I needed her attention now, more than ever. Only she wasn't listening. She was talking just like Goodman, Simon, or the warden.

"Oh never mind!" I said. "I thought I could talk to you."

"You can talk to me," Sherry said. "You can always talk to me. But it doesn't mean you'll always hear what you want to hear."

"You're all just a bunch a homophobes."

A bunch of what?"

"Homophobes," I repeated. "Homophobia." I read it in the book Paul gave me.

"I'm not afraid of homosexuals," Sherry said. "And I don't dislike them either, but the rules are the rules, and the issue is not whether anything is wrong with being gay. The issue is—the enforcement of rules and your willingness to accept responsibility."

"Forget it!" I stormed out of the office.

How could she be so callous? She was probably taking Simon's side because she had to, and I didn't want to hear it. I felt betrayed by her, and I didn't care if she reported me, or wrote me up. I wasn't going to listen to any more of her bullshit. What made me think anyone inside would be different?

"You always have a choice," she had said to me once, after Paul and I beat up Reese with our locks. "You can let what happens in here harden you up— or soften you. And only you can decide that. But take a good look around. Which one do you think will take you further?" She obviously knew what we had done, but neither of us would discuss it with her directly. Besides, she knew we would never admit it, so we talked around the matter without putting either one of us in an uncomfortable spot.

Paul's lips tasted sweet, but his stubble pinched the skin around my mouth reminding me of old times under his bed. When Slide Step first kissed me, I had asked if he wouldn't do it again. I didn't like kissing. I told him about the girl I had once dated in seventh grade and the time she stuck her tongue in my mouth after a dance. It grossed me out. Slide Step understood. But now that Paul was doing the same, I was able to surrender to it. In fact, I loved it. He was holding the back of my head while caressing my neck. When I opened my eyes, I was expecting to see his shut, but they weren't. He was staring at me intensely, and it drove me wild. Paul was the first person who made me feel I could do no wrong. He even liked it when I acted like a geek and embarrassed myself. When he nibbled on my lip, I felt my dick grow.

We were lying beneath the junipers next to the gym. It was cold outside, and an occasional pine needle cut through my jeans. They were sharp, like his chin, which scratched a light trail across the skin of my stomach. He had been sucking me for what felt like an hour. He caught my load, as I exploded, and continued sucking. My breath was racing as fast as my mind, but in those few moments, I felt as if I had transcended the barbed-wire fence that surrounded us.

Paul was in D-unit, and I had been moved to C. We waited a few weeks and asked if I could be moved to D; meanwhile Paul asked about C—but we were both told no.

I took Jake on as my man. I didn't have a choice, and Paul was being pressured as well. Something happened to him earlier in the day, but he didn't want to talk about it.

Paul scooted up beside me against the wall and took my hand. "I just can't take it no more," he said. His eyes glassed over. "I've been down a long time."

We sat there silently—holding each other's hand and listening to inmates come and go from the gym. "You know, before coming to prison," Paul said. "I'd never harmed anyone physically. I never even considered it. People don't realize how difficult it is to keep your mind when you're in an environment where at any moment you might be assaulted. It's a bad way to live."

I squeezed his hand.

"In order to survive, you have to become an animal just like everyone else, because the only thing they respect is violence."

"I wish people on the outside knew what went on here," I said.

"Shit. We're convicts," Paul said. "Nobody cares about convicts."

I looked up at the sky through the trees.

He was right, but it still didn't seem right.

"You'll be out in a year or so," he said. "I still have a long time to go. I'm just tired, you know?"

I looked at Paul and nodded.

The consequences of what we were considering had not occurred to me.

We had devised a plan of escape. On the face of the inside fence, was a tightly woven metal mesh that ran about halfway up. It prevented hands and feet from being able to climb it. And the rolls of constantine wire created an extra hurdle. But the gun tower on the corner fence, behind the gym, was often unmanned.

Paul and I discussed our route as we hid in the bushes and watched for movement in the tower. "I'm not sure I can climb the fence where the mesh is," I told Paul.

"I'll be right behind you," he said. "I'll give you a boost."

Paul had taken forks from the kitchen and rolled tape around the handles to give us something to grip. "But what if they bend?" I said. "You're not tall enough to boost me."

"Don't worry," he said. "You'll make it."

"Maybe we should wait and go over the gate to the rec yard, then scale the other fence in back." The fence that enclosed the recreation yard was different from the others. It was a single rather than a doubled fence, and the gate to the yard didn't have any mesh on it, so we could climb it easily—without having to use the forks.

"Yeah, but then we'll have to climb the outer fence in back," Paul said. "And that one has the mesh."

"So what," I said. "If we wait and go on a foggy night, the guards won't be able to see us. So we can take as long as we need." There was another tower, along the back line of the yard, but that was only manned when inmates occupied the yard.

Paul looked at me and considered it.

He leaned back against the building, nodding his head. He looked relieved.

"We can slip out our windows in the middle of the night and meet over here." He pointed to corner of the gym. "Or better yet, I'll come tap on your window. I know how you like to sleep."

A couple of days later, when they were late clearing the morning count and called my unit to chow, I looked for Paul but couldn't find him. Certainly, the fog hadn't made it easier to locate him.

"Hey Tim!" an inmate shouted. "Your boy broke camp last night."

I stopped in my tracks. He did what? Suddenly, it made sense. The fog, the delayed count, they were off by one. I couldn't move. Several more inmates walked past, "He made it, Dawg. He got away!"

He was supposed to come get me! How could he leave without me? I'd never felt so abandoned, not even by my family.

"You should be happy," one of the inmates said.

He had waited for the perfect night. The fog was so thick the guards couldn't see the fence. It felt like a gunshot had crackled from one of the towers, and it hit me squarely in the chest. I couldn't breath. I looked over at the gates next to the gym to see. The barbed wire drooped at the top. I just couldn't believe he was gone.

I even watched and waited as the last of the white guys straggled out of D-unit. Naturally, Paul wasn't there. "He made it!" someone cheered. It was true. Paul was gone.

I went back to my cell and cried. Now I was *truly* alone.

A few minutes later, I was called to Unit Manager's office.

"I'm sure you're aware," Fitzsimmons, the ARUM for C-unit, said. "King escaped this morning. They've asked me to see if you know where he is?"

As if I would help them. Fitzsimmons was just like the others—a pompous prick who didn't give a fuck about Paul or me. They couldn't stand that we were happy together. Fags weren't entitled to happiness. Even inmates who raped the boy they kept weren't separated. If it weren't for these bastards, Paul would still be here. Well, fuck Fitzsimmons, and the rest of these motherfuckers. But I couldn't say that and jeopardize myself, so I simply shook my head no.

He started to say something, but stopped himself. "OK then. That's all."

I went back to my cell laid on the bed. I faced the wall, blocking out everything else, as I did the next day and the day after that. I had classes to attend, but I didn't care. A letter slid under my door. I didn't bother to get up. I left it there on the floor.

"C'mon," I said to Randy. "Please?"

"No way."

Randy was the best tattoo man in the prison. I wanted him to put Paul's name on my arm or shoulder, but he wouldn't do it. Yet he did everyone else's tattoos. He had taken apart an alarm clock, and attached a sharpened piece of guitar string to the hammer that rang the bell. Once wound up, the hammer went back and forth, puncturing the skin. He dipped the "needle" in ink that was made from torn-out pages of a Bible.

"You'll end of up regretting it," he said, "and you'll blame me."

"No I won't," I pleaded. "I really won't."

"I know how you're hurting right now, Tim, and I'm not going to do it."

"Fine," I said, and stormed back to my room.

The next day, news of Paul arrived. But it wasn't from the guards and administrators. They wouldn't tell us anything. We found out instead from a Grand Rapids newspaper. On the front page was a picture of Paul, leaning face down over the hood of a police car. According to the paper, he had broken into a house near the prison, tied up a young woman with a phone cord, stole her car and then headed toward the state line. He asked for directions before he left, so when she untied herself—she called the police, described the car he was driving, and the direction he was headed in. The State Police caught him in a roadblock. He was charged with breaking and entering of an occupied dwelling, armed robbery, car theft, and escape. He was taken across the valley to the Michigan Reformatory and was thrown in the hole.

I didn't know what to feel when I saw the back of his ponytail in that picture. Whereas once I couldn't believe he'd left without me, now I couldn't believe he had been caught. All I could think about was all the time he was going to get.

"Ten years minimum," one of the cons said. "They gave him a dime the last time, so the judge will give him at least that much."

Another con pushed his way in to look at the paper.

"No way. They'll give him twenty. They double it the second time around."

"Ain't no good time either," the first guy said. "The motherfuckers done took that away. He ain't never getting out."

"Stacked!" One of them shouted. "They'll stack it on his first sentence, so he'll have to finished serving that time before he begins the next."

That could have been me with him—facing all that time, but all I cared about was being back together with him. No matter if it meant twenty more years in prison. He wouldn't have gotten caught if had taken me with him. I wouldn't have let him be so stupid as to ask for directions and then go that way. How dumb could you be? That wasn't like Paul. Hello, Police? I've just escaped from prison, I'm driving a stolen car, plate number: *I'm a big fucking idiot*—and I'm traveling on Route 66 headed right at you.

I wrote him a letter and asked him why he had left without me.

Two days later, I was summoned to the Control Center. Mr. Curtis, the Deputy Warden, was holding the letter I had written to Paul.

"Are you sure you don't want to talk about this?" he said.

He was placing me in administrative isolation pending a security reclassification hearing. This was standard practice when they had information that an inmate was planning to escape.

When I had finally read the letter had been slipped under my door, a few days before, it was from Paul. He sent it to me the same day he left—apologizing for leaving without me.

"I didn't come get you," he wrote, "because you don't have that much time to go. And I needed to do this on my own. You know how to do your time now. But please know, that I will always love you."

The letter Mr. Curtis was holding was my response.

All incoming mail was screened for contraband, yet out going mail was sealed and private. When I mailed my letter to Paul, I hadn't considered what happens at the other end. My letter was screened when it arrived at M-R. They sent it back.

"You wrote some pretty heavy stuff in this," Mr. Curtis said.

I didn't know what to say. I was embarrassed about what I had written, even though I couldn't remember most of it. I was trying to express what was tearing me up inside. I remembered telling Paul how I missed him and would give anything to be with him—including going over the fence myself—just to see him again.

"I don't believe you really intended to escape," Mr. Curtis said. "But I have to lock you up pending a hearing. It's standard procedure."

Not only couldn't I see Paul, now I couldn't communicate with him either.

"I'm assigning the Inmate Advocate to work with you. The outcome of this has consequences I'm not sure you're capable of understanding."

Mr. Curtis was an African American, and like Miss Bain, he surprised me by seeming to be kind.

They moved me back to A-unit, and into an isolation cell. A few days later, the Inmate Advocate came to see me. The guard unlocked my door and brought me down to the card room. The housing unit was empty with most inmates away at their assignments.

Miss Brown smiled, as I sat opposite her, and then waited patiently as I swapped chairs. The first one had a crooked leg and wobbled slightly.

"I had a hard time getting comfortable myself," she smiled.

I didn't know who to trust anymore, so just nodded politely.

"Sometimes, when you find someone else who doesn't belong—it's as good as belonging yourself," she offered. "I know this isn't easy to talk about, but we have to get you prepared for your hearing. The consequences could be serious, and . . ."

"I don't care," I said. "They can increase my security or do whatever they want." And I meant it, too. For once, I spoke the truth of my feelings without fear of the consequences. I had Paul to thank for that.

"Do you have a cigarette?" I asked.

"I don't smoke," she said.

Of course she didn't. She looked too straightlaced and reminded me of a vegetarian character from one of Paul's novels. She wasn't wearing a wedding ring either. For a moment there, I wondered if maybe she was gay. At least that would've given us something to talk about.

"I don't have anything to say," I said.

She looked toward the guard's desk.

"I'll be right back," she said.

She closed the door behind her, and I put my head down on the desk.

Whatever they were going to do, I just wished they'd hurry up and do it. It didn't matter anymore.

The door opened again, and I heard her enter. She placed something on the table and slid it across to me.

It was a journal, with a black and white cover—similar to the one I was given when I first went to work for *The Oracle*. I looked up and saw Miss Bain standing there.

"I don't think Paul would have wanted to see you self-destruct," she said.

"Hey Miss Bain." I looked down at the floor. I'd not seen her since storming out of her office the day she bawled me out. It was nice to see her, but I was embarrassed by how I must have looked.

She sat down opposite me at the table.

"You look like you could use a shower," she said.

In spite of myself, I smiled at her.

"You miss him, don't you?"

I nodded.

She nodded back.

She placed a pen on top of the journal and slid it closer to me.

"I know, for me," she said, "I can sometimes write about things I'm not able to verbalize. Maybe you could start by writing about what he meant to you, Tim. Something seems to awaken inside of you when you write, so let it speak to you."

I sat in my cell for several days, before I picked up the pen. Yet when I did something really did seem to take over. I wrote about how I felt prior to coming to prison, and what it was like for me when I first arrived there. I put into words for the first time what it felt like to be drugged and raped and forced to get a man. How Slide Step took care of me, and how I was devastated to learn he might have been the one who set up the attack in the first place. I wrote about my experience in county jail and how the probation officer hit on me. "You probably won't believe this," I wrote, to whoever might one day open the journal and read its contents, "but it happened, so I don't care what you think." And then I wrote about Paul and how I had never known anyone similar to him before. Paul was like me—he was gay. He liked what I liked and felt the same way I did about most things. He had been raped, just as I had been, but had learned how to deal with the memory of it. I told how he helped me when no one else would and how he taught me to survive in here. I wrote about how, after having sex with him, for the first time in my life—I no longer felt alone in the world.

Recalling all of this was enormously difficult. Beyond the painful thoughts I forced myself to summon up, I was made to stay "present" through the writing process. Not zoning out or detaching myself from the deep wounds that up till then had held me back. Like my dad, I retreated inward, to that place where a small part of myself was kept hidden from the rest of the world. Somewhere safe.

Reluctantly, I let the inmate advocate read it. When at last she'd finished, she looked at me with a gentle smile, knowingly. Something in her expression told me that she understood. Finally someone understood. I came out and spoke the truth of my feelings and someone at long last understood. The feeling of being seen and heard for who I really was overwhelmed me.

That afternoon, the Classification Committee released me from isolation.

The following day, I went back to work. Miss Bain had made sure I was reinstated.

"You have a lot to catch up on," she said.

I took some folders back to my desk and sat down. I noticed the calendar. The day Paul escaped had been March 3, 1979. Exactly one year since I first came to prison.

34

I Will Arise and Go Now

*I stood near the dugout, swinging the two bats together at the same time.
This was how Little Leaguers warmed up when it was their turn next to
bat. Holding two at a time made it easier when I stepped to the plate
with one. I took a practice swing and then another. Suddenly, something
inside of me said, "You're going to blast that ball right out of here."*

*I'm not sure why that happened, but I believed that voice and swung
at the very first pitch. The bat let out a crack, and the ball set sail for
deep center field. The kids were playing shallow, expecting me to pop up
or strike out again. The ball flew over their heads.*

*When I came around third, the coach was waiving me in and my
teammates were cheering at home.*

*I don't know who or what it was that spoke to me that day, but it
didn't matter. I believed that voice, and it worked!*

Time passed slowly after Paul left. My days dragged by, each one much like the
other, until days had become weeks and weeks became months, turning finally
into years. I settled into a routine and struggled to keep my sanity as I watched
my body slowly change—filling out some, and finally developing muscle.

I was glad I wasn't sent to the Michigan Reformatory, Gladiator School,
to be with Paul. I remained very afraid of the place. When a prison riot broke
out over there, many of the gay men and boys were gang raped. Paul told
me he had escaped being victimized himself, because he brandished a shank
and kept moving until the National Guard came in and quelled the disturbance. My brother Bobby was spared as well, though all of his belongings
were destroyed—including the new television my parents had bought for

him. The gangs were prevalent at M-R, and it was no place for a boy like me. Bobby toughened up some, even more than he'd always been, and he learned how to survive on his own. Paul just got someone that he could control—to take care of him.

I worked for Miss Bain for a couple more months, but she was promoted to Treatment Director and transferred to another prison. I was happy for her, but at the same time devastated. It felt like another abandonment. In hindsight, I believe Miss Bain was aware of this because of how well she handled the transition. She assigned me as a clerk, in the kitchen, working directly for the Food Services Director. It was a position that was demanding and carried a lot of responsibility. So I had some time to adjust before she left.

To keep others from messing with me, I hooked up with Jake from the inmate store. I moved to D-unit, where he was housed, but that only lasted for a couple weeks—the Administration had me moved, because we were spending too much time together. Once I was moved to another unit, the other inmates started pressuring me again. Jake had respect among the other inmates, but it was difficult being separated from him in another unit.

I sat back and studied the inmates, like Paul had taught me, and looked for someone else that I might be able to control. But I still hadn't figured it out, so I stayed with Jake and learned to navigate the pressures. Balancing when to get Jake involved with someone who was pressing me, and when to just ignore troublemakers who were giving me a hard time. In exchange for his protection, I hooked up with Jake in the projectionist booth once a week during the inmate movie. Jake was as gentle as he could be, but he wasn't Paul, and he wasn't Slide Step.

After Sherry left, I sent several "kites" requesting a transfer to another prison—thinking it might be different somewhere else, but the only other medium-security prison for inmates who were under twenty-five was The Dunes in Kinross, Michigan. But The Dunes was made up of dormitories and, according to the policy at the time, homosexuals could not be housed in dorms.

Ever since I beat that ticket on a technicality, I spent time in the law library studying the Department of Correction's Policy Directives. I was fascinated by them and once again entertained the fantasy of one day becoming a lawyer. There was something empowering about knowing the rules and regulations as well, or even better, than some of the staff. And that's when the idea hit me.

That evening, on my way back to my cell, I picked up a stack of official grievance forms from the guard at the front desk. Warden Handlon hated grievances, so I started filling them out for anything I could think of—no matter how frivolous they might have been. I wrote one for not being allowed to walk on the grass, and another for how homosexuals were discriminated against in housing. And then another for not allowing magazines to be sold in the inmates store that depicted homosexual acts—even though the magazines they did sell like *Playboy, Hustler,* and *Penthouse,* routinely showed spreads of lesbian action. It was male homosexuality they were outlawing; yet they looked the other way if it were women. I filed another grievance for the types of inmate movies they were choosing, and for Warden Handlon's refusal to allow a Prisoner's Progress Association. Anything I could think of, I wrote a grievance. Then I dropped them all in the box, smiling to myself at the thought of the warden seeing them appear on his monthly report.

Two days later I was called up to the Control Center and when I arrived there, two guards were dispatched to my cell to pack up my belongings.

"Bag and baggage," Mr. Jackson, the Administrative Assistant Warden, said to me. "Warden Handlon has ordered you transferred."

"For what?" I said, sounding innocent.

"For protection," he said. "In one of your voluminous grievances, you stated that you were in fear of retaliation from the guards or other inmates."

"Where are you sending me," I asked.

"M-R," he said.

"M-R! You can't send me to Gladiator School! And you can't increase my security without a disciplinary reason for doing it. At least not without an Administrative Hearing, *beforehand.*"

"For protection, we can," he said.

"And if anything happens to me over there you know I'll sue," I said.

Mr. Jackson just looked at me.

"If you're really doing this for protection, why don't you send me to Riverside?"

"You'd go to Riverside?" he asked.

"Hell yeah," I said. "I've been begging to go there ever since I got here."

"Wait right here," he said.

Mr. Jackson went into the next room, and I could hear him speaking to someone in a hushed a tone. Then he returned.

"OK," he said. "You're going back to Riverside."

I tried, unsuccessfully, to keep from smiling.

Two hours later, I was once again crossing the yard of Riverside Correctional Facility, where the sounds of radios bellowed from all directions. I heard steel weights being dropped on concrete, and the familiar smell of earth and spring was in the air. If the place hadn't changed much, I surely had. I walked with a cat in my stride and few inmates on the yard even bothered to notice me. I was no longer a fish.

Once inside 10 Building, I breathed a sigh of relief when the guard took me upstairs to the second floor. And that's when it occurred to me. What if he wasn't here anymore? I stopped and stood in the hall. The guard, who was escorting me, turned around and looked at me.

I knew Riverside wasn't necessarily the best place for me. It was a close-custody prison, with guys who may not ever get out. And it was where the first of my rapes had happened. But at least Slide Step had protected me after that. And at least in here, there was someone who seemed to care about me. But what would happen if he were no longer here? Foolishly, I hadn't considered that possibility earlier, when I started executing my plan by filing all of those grievances.

I would learn later that at about that same moment, an inmate on the other side of the building ran up to Slide Step and told him, "Wait till you see this bad motherfucker who just walked up in here!"

Epilogue

It's my last night in prison and I sit in my cell hoping I will be able to sleep. My stomach felt nervous all day, and I couldn't eat. The thought of being released was exhilarating, but it was also scary. I didn't want to mess up again, like I had twice before. I was in a minimum-security camp for parole violators.

I remembered Miss Bain once say that if we're not careful, inmates can become institutionalized. We develop a learned helplessness, where we become almost dependent on the structure and security of prison. It seems counterintuitive, yet it would explain why guys were always coming back. Prisons are awful places, but you learn to adjust and after a while it becomes a way of life. I thought of the old timers I met at Riverside, the ones who were doing life on the installment plan, and drinking paint thinner and Mountain Dew. I was not going to become one of them.

I remembered how frightened I was the first time I got out. I was sent to a correction center in downtown Detroit, and as I stood at the corner of Clark and Vernon, I was afraid to step off the curb when the light turned green. It was as if I had forgotten how to cross the street—afraid I'd be run over by the busy traffic. They had given me a food voucher for a Coney Island, which I couldn't eat. And then I remembered the despair I had felt, just a few weeks later, when I realized how hard it was to make it in the free world.

Job prospects were difficult enough with the economy in a recession and the auto industry in the dumps. But then having to take a Department of Correction's job search verification form with me—to every place where I asked for an application—did wonders for getting me hired. I couldn't believe how quickly my dreams all seemed to vanish. At one point, I felt like I was more content inside prison than I did in the outside world. At least while I was in prison I had something to look forward to. On the outside, I had nothing. And worse—I didn't have a clue how to go about getting it.

I violated my parole by getting drunk and running away from the Correction Center. When I came back, the parole board gave me a six-month flop, which I was just finishing. But this time it was going to be different, I was determined to make it out there.

This time through was no easier than when I had been a fish, because everyone knew my story. I wouldn't punk up with anyone by choosing a man. I wasn't going to be anybody's fuck boy any more. At least violence was less of a threat here, since most of these guys too were waiting to be paroled soon.

I stayed calm, even when someone pounded on my cell door and hollered, "Good night, faggot!"

The guards were now flashing the lights for lock-down for the night.

"We'll get you next trip," another inmate yelled.

A few nights earlier, a black guy had tried to corner me in the bathroom—him and three other guys. As had been the case with Moseley, I walked a fine line—because any fights or complaints that might occur in my final days could delay my release. All the inmates knew that, so some took advantage of the situation. Even so, I was not about to let myself be victimized again. I'd grown up at least that much. Luckily, I saw the others hiding in the stall before they were able to grab me.

"Next time, Baby Boy," the inmate shouted. "That ass is mine!"

That was Carlton; he was on the ride-out list for 7 Block. The board flopped him for having drugs in his urine. He had been out of prison less than thirty days.

The guards pulled the release breaks, and the lock engaged in my door.

I dropped to the floor and did some push-ups, which helped me to vent my anger. It was my last night, in this inverted world, and the rage from my time in prison had swelled inside of me. It had been four years since I first came here. I was locked away between the ages of seventeen to twenty-one years old. So while some kids were away at Penn State, I was sitting in the state pen. It was some education.

When I first went in, I spent most of my time checking out from what went on in here. That had now changed. I struggled to remain present. But being present all the time had its drawbacks. It made me paranoid for one, and the cumulative effects of all that adrenaline can wreak havoc on your body's nervous system. Instead, I found another place—an in-between world—where I stood with my eyes wide open and my feelings locked away. It was as if an invisible force field surrounded me and nothing could penetrate it. Inmates could call me whatever they liked—faggot, snitch, punk-ass-bitch—but they weren't going to put their hands on me. Not if I could help it.

I was still on the floor, when I sensed someone watching me. It was the guard, Hughes, who had stopped in front of my cell. His eyes, like his hair, were old and gray. He had been indifferent to me since I first arrived, and even now, had a half-smirk on his face as he looked down at me.

"Good luck tomorrow," he said. "I hope you make it."

Then he said something I hadn't expected.

"You don't belong here."

They were simple words, plainly spoken, and yet they rang in my ears. The door at the end of the corridor squeaked open and then closed behind him. Perhaps it was an accumulation of everything that had come before, but what he had said triggered something inside me. I began to bawl uncontrollably. I didn't belong there, and all along I knew it. I tried to muffle the sound, but couldn't suppress the noise. Nor did it matter anymore.

"Yo!" an inmate yelled from down the hall. "Who the fuck is that?"

Another voice hollered, "Someone needs to give her a dick!"

Fuck 'em all, I thought. They could drown in my tears for all I cared. The rage, pain, and sadness escaped from me like a broken pipe, releasing all the pressure of emotions that had been suppressed so long that I had grown numb.

I lay there on the floor, curled and still, soothing my face against the cool metal bedpost. At some point, I had grabbed my pillow and hugged it like a baby as I sobbed. Then almost as suddenly as it had started, the tears stopped and my body calmed itself.

When I had shut down over the years, I had blocked out anything that hurt me or might have hurt me. At the same time, in doing so, I also locked something else in—stuffing it deep within myself. For a split second I caught a glimpse of who I truly was. It was such a brief simple moment—triggered by what that guard had said: "You don't belong here."

I got up off the floor and tossed the pillow on the bed. I threw cold water on my face and stared at myself in the scratched-up mirror above the sink. Then something unexpected happened. I got down on my knees and placed my hands together on the bed.

I could not believe what I was doing. It had been years since I had gone to mass. I felt as cut off from the church as from my family. God, it seemed, had abandoned me around the same time as my mother. But now I was down on my knees, and looking for answers. "Please God, just give me an opportunity, and I'll do the work."

I didn't know where my words were coming from, but I had heard someone say once, that only when your whole being becomes a prayer will God listen to it. I wasn't asking for anything so much as I was making a promise, a pact maybe, and not even with Him, but with myself. I had hit bottom and became willing to do whatever necessary to put the life I had known in the past. "Just give me an opportunity, and I'll do the work."

This was my last night behind bars.

The next morning, on May 3, 1982, I walked out of prison for the last time. And as I left there—I left as a man.

Epilogue

On June 1, 1984, I was discharged from parole. To date, the only run-ins I've had with the law have been minor traffic tickets. (I paid both fines immediately.)

My dad quit drinking for ten years. Sharon said they were the best years they ever spent together. They currently split their time between their home in Michigan and Texas, where they bought a trailer and retreat to in winter.

A year or so after my release, I came home for the holidays with a boyfriend. This was my first trip home with a guy and the first time my family had to face my sexuality head-on. To my surprise and delight, it was Sharon who stood up and said that anyone who had a problem with me—would have to deal with her.

In April, 2001, my brother Rick died from a drug overdose. He was forty-five and on parole at the time.

My stepbrother Bobby served nine years for the armed robbery he and my brother Rick committed together. He now lives in Michigan.

Claudia, my ex-girlfriend, had a miscarriage. I never heard from her again.

Slide Step is still in prison. His discharge date is 2021. I never asked him about what Paul had said. If he had set up my initial rape—I didn't want to know it.

The Oracle won an national penal press award. None of the original inmates who worked on the newspaper, upon their release, have returned to prison.

Warden Handlon retired from the Department of Corrections. He died a few years later, and the Michigan Training Unit was renamed The Richard A. Handlon Training Unit.

Sherry Burt made warden after thirteen years in the department. We've kept in touch, and she plans to retire soon.

When Paul was sentenced for escape, burglary, armed robbery, and car theft, his victim appeared in court. She asked the judge for leniency, citing how polite and apologetic Paul had been to her. Nonetheless, the Judge gave Paul ten additional years, to be served consecutively to his original sentence.

In the fall of 2002, while I began work on this book, I discovered sadly that Paul was still in prison. I wrote to him the following letter:

December 5, 2002

Dear Paul:

So here it is, almost twenty-five years later and you're finally hearing from me. I imagine this letter will come as quite a surprise. Yet even after all this time, I've never stopped thinking about you.

I tried to visit a few years back, but they had changed the rules and I couldn't get in to see you. I was all checked-in and it wasn't until the woman at the front desk told me to place my all my belongings in a locker that she noticed I wasn't on your list of approved visitors. I had stayed in a hotel the night before and was so nervous about seeing you again that I hardly slept.

I'm not sure why I didn't write to you after that. Perhaps I wasn't ready to deal with whatever feelings may have come up as a result. I was also a little afraid you might not remember me. Though you played a major role in my life, I realize you've been down a long time and I may not have been as significant in your life as you were in mine.

I assumed you were released after that, and I had no clue how to find you. I located you this time on the Internet. The Dept. of Corrections has a tracking system that's open to the public. It even has a nice digital picture. You've aged some since we last parted.

Enclosed is a picture of my family and me. As you can see, I look older as well. I'm the one in the middle with the (premature) gray hair. I've lost some weight since then—but I'm still a lot heavier than I was at seventeen. The good-looking folks next to me are my partner Tom and our daughter, Annie. We've raised her since she was in the 2nd grade; and we adopted her a few years later. She's fifteen now and growing up fast.

We live in a small village on the east end of Long Island. It's a remarkable place. Tom and I are openly gay and we're very active in our community. In fact, Tom ran for school board last spring and came within 16 votes of winning. He was up against three tough incumbents. It's wild how different life is from the Midwest and the 1970s. Our Mayor is a lesbian, but it's never been an issue. No one really cares. Unfortunately, I think she's a lousy Mayor.

I retired recently from the software industry. I got into computers when I moved to New York in 1982. I went to college at night and got my bachelor's degree in computer science and marketing. I rode a couple of waves in the software business and was in the epicenter of the dot.COM bubble burst in 2000. It was a lot of fun and I did well, but it also aged me. I was running U.S. Operations for an Israeli software company until this past summer, when they started to insist I travel to Israel a little more often than I wanted to. The last trip I made was in August, when a bus bombing occurred within a mile of my hotel. That was it for me. I decided there's more to life than living on airplanes.

Tom and Annie are glad to have me home and I'm enjoying not traveling as much. I've taken up writing and I've gotten involved with a human rights group. I want to spend the next chapter of my life working on something more meaningful than selling software. I'm currently writing a book about my first love and some of the darker days of my youth. I was doing research for this when I found you on the web.

It saddened me deeply to see how much of your life has

been spent inside, Paul. My heart broke for you, all over again. It seems only a moment ago that you were that eighteen-year-old kid who slipped inside my life and taught me how to celebrate who I am. I miss that kid, that friend, that lover and mentor who made such a difference in my life.

It's hard to try to put into words all that I'd like to say. There are so many ways in which some of the things you taught me, I have been able to work in my life in positive ways. Thank you for that, Paul. I want to tell you how sorry I am that you are still there. But I don't want to press your bit either. I can't imagine what that must feel like.

Please understand that I'm very happy in my life and with my family. I would not change a thing. I recognize that who you and I were, twenty-five years ago, is a world and a lifetime away from where we're each at in our lives today. But I wanted to take a moment to say hello and to honor what we shared together.

Whenever the song "Always and Forever" comes on the radio, no matter where I'm at or what I am doing, I stop and think of you. I remember when you sent me those lyrics shortly after you escaped. I think about what you meant to me and about that wonderful period when I fell in love for the first time. I think about how you helped me put aside my shame and rejoice in who I am. It was the first time that I no longer felt alone in the world. And though I've enjoyed a few successes since, there has never been another experience like that time and space that you occupied in my heart.

I came across two fragments of poems that best express these thoughts:

Stone walls do not a prison make, nor iron bars a cage;
If I have freedom in my love, And in my soul am free,
Angels alone that soar above enjoy such liberty.

But though my wings are closely bound, my heart's at liberty; My prison walls cannot control, the flight, the freedom of the soul.

In spite of our circumstances and the repressive world we were confined to; you helped free my spirit and liberate me. I hope you can see this in yourself and that in some small way this may help you. You're a wonderful man Paul, and life has not been kind to you. I pray that better times lie ahead. And above all else, I wish for you to know how much you have lived freely and joyously in my heart these last twenty-five years. This will never be contained, subdued, or silenced by anyone and anything.

Always and Forever,
Tim

I didn't know if I'd ever hear from Paul or even if he received my letter. But contrary to his warning that I'd forget about him, I never have. It's been twenty-five years since I had last seen him, yet the pain and memory of those experiences are as vivid to me now as they were back then. The thought occurred to me that the only difference between Paul and me was that he didn't come knocking on my window the night he escaped.

My Dear Tim:

I wish I could explain how much you brightened my life today. There have been very few truly exciting moments in my life, since I last saw you, but opening that letter and reading your beautiful words has been very special.

I'm in the prison hospital right now. I had a quadruple by-pass on December 6th. I am very tender all over but getting stronger each day. I am not as articulate as you are, but I hope I'm able to express how truly proud I am of you. I have thought of you many times over the years, and I never once doubted that you would do good things in your life.

I could never forget you Tim. I remember that wild curly hair that you could not keep out of your eyes and the quick intelligence that always made me proud of being your friend. I remember so clearly when we first met, you were being pursued by (Slide Step) and I lusted after you each time I saw you. Then we went to MTU and fell in love. You are the only man I have ever loved and that is OK with me.

A lot has happened in my life since I escaped on March 3rd, 1979. They gave me 10 to 20 for that escape and burglary and stacked it on top of the 10 to 20 I was already serving. In 1983 I got caught with a knife and they added another 2 to 5 year sentence.

I did get paroled in August 2000; I was out until September 12, 2001. I'm now back on a parole violation because I stopped reporting to my agent; dumb move on my part. I'm on my second 12-month flop. I've been on the street for one year since 1975. I'm not complaining just counting the years. My own actions are the cause of my prison stay.

I have not been involved with a man in over ten years; when I went home in 2000 I met a lady and I have a beautiful relationship with her. For the first time since I left your side, I found someone who truly loves me. I hope that you can some day meet her. She knows nothing about my sexual past, though I will tell her. But that's OK, because she would not question my friendship with you and nothing in this world could change the fact that you are one of the very few people on this earth I have ever truly loved or trusted.

You have a beautiful family, I can see the love and warmth in your faces; I am glad that your life turned out well and that you never returned to this madness. But I never doubted you would. I knew that you were better than all those people around us, including myself. And I'm so glad I didn't take you with me on that stupid escape.

As crazy as it may seem, I mentioned you to someone about a month ago. An old friend and I were walking the yard and talking about years past (He has been down 25). Well the subject got around to "the finest motherfuckers we ever met," (smile). I went on to describe a tall slim kid with a mass of curly hair, long legs, a plump butt and the sweetest lips God ever made for kissing.

My mind keeps flashing back to the time we spent together. I remember being in the field house with a hundred people around us. I looked across the room into your eyes and we both just smiled because the love was so strong.

I remember so clearly the first time we made love, we were under my bed and we used shampoo (smile). We both had dry skin for a week. I can remember sitting and talking for hours, and how difficult it was for you at first to have people know that you were gay, but after awhile you realized that only you can live your life.

Life was not a party then. I can remember us going after a

guy with a padlock because he would not leave us alone. But our bond just grew stronger and stronger. I have never stopped loving you and I never will; our lives are different now and we both have other people in our lives, but we can still be dear friends and hopefully become a part of each other's lives.

I must have read your letter 20 times by now; it is so great to hear from you. I have wondered over the years what had become of you. I see people all the time who have been home 4 or 5 times and some that have been here as long as I have.

Tim you are always going to be a part of my life, thoughts of our beautiful relationship have carried me through many lonely and depressing years. I almost died the day after Thanksgiving; I had a series of heart attacks that lasted 12 hours. I didn't even realize I was having heart attacks until the pain became so intense I couldn't draw a breath. They rushed me to the hospital in Newberry, Michigan (I was at a medium security prison there).

From there I came by ambulance to Marquette General, it was not until the sixth that I was stable enough for by-pass, but I am doing much better now, except I am sore as hell (smile). I will be in the hospital ward here in Marquette for a few more weeks then probably go back to Newberry.

I will have a Parole Board interview in about June of next year, I am pretty sure they will let me out, I will parole to my lady friend, from there I really have no plans.

To tell you the truth Tim, the thought of going back to the free world scares me. I'm not sure I can make it as a free man. I know that sounds crazy, but prison is all I know. I have been locked up since I was ten years old and the world out there is not normal to me. I have common sense and can learn anything but it is kind of late in the game to start from scratch and have anything for old age. If I had gotten out ten years ago, I would have stood a better chance. But I will get out and give it my best shot, I won't ever do anything to bring me back here, I know I would die in here if I came back.

I'm lucky that I have a good woman who loves me dearly and will stand by me; I'll make it in the free world.

Tim I have felt so lonely, afraid and depressed since my heart attack that I have just been floating along in a fog. And then I got your letter and it made me smile, cry and then realize that life is not over because of this heart attack. I can get my strength back and get back into life.

Thank you Tim for giving me the spark I needed. I also want to thank you for sharing your feelings about our relationship years ago; I had no idea that I had such an affect on you. And although I know it's your basic goodness and intelligence that have brought you the success you have achieved, I truly appreciate your offering me some credit for helping you through.

I remember sitting in the hole at M-R after my stupid escape; writing you long letters and awaiting your replies.

So you are going to be a writer. I can't wait to read your first book; maybe someday you can help me write the story of my 28 years in prison.

Well Tim, I have rambled long enough. Thank you for brightening my life once again. I wish you and your family the very best for the holidays and the coming year. I am enclosing the address and phone number I will be paroling to. Please write again if you find the time.

Always and forever,
Paul

Afterthoughts

Early one morning, recently, I drove south on the Bridge/Sag turnpike in route for my morning coffee fix. It was late autumn, and the leaves had turned brown and were gently falling. Two miles out of town, about halfway between Sag Harbor and Bridgehampton, I passed a couple of crack dealers lingering on the side of the road. One of them looks familiar and slightly nods. I keep going. It's one of the few African American communities nestled among the Hamptons—Bridgehampton, East Hampton, and Southampton. It's mostly poor and seems out of place in a region that houses some of the most expensive real estate on the eastern seaboard. I'd heard locals refer to this stretch on the turnpike as Lionel Hampton.

Some things, like racism and marginalization, never really change much. It just isn't as overt as it once was.

When I reach Route 27, I turn right and pull into a Starbucks, where I'll order my caffé latte, like I do every Sunday morning at 7:45. It's a crucial stop on my way to my morning meditation meeting at the Wainscot Chapel.

I'm feeling particularly vulnerable this morning, and in need of a meeting. I had given an interview on CBS News on Logo, and the network had been running the story throughout the weekend.

"Why am I doing this?" I say aloud.

I often talk to myself when I'm alone in the car. Most people, who see me doing this, would just assume I'm talking on a speakerphone, but I find it an opportune time to speak my thoughts out loud.

For the past several years, I've been an advocate for prisoner rights. I sit on the board of Stop Prisoner Rape, a human rights group that's dedicated to ending sexual violence against men, women, and children in all forms of detention. I visit a dozen of cities a year in my various advocacy work. Mostly, I just share my story to help put a human face on the issue.

A few weeks earlier, I testified before the National Prison Rape Elimination Commission, and the *New York Times* ran my story nationally. I also wrote a *Times* Op-Ed piece, titled "Unsafe Behind Bars," and everyone in my community seemed to have read it. Before this, very few had known I'd been to prison. I was putting myself out there in a very public way, and I was starting to doubt why I'd done it in the first place.

I had had it all—a successful career in the software industry, a Senior Vice President title, and a comfortable six-figure salary that went along with it. My past had been clearly behind me. I was a kid then, and who I was at that time had nothing to do with who or where I was at today. But ever since I walked into a video store in Manhattan and saw some kids laughing at a depiction of prisoner rape on the TV monitors—I decided it was time to do something. In short, I became a human rights advocate dedicated to ending sexual violence in prisons.

But now I was feeling fearful about my future and doubting the sanity of that decision.

"Are you sure this is what I'm supposed to be doing?" I said out loud.

I could almost hear the doors slamming shut behind me—to the privileges and respectability I once enjoyed as a software executive. Now that my prison history was public knowledge, what kind of future could I hold in the corporate world?

For twenty-five years, I have kept my end of a bargain I had made with God. If he gave me the opportunity to do the work, I would do the work—no matter what it was.

"Are you sure, God?" I said again. "I'm afraid, and I'm not sure I can do this. Can you send me a sign?" Though I felt a little silly hearing myself say that, because if it were signs I were looking for—all the opened doors in front of me should have been the clearest indication that I'm on the path I'm supposed to be on.

From the moment I decided to write a book, people came from out of nowhere to help me. The Ashawagh Hall Writer's Workshop, in East Hampton, for one, adopted me as if I were their relative. And my friends at Stop Prisoner Rape elected me to their Board of Directors—and most recently I was voted President of the Board. Every other day, it seemed, I was being asked to help out here and there—so much so that it was becoming difficult to finish my book—which had already taken over three years to complete. I worked as a consultant to the U.S. Justice Department, as they set up the staff of the National Prison Rape Elimination Commission, and I helped coordinate their first public meeting held at Notre Dame Law School. The U.S. Bureau of Justice Statistics invited me to provide input on the survey instruments for the first-ever national inmate study of the prevalence and incidence of prisoner rape in the United States. And I worked with the National Institute of Corrections on an inmate orientation video that is available to all new incoming prisoners in the United States on how to avoid prisoner rape and staff sexual misconduct.

The first time I spoke out publicly was in support of the Prison Rape Elimination Act, the first-ever federal legislation to address the issue. When I stood on Capitol Hill and told my story, I stood next to Linda Bruntmeyer, whose seventeen-year-old son had been repeatedly raped by Texas prison gang members. And then after prison officials refused to intervene—he hung himself in his prison cell. Like my friend, Grasshopper, he had been sent to an adult prison for starting a dumpster on fire. Thinking back on the despair I had felt before Paul entered my life and taught me some survival skills—it could have easily been Sharon who was standing there, preparing herself to tell her son's story of rape and suicide.

I went inside Starbucks and ordered my venti nonfat latte and a blueberry scone. It was a long way from the three powdered donuts in a waxed-paper bag and a carton of milk left resting on a cross-section of bars.

As I waited in line for my order, someone behind me said, "I saw that guy in the *New York Times*. He's that guy who was raped in prison."

Being a poster child for prisoner rape was not high on my list of ambitions. But I have spent many years in therapy, dealing with post-traumatic stress disorder and the residual effects of my rape trauma syndrome. It took almost a decade of therapy, before I could even talk openly to my therapist. For a few years after my released from prison, I was like a walking time bomb with anger and rage. But now, after eighteen years of recovery and therapy, I follow a spiritual program that believes that no matter how far down a wrong path someone may have gone, or how far they've fallen, others can benefit from knowledge of that experience—especially if that experience led to redemption.

I turned around and smiled gently at the guy who made the comment. I could tell by his look, that my smiling at him made him uncomfortable. I had been told before, that meeting me was sometimes disconcerting because I hardly looked like an ex-con.

Behind him, on the *New York Times* rack, an article caught my attention. It was the first in a series on teenagers behind bars who were jailed for life for crimes committed as teenagers. The caption read, "To More Inmates, Life Term Means Dying Behind Bars."

My friends at Human Rights Watch were releasing a report on how a growing number of teenagers who were ending up behind bars were never getting out. On the cover of the newspaper, were two mug shots of Jackie Lee Thompson. The first picture had been taken when he went in to prison at age fifteen, and the other shot was recent—age forty-nine—after having spent thirty-five years inside.

I stood there transfixed by the mug shot of the fifteen-year-old boy, side by side with his foty-nine-year-old self. No matter the time difference, the eyes were the same in both photographs. Only the expressions were different; the fifteen year old appeared frightened, whereas the forty-nine year old looked lifeless and sad.

That was me at seventeen and that could have been me today. Like Paul, Slide Step, and all the others, I could have easily spent the past twenty-five years of my life behind bars. What really separated us other than circumstances?

I walked out of Starbucks, forgetting my latte on the counter. I drove to my meditation meeting in Wainscott, tears rolling down my face. It became so clear to me what I'm here to do.

Once again, God had given me my sign.

According to the U.S. Bureau of Justice Statistics, we housed over 2.2 million prisoners in the United States—more than any other country in the world. And an estimated 13.5 million more pass through the justice system each year. Including over 100,000 teenagers who are housed in adult facilities.

Sexual violence is a crime that preys on the vulnerable. In some states, children as young as fourteen have been sentenced to adult facilities, and in many cases, they fit the profile of likely sexual assault victims because they are small in stature and inexperienced in the ways of prison. According to experts, teenagers in adult facilities are five times as likely to be sexually assaulted than young people housed in juvenile facilities, and eight times as likely to commit suicide. But while certain characteristics like age, sexual orientation, or physical appearance can increase the likelihood of rape, anyone can be a victim of sexual violence behind bars. Male, female, transgender, young or old, gay or straight, black or white, physically weak or strong— anyone. It's up to corrections officials to take steps to prevent it. Stephen Donaldson, the former President of Stop Prisoner Rape, was an antiwar protestor, with no prior history of criminal activity. He died of complications from AIDS, which he believed he contracted as a result of his rape.

And today, when HIV rates among prisoners are estimated to be five to ten times higher than the rest of the population, the risks are even greater.

Most people who want to be tough on crime don't care what happens to inmates. But they should care, because 95 percent of all prisoners are eventually released back into society, indelibly marked by the violence they have seen or experienced.

Up until recently, corrections officials have not been doing enough to curb this violence. Prisoner rape occurs most easily when guards aren't around to see or hear it. Inmate populations are continuing to grow and this makes policing prisons and jails even more difficult. Insufficient staffing and outdated facilities where observation of inmates is limited contribute to an atmosphere that makes it harder for authorities to protect vulnerable prisoners. There's no question that jails are short of money, but there are steps that can be taken to protect inmates from being raped. Staff training, inmate orientation, and assignment of prisoners by crime and by propensity to violence are a few examples. By not stopping and prosecuting sexual offenders in prisons, we are in effect legitimizing the act.

Being gang raped in prison has scarred me in ways that cannot be seen or even imagined. My shame, low self-esteem, self-hatred, deep-seated rage, and inability to trust went unabated for years. To drown out the painful memories, I went through a period of heavy drinking and drug use. Even after years of therapy and recovery, I still occasionally awake at night in cold sweats, crying. I'm remorseful about the actions of my youth, and I accept full responsibility for the choices I made, but no matter what crime someone may have done, no one deserves to be raped.

When President Bush signed the Prison Rape Elimination Act of 2003, Congressman Frank Wolf (who sponsored the bill in the House with Congressman Bobby Scott) sent me a personal note that read: "Hopefully the work we have done will save another seventeen-year-old from suffering the same fate as you did."

I am a survivor, but my story is far from unique. I speak for the estimated hundreds of thousands of voiceless inmates whose personal stories will never be heard, whose life-and-death struggles behind bars will never be known. In giving voice to other survivors, I'm also taking back the voice that was stolen from me when I was seventeen years old and remained lost to me for many years. I have reclaimed that voice and with it strive to shatter the walls of silence that keep survivors incarcerated in their own personal prisons of despair, shame, and alienation.

Fish is my story, it is our story.

Acknowledgments

First and foremost, to Marijane Meaker and The Ashawagh Hall Writer's Workshop: I could not have completed *Fish* had it not been for your guidance, compassion, and loving support. Even as my life felt like it was unraveling—you encouraged me to keep writing no matter what. To Jess Gregg (*The Tall Boy*, Permanent Press): You have been a mentor, a guide, and at times—a firm, loving father. Vince Lardo for his generous time and advice. To Laura Stein, Lynn Blumenfeld, Bob, Ed, Helen, Tom, Rob, Aurrice, Vivian, Betty, Meredith, Annie, Amanda, Wendy, Annette, Susan, Debora, Jim, Glynne, Barbara Ann, John, Leo, and Stacy. My inner boy thanks you with all of his heart.

Special thanks to Jim Fox, for his friendship and legal counsel, and to Tom Fallon who brought us together. To Scott Manning, my hardworking publicist, and Dr. Diane Austin, who was the first to read the entire manuscript and offer her clinical insight. To Robert Gatto, Lovisa Stannow, Kathy Hall-Martinez, Lara Stemple, Cynthia Totten, and my friends at Stop Prisoner Rape who also provided feedback. To Laurie Van Rooten, who believed in Fish nearly twenty-years ago, and who never stopped asking me when I was going to sit down and write it. To my friends of Bill W. who help me build the foundation upon which I live a sober life. And to my Higher Power and salsa secreto.

To my close friends and family, who helped hold my world together as I lowered myself down into the emotional abyss of darkness: I could not have been able to report back from any of those places, had you all not been there to help hoist me up again.

To Don Weise, my good-looking, sexy, and talented editor, who first heard about *Fish* over dinner and championed it with all of his passion. He understood what I was trying to do, and applied his gifts in all the right areas. If we help change the world of just one vulnerable inmate—Don is in large part responsible.

And last, to the hundreds of thousands of men, women, and children who end up behind bars every day: No matter what someone has done—no one deserves to be raped.